THE
WILD-HORSE
RIDER

Jim Sypult

THE WILD-HORSE RIDER

The Wild-Horse Rider

Author: Jim Sypult
Editor: Sharron Sypult
An Historic Memoir
Personal Accounts: Players, Coaches, and Friends

Cover and Book Design: Paul Cowan, Iconix.biz
Cover Photo: Matt Beitzel, Methodist University Archives
Photo Credit, page 140: Methodist Athletic Department
Bicycle Painting, page 245: Cathleen Campbell
Lion Head Icon: vecteezy.com

ISBN: 9798542660929
Printed in the United States of America

First Edition: August 2021

For Jim — my love and lifemate —
whose voice is the soul of this book.
You left it all on the field, babe!

ACKNOWLEDGMENTS

I AM GRATEFUL TO MANY people who made this memoir possible: Mom, the crème de la crème and personal cheerleader; Jill who urged me to print her father's stories unsanitized and in full; Laura, my niece and kindred spirit who comforted me through an acute loss; and Scribblers, a Hilton Head Island writing club and catalyst for Jim to record his stories.

Sansing McPherson, my critique partner, CMS czarina, and project godmother whose wit, writing skills, and publishing experience are appreciated more than I can say. I'll always value confabbing during the pandemic, discussing libel and consequence of disclosing family secrets, grappling with football terms and the f-bomb, and pondering weighty issues such as whether to use *big balls* or *iron testicles*.

Rhyan Breen, a Wild-Horse Rider I taught in an appreciation of literature class who in turn taught me that truth is a defense to libel. He and other players were ideal students in class ... and not just because of my direct link to the head coach. Rhyan's legal advice was critical to this memoir.

Dave Eavenson, MU's athletic director and vice president, also a Wild-Horse Rider and former student. He shared a remarkable coaching experience and camaraderie with Jim and will always be family. If the need arises, I know I can call on Dave. He told me once what Jim would say if here: "Get up and go on." I'm trying to do that.

The Wild-Horse Riders, who helped tell the Jim Sypult story and in so doing told their own — what they were, what they said, what they felt. They connected on a deeply personal and emotional level, uniting in spirit and brotherhood — the depth I could not plumb. I so appreciate their advice, tributes, and encouragement to produce this memoir.

Jim Sypult, my lifemate and truest friend whom I will love forever and a day. I share his story to lift spirits, pay homage, and celebrate this remarkable man who set the standard for character. I can still hear him telling stories, see the magic in his eyes, and feel his luminous, larger-than-life presence. He challenged us to be our best selves and lived life as a Wild-Horse Rider.

CONTENTS

PREFACE

*T*HE *WILD-HORSE RIDER* HAS NOTHING TO DO WITH HORSES. Not a whit. It has to do with a college football coach and a fiery speech during a 0-10 season.

Make no mistake, this is a story about winners. It's about Coach Jim Sypult who told "The Wild-Horse Rider" story and hundreds of former players who retell it. It's about a singular time in their lives when youth and experience meld into manhood.

You may wonder what a motivational speech has to do with horses. Let me explain the metaphor: A wild-horse rider prepares for whatever's ahead and steps up and makes the play. No matter the obstacle, he performs, overcomes, and changes the game. He's a leader, a role model, a *winne*r. This mythical figure could be a woman ... but not in this book.

The Wild-Horse Rider Speech was born late in a game during a rain break when Coach Sypult smashed his clipboard on a barbell rack to get everyone's attention. The room became instantly quiet, and a quarterback dodged the airborne shards. The coach eyeballed his team, and then the words flew from his mouth — spontaneous, unscripted, inspired. His voice and personality held them — mesmerized — in a moment in time that was timeless.

"There are five types of people," he shouted. "Doctors, lawyers, fighters, *fuckers,* and wild-horse riders." The f-bomb caught everyone off guard as it isn't in the Bible and is, therefore, out-of-bounds. With raw emotion, intensity, and impact, Coach Sypult described each of the five types. He wanted to go to war with fighters and wild-horse riders, not fuckers—aka fuckups. He rose to the occasion as he had so many times before, but *The Speech*, as well as the way he told it, was one for the ages. It became a legend and is even more legendary as years pass and it's retold to other squads and crowds — a ripple effect.

At the giddy-up, I *must* explain the hyphen (-) in the title — not to be confused with a dash (–). The teensiest difference but very different. Similarly, a *wild horse rider* (no hyphen) is a horse rider who is wild, while a *wild-horse rider* (hyphen) rides *wild* horses and is not wild ...

although he could have a *wild* streak. That's as clear as mud at the bottom of a pileup in a downpour. Let me give this another ride. The horses are wild and untamed, not the rider. The rider is daring and fearless, admired and respected. He rides wild horses figuratively, not literally. I'll get off my high horse now, but the hyphen makes a difference ... to an academic, if no one else.

I may depart from the literal use of words now and again. Relax, I'm just the editor and will not be saying much ... except in this introduction. So what's an English professor doing in a story about a rugged, hard-nosed sport like football? Well, I do love a good story, and this storyteller who had a keen sense of humor caught my fancy.

Since the day we met, I loved Jim Sypult. He loved me ... and football. Not sure which he loved more. I was walking up the steps at East Fairmont High School in West Virginia when someone called my name. I turned and saw a tall, handsome guy with broad shoulders, a buzz haircut, and a winning smile. Be still, my heart! When I talk about

"Since the day we met, I loved Jim Sypult. He loved me ... and football. Not sure which he loved more."

Jim, I tend to rhapsodize like some Wild-Horse Riders unabashedly declaring love on *Facebook*. Clearly a touchdown.

Anyhoo, Jim and I were immediately drawn to each other like

magnets. We were alone in a room full of people. Make that alone amid the crowd outside. He was as fine as all outdoors. Sweet tastes and appetites. Delicious in deliciousness. Intoxicating, and I'm not a drinker. Whatever it was, it just was. I was fourteen, and he was fifteen. Salad days yes, indeedy!

"You want a bite of my candy bar?" Jim asked in his deep voice. I don't remember my answer. I only know "The heart wants what it wants." (How often does Emily Dickinson appear in football annals?) He went home and told his mother he met the girl he was going to marry.

Some things are just meant to be. Jim was my first date, my high school sweetheart, my Prince Charming. He looked and sounded like Rock Hudson, the quintessential movie star at the time. I became Jim's girl and wore his football cleat on a chain around my neck. It was an actual football cleat, announcing to the world that we were going steady.

Jim was the starting quarterback, and I, the head cheerleader. He starred on the football field, basketball court, and track, and I cheered him on. I cheered for the EFHS Bees and then WVU Mountaineers, Davidson Wildcats, and Methodist Monarchs — as well as Tigers, Minutemen, Falcons, and Blue Raiders.

I wore their colors and cheered until hoarse. Once in Rome, Italy, I was the *only* fan in the stands cheering for our team, the Towers of Bologna. I had years of experience, made quite a spectacle of myself, and can only imagine what the Italians thought because I couldn't understand what they said. It was *Italian*! "It is better to be looked over than overlooked." Yep, now I'm quoting Mae West.

To continue, ours was a storybook romance, and our love was rare, sacred and sensual, beyond measure and reason. "Love rules without rules," an Italian proverb. Be forewarned, I will wax lyrical on occasion. Jim kept journals, loved to read, and told excellent stories — soft spots for me. He was naturally funny and athletically built — a hunk! And his handwritten notes won my heart. We were lovebirds and married very young. We grew up together, played house for fifty-three years, and had a real partnership when it was uncommon. All we ever wanted was a house with a white picket fence.

Wait! Jim also wanted to coach, and I wanted to go to school. I never intended to spend decades in front of a desk or behind one.

One path led to another and then another, as in a Robert Frost poem. One of Jim's old girlfriends saw no reason for me to go to college even though she did. An unmarried professor told me I was selfish to pursue a degree instead of being a domestic goddess. A coach's wife wondered why I wanted a doctorate degree. Jim pooh-poohed them all as only he could and encouraged me to pursue my dreams. He was very much about dreams.

One of Jim's dreams was to play football at WVU. He earned a full scholarship, started all four years, and was chosen team captain. His WVU stardom only cost him a few concussions, front tooth, and separated shoulder. I worked as a secretary in the English department and sustained no injuries other than my liberal arts leanings.

We lived a frugal life, not by choice, which didn't matter because we were in love, a love as deep as the sea, as infinite as the sky. Once Jim even sold his blood to buy me a Christmas present. Sigh! I couldn't cook, so he learned to cook. When we held hands, players watched. He defended me in a sexual harassment case — another story, another time. He supported, counseled, and protected me — as he did everyone. In telling about us, I'm telling about Jim as we were inextricably bound like football and fall.

Jim grew up in a coal-mining community in West Virginia. He overcame family, teacher, and academic prejudices, following his heart as to what was right and wrong, teaching his truths to teams, coaches, and others. He represents the soul of America, and his story is the unequivocal American story rooted in the great American sport — football. Granted, I'm partial, but it's true.

Off-season, Jim got up before the sun, prayed, read, and wrote in his journal. He then devoted himself to long days of recruiting, spring ball, and whatever problems that popped up like a windstorm. In season, I rarely saw him. He was married to his job and learned to live with little sleep and exhaustion. I learned to share him, becoming a proverbial football widow.

As a boy, Jim admired a fictional character named Chip Hilton, a leader and fiercely competitive figure in a series of books for adolescent boys written by Clair Bee. Chip excelled in sports, demonstrated good sportsmanship, and encouraged his teammates to play their best. He was a gentleman and everything Jim aspired to be: decent, honest, ethical, resilient, and humble. Stories have the power to make us who we are — spoken like a dyed-in-the-wool English professor.

Coach Sy, as he was known, was a man of courage and conviction, a formidable opponent who led by example, working harder than anyone in an all-in approach, no job beneath him. The chips-down, ultimate guy, selfless, and proud but disarmingly humble. Coach Sy instilled the highest values and always did the right thing. He didn't lie, cheat, or steal — a code of behavior he taught his players. He might have stretched the truth or borrowed a joke or two, but he never cheated — not even on taxes.

"Jim coached our daughter in tennis ... or tried to."

Coach Sy trusted others to do what was right. He loaned money to a player who never paid it back. He expected administrators to be honest and ethical, but some didn't perform well on game day. He allowed an American running back on his Italian team to go home, believing his player would return to finish the season. Never fear, I won't mention your name, Spark Clark from Ohio.

Those who made the Dean's List, Coach Sy invited to our home for a spaghetti dinner he prepared himself, using Annie Lavoretti's meatball and sauce recipes. He served pancakes to his Italian players who were clueless as to what they were. When we won the conference championship, he and his coaches celebrated with a phenomenal filet dinner and stories, the fun superseding the Super Bowl playing in the next room — not hyperbole.

"Humor," he said, "has always served me well in difficult times," of which there were many. Coach Sy soldiered on despite letdowns and uphill battles, and we did what the French do during the darkest hours — *dot, dot, dot* (a *Momma Mia* allusion)! When he wasn't selected as the head coach at Davidson College, he found a way to move on. *Dot, dot, dot!* One fabricated incident and unfounded attack on his reputation brought him close to circling the drain. But his spirit, his indomitable spirit, prevailed ... as always. *Dot, dot, dot!*

A teacher, spiritual leader, and football guru, Coach Sy was born to lead, born to inspire, born to coach. He was demanding yet loving. He even coached our favorite (and only) child in tennis ... or tried to. Sometimes tears flowed after a rigorous training session or grueling practice, but sweaty hugs followed. At thirteen, she was the No. 1 seed on her high school tennis team.

As for people skills, Coach Sy's were exceptional. He had dignity and gave others dignity. He believed in us and made us believe in ourselves. Everyone loved him, and he loved everyone — well, almost everyone. His faith in God gave him strength, and football, a game he called "the greatest ever invented," gave him joy. He took pride in his football family and their accomplishments, and he relished the success of an unlikely winner, a dark horse.

Under Coach Sy's leadership, the players bonded and became brothers and champions on the field and in life — *winners* in their hearts and minds. They echo his spirit in what they say and how they live. His character became their character; his words and stories, their own. Exaggeration? You decide.

Never underestimate the power of stories, friends. Stories have power — power to inspire, heal, and teach us to care; power to make us brave, hopeful, and happy. Coach Sy knew how to tell a story and captivate an audience. He just knew. He spoke with ease, made shrewd observations, and laced his stories with life lessons. *The Speech* and his other speeches were riveting and resonated with all who heard. And his stories generated this book.

Take it from this horse's mouth, "The Wild-Horse Rider" story transcends the gridiron, and so does the storyteller. The man, the myth, and the message come together in one — Jim Sypult, the original Wild-Horse Rider.

I urge those buckaroos and equestrian enthusiasts expecting a story about cowboys to join this journey of a true rough rider and his followers. Teddy Roosevelt's Rough Riders were a cavalry unit accustomed to riding unbroken horses — an apropos allusion if ever there was one. Plus, Coach Sy read extensively about Roosevelt and likely alluded to him on occasion to fire up the troops.

"We were inextricably bound like fall and football."

This memoir is a collection of Coach Sy's essays, essays that begin with his childhood and are told from a child's perspective. His voice changes as he evolves into a man of integrity, pride, and vision. After he retired from coaching, his subjects expanded to Colin Kaepernick, tennis, and even beauty.

Jim Sypult was no ordinary man, and our life together was anything but. He led, and people followed. He talked, and others listened. He told stories, and he held us captive. He made us laugh and kept us laughing. He meant so much to so many, and those who knew him were absolutely devoted.

Called the *Father of Methodist Football* in Fayetteville, North Carolina, he was an amazing storyteller, exceptional motivator, mentor, father figure, iconic coach, and superhero with a whistle and a stopwatch. He laughed hard, loved hard, and lived hard. His life was meaningful, and he had a towering, lifelong impact. I'm not gilding the lily here (Shakespeare).

My goal is to honor Jim by sharing his stories and those told by others who, by the by, called me *Dr. Sy* and *Momma Sy* — some still do. The Jim Sypult story is extraordinary — as was he. I hope these pages lift spirits, provide an escape during difficult times, and find favor with football fans, coaches, and, most especially, the Wild-Horse Riders.

1
ROOTS AND WINGS

Jordan, West Virginia

I WAS BORN SEPTEMBER 22, 1945, to Virginia Isabelle and Carroll Robert Sypult. Dr. Hickson delivered me, and he delivered my daughter twenty years later. Same guy. Hickson came to Jordan from the city once a week to doctor those with ailments. He had an office connected to our house, and my mom served as his cleaning lady and receptionist. Obviously, he was very close to our family.

Mom was the child of a single parent. In the 1920s, those born out of wedlock were labeled and ostracized even though nearly every family had illegitimate kin. They hid the truth like a criminal record or X-rated magazine. Mom carried this shame her entire life believing everyone talked behind her back even though very few even knew, including me. Her maternal grandmother, only known as Grandma Jones, raised her, but my mom was extremely loyal to her mother.

In addition, my mom's stepfather sexually abused her, another matter I did not know as a child. Mom was emotionally unstable and had many physical illnesses. I realized why when these family secrets were revealed later on. Sometimes people blame themselves for what others have done.

According to family stories, my mom's stepfather was a self-educated engineer. He died before I was born, so I grew up believing he was a good man; in actuality, he was a real turd.

"People aren't completely worthless," my dad always said. "They can always serve as bad examples."

Dad was a real character, nicknamed *Blackie* because of his dark complexion and *Peaboggie* for some unknown reason. He loved sports and worked hard at a young age. He drove trucks and was a delivery boy for a grocery store.

My Grandfather Pete was a strong disciplinarian and well-respected. He was a foreman in the mines and expected his boys to work. Rumor was he once owned a wildcat mine and lost it in a card game. Grandpap and my great Uncle Ernie owned a trucking company, Sypult Brothers, that delivered coal to homes. He also had part ownership in the Fairmont Pirates, a minor league team in town. My Uncle Clyde played first base on that team and was pretty good. Grandpap drank too much, chewed tobacco, smoked cigars, gambled, and reportedly chased women. Dad followed suit. There were good and bad examples, and the bad often set me in the right direction.

The day I was born my father said, "It's another quarterback." In my baby book, he wrote, "Another Football Player," a moniker that would become my destiny. Mom lovingly wrote, "A long, happy life for Jimmy." Dad loved the game, and his lifelong dream was to coach football which became my dream as well.

Football actually was a factor in my parents meeting. Dad was a second-string center for West Fairmont High School. He played for a legend, Bizz Dawson, and decided to drop out of school in his last semester so he could return the following year and compete for a starting position. That's how much he loved football. Unfortunately for my dad, upon his return to school, he discovered he was beyond the age limit and declared ineligible. Fortunately for me, my mom entered school that fall as a new student, and they hooked up somehow and married soon after graduation.

Dad did indeed coach a little football. He formed an independent, semipro team of pickup guys who still wished to play after high school. They were a ragtag group. Dad secured funds from local merchants to pay the expenses. Each jersey had a name of the merchant on the back. (I still have one of those jerseys.) Dad told tales of housing players in the basement the night before big games to prevent them from getting drunk. I suspect he wasn't always successful in this endeavor.

On one occasion, the team traveled to Moundsville to play the inmates at the state prison. They played the game (I know not who won), and afterwards, his team climbed on the bus for the return trip home. One big problem: Not all the inmates were accounted for. The bus was thoroughly searched and not allowed to leave until the inmates were found ... hours and hours later.

Dad delivered groceries for a store owned by Consolidated Coal Company in Watson, West Virginia. All those stores were known as the "company store." He drove a truck and home delivered groceries to the miners' families in the area. Soon he was awarded a position in Jordan, a new community that had just opened a mine.

Dad was the manager, butcher, postmaster, furniture salesman, Boy Scout leader, and church deacon in the Presbyterian Church. Miners were paid in scrip, a substitute for money, that could only be used to purchase goods in the company store. It was pretty regular that a miner overspent his salary and asked dad for an extension. During those times, one hit song, "Sixteen Tons," depicts the miners owing their soul to the company store.

We lived in a prominent house that had the *only* indoor bathroom and running water. I suspect the water was polluted because we still pumped water for consumption from the pump outside. Everyone else had outhouses for bathrooms except for the doctor's office attached to our house. Outside on the front yard, an honor roll was constructed to pay homage to those soldiers killed in action during World War II. Quite a number from that small community had lost their lives.

Next door was the parsonage. The Presbyterian Church sent missionaries to these small mining communities. These clergymen were centrally located in Jordan but reached out to several communities in the area. The entire community participated in building a wonderful church on the edge of town. Three clergy families lived there during our stay in Jordan: The Rev. Dillion (*Preach*) and his wife Peg. They left and served for many years in India. The Rev. Tom Moffet and his wife, Meg. They left, and Tom served in the inner city of Chicago and Cleveland, I believe. The Rev. Ed Towne left the ministry, divorced his wife Sally, and taught theology.

You might wonder how I remember these people so well who were part of my life before the age of nine. Short answer: Mom was great friends with these people. They babysat me. I even slept in their beds with them! When they left Jordan, my mom, a faithful letter writer, stayed in contact throughout our lives. When my mom died fifty years later, these three ministers traveled from New York, Cleveland, and Chicago to officiate her memorial! It was a wonderful tribute to her memory.

The church was important in my daily life: Sunday school, Vacation Bible School, church service, dinners and picnics, and construction of the church. Everyone participated. I remember feeling pretty important when the preacher mentioned "the disciples." I thought he was talking about my uncles Frank, Cotton, and Clyde: "da-Sypults."

I had a sweetheart in the sixth and seventh grade, and she was Italian. Apparently, no one took notice, and I was off the hook for this family transgression. Years later, I took a job coaching in Italy, and my daughter married a Jew. There must have been a lot of grave-turning over these two collaborations.

Another thing alive and well was sports. We played basketball on makeshift goals and football on the slate dumps — tackle too. The missionaries would organize trips to the Mountaineer Mining Mission on the other side of Morgantown where we could swim in the pool and shoot baskets in a real indoor gym. We also had a church league and played games on Saturday in the girls' gym at the high school. I was too young to play, but at every timeout, I tried to impress the crowd (mostly parents) with my shooting prowess. At the top of the hill was a baseball park developed by the community. In the spring and summer and on Sunday (the miners' day off), baseball games were organized against neighboring communities such as Catawba and Rivesville. Families would pack picnic lunches and climb the hill to cheer on the local guys.

My brother, Robert, was ten years older than me. He was in high school when I was five or so. He played football, basketball, and baseball at East Fairmont High. Dad took me to every football and basketball game and some baseball games. Robert was my hero, and his teammates were my idols. Carl Baker and Tommy Moore were saints to me. Robert shared quarterback duties with a fellow named Dick Hinbaugh. Naturally, I thought Robert was the better of the two, and Hinbaugh was like Darth Vader to me. Actually, he was a pretty nice guy. After games, my dad and I would go to Mazza's (pronounced *Mazzi's*), the local high school hangout, and eat hot dogs. Life couldn't be any better.

Jordan was Mayberry and Opie and paradise all wrapped in one. We played marbles anywhere we could find a smooth spot along the dirt road. My marbles were sacred, especially my *steely* which couldn't be moved by any attack with a glass marble. I had my first fight playing marbles. One of the boys stole my favorite marble, and I went home crying. Dad met me at the door and inquired as to what my problem was. When I informed him about the stolen marble, he sent me back to retrieve the stolen goods.

"Go kick his ass, and don't come home without it. A Sypult doesn't allow anyone to steal from him." It was a lesson in Sypult pride.

Remember I was about five years old. So out I went and confronted the kid. "Give my marble back, or I'll kick your ass," I said. The kid stood up and punched me in the nose and made it bleed. I couldn't go home, so I just stayed outside crying not knowing what to do. At dark, my mom searched for me and brought me home with a strong reprimand for my dad. Fighting was never my strong suit.

We rode our bikes on the dirt roads marred by potholes that were occasionally repaired with gravel, and we hit deep ditches filled with rainwater that made for challenging obstacles. We raced each other. We wrecked our bikes. We got cut up. We had a grand time.

Of course, we played cowboys and Indians. I had three good buddies: Gary, Sonny, and Kenny. Sonny's parents had a black maid named Lucy. One day we found Lucy's lipstick and decided to use it to paint on war paint. When I got home smeared with lipstick, my dad wanted to know where we got the lipstick.

"From Lucy," I admitted.

"You're going to turn black in the morning," my dad announced. Convinced I was changing races, I stayed up all night studying myself in the mirror.

On another occasion, Sonny had stolen a *porn* magazine from his dad. After studying the contents, we decided we would *fuck* Lucy. Remember, we were five. Early sex education. Sonny was chosen as spokesman. She was in the kitchen when we arrived.

"Hey Lucy." Sonny nervously asked, "Wanna fuck us?"

Lucy turned, grabbed Sonny by the back of his jersey, turned him across her lap, and proceeded to whip his ass. It scared the, well, it scared the *fuck* out of me. We all lived in fear the next couple

"We played hide and seek, red rover, and kick the can until well after dark. And we told stories, some true, some almost true. It was paradise."

of days because Lucy threatened to tell our parents — although she never did.

We walked on the railroad tracks, threw rocks into the Monongahela River, watched the miners cross the river in the ferry returning from work and go to Drummand's, the local bathhouse and tavern. We played hide and seek, red rover, and kick the can until well after dark. We built roadblocks out of leaves in the fall and upset outhouses on Halloween. And we told stories, some true, some almost true. It was paradise.

Then the coal company announced the mine was closing, and my dad got transferred.

Paradise Lost and New Beginning

I was in the third grade when my dad was moved to a company store in Rivesville. Mom didn't want to move there, so they rented a house in Fairmont. Of course, I was unhappy about leaving my precious life in Jordan. I would have to transfer to East Park Elementary that was much larger than my previous school. Instead of three grades in one room, there were three rooms of third graders! I also went from the top of my class to the bottom. I was way behind the others and had little time to catch up. I was not even close to the other students in math. I was miserable. I missed Jordan, my friends, and Mrs. Reed.

And so I took action: I played hooky. Every day I would leave home, and instead of going to school, I would shoot baskets in a neighbor's yard. I hid a basketball in the bushes and spent the day on the basketball court. I played basketball for a few weeks and woke up one day with an ear infection. My parents took me to the doctor, and I was admitted to the hospital for surgery.

Mom called the elementary school principal to inform him I would be missing school for a couple of days. The principal in turn informed my mom I had not been to school for a couple of weeks! I was caught. I was now far, far behind in school. The school wanted to hold me back and repeat third grade, but my parents convinced the school to promote me. In retrospect, athletically, I would have matured an extra year and been stronger and better at sports.

On I moved to fourth grade and Mrs. Frum. All I recall about this teacher is getting smacked across the palm of my hand with a ruler for answering questions incorrectly. It was not exactly positive motivation.

Fifth grade was the low point. Again, I was still at the bottom of the class. One day during gym, we had a relay race dribbling a basketball the length of the floor and back. This I could do. I flew down the floor and back and instantly became a hero to my classmates. Back in the classroom, my classmates were praising my exploits when the teacher, Mrs. Findley, told the class to be quiet.

"Jim," she said, "dribbling a basketball is fine, but you'll never amount to anything else."

I was hurt. I was embarrassed. I was mad. For the first time in my life, someone really pissed me off, and I was motivated to prove I was better than I was being judged — a life lesson. I would show her and the rest of the world she was wrong. I wrote ol' Mrs. Findley a letter saying she didn't know anything about me and had no right to judge me. Letter writing expressing my anger would get me in trouble many times in the future. I've learned it is better to write the letter and not send it until I had time to think about it — another life lesson. Mrs. Reed (remember my first-grade teacher?) made students feel good about themselves. She was so positive. Mrs. Findley, on the other hand, made me feel bad about myself.

Why would a teacher say such a thing? Education is about positive learning. Motivation is encouraging students to learn through intrinsic desire. This teacher set me on a path of "I'll show you" instead of "I love you, and I love learning." Big difference. I faced negativity more than once in my life. I had some really positive teachers and coaches who were wonderful educators and motivated me with the idea that I was capable of doing anything I set my mind to. Thank God for those role models.

Teachers and coaches can make a huge difference in kids' lives by the little things they say and do — another lesson and a turning point for me. I guess, in a way, Mrs. Findley woke me up. I have since forgiven her for her remark. Later, I would experience others who said similar unkind words, and I admit their remarks disturbed me too. Maybe it was just learning to deal with criticism and disapproval which always upset me. On the plus side, her remark made me sensitive to words that hurt others and appreciative of positive feedback.

Life got better in the sixth grade. I had a new teacher, Mrs. House, who elected to call me *Sy*, a nickname that stuck. She also discovered I needed glasses. I sat in the back of the room most of the time because seats were arranged alphabetically. The *S's* ended up in the far back, and I couldn't see the blackboard! My grades improved dramatically when I got glasses and could see. Who knew? Small things can make a big difference.

Most importantly, the basketball coach, Joe Ross, discovered my basketball ability and put me on the team reserved for only seventh and eighth grade students. I would be the only sixth grader on the team! Every day I was excused early to attend practice — a big deal. Coach Ross was a burly Italian with dark, curly hair and a volatile temper. He was gruff and demanding but very dedicated and expected his players to act like gentlemen and play hard. He was talking my language. I loved the guy, and he gave me a sense of importance. Now I felt like somebody who just might be somebody. I wanted to excel, and a coach came forward to give me a chance. Positive motivation. It turned my life around and could do the same for others. Moreover, I began to see athleticism as a talent and gift to be valued.

I had a girlfriend now based on a relationship that started on the playground. She was selected as the queen, and I was named the king of the playground. I started walking her home every day and holding her hand. She was a cute Italian girl in the seventh grade — a year older. I was dating an *older* woman! She would remain my girlfriend until she started high school.

My seventh and eighth grades breezed on. I was the star of the basketball team and served on Boy Patrol. I made pretty good grades and was popular. I still got some negative feedback from a couple of teachers, Miss Prickett and Mrs. Satterfield, who said I would not amount to anything unless I developed other interests than sports. I was doing pretty well, so their remarks didn't really bother me ... although I was still sensitive to the criticism.

As a general theme and question, I still cannot understand why an educator would say anything negative about a student instead of offering positive and supportive feedback. I wasn't a bad kid. I wasn't a troublemaker. I was just a regular student in the middle of the pack educationally and a better than average athlete. Shallow and misguided teachers are detrimental to our educational system. They label students. Once labeled, students are in for a hard time.

A real hard time came at the end of my eighth grade year, and being a labeled kid had nothing to do with it.

My playground girlfriend had moved on to high school, and that move had severed our relationship. I started dating another girl, Dottie. Walking her home and carrying her books constituted the dating. She was a little loose, a little slutty, and she introduced me to some education I didn't really comprehend. I didn't understand what showing me her "kitty" meant, but I was all for it. Anyway, nothing happened, and she broke up with me.

One night, my friends and I went to a dance at the local YMCA. I danced with Dottie that night because she asked me. I thought she was a little too intimate, especially since she had broken up with me. After the dance, my friends and I were waiting for my father to pick us up and take us home. I was standing on the sidewalk when this older, much bigger guy started prancing around asking us if we had seen a tall, ugly kid with glasses. This bigger guy, Ronnie Masters, was recently released from reform school and was two or three years older than we were.

Unknowingly, I was the tall, ugly kid with glasses. Suddenly, out of nowhere, and I didn't see it coming, Ronnie sucker-punched me in the mouth. I went down to the ground shocked, confused, and cloudy of thought. I tasted my blood for the first time, a taste I didn't like, and my mouth was cut pretty bad. I got to my knees and made a big mistake. "You'll pay for this," I said to Ronnie. "I'll have you sent back to Prunytown" (the reform school location). Pissed even more, he uppercut me under the chin.

My buddies didn't come to my rescue, but they gave me good advice: "Stay down." I did, and Ronnie left with my ex-girlfriend in tow.

Dad arrived and asked me what had happened since I was bleeding. "Oh, Mr. Sypult, Jim really got his ass kicked," they squealed with excitement. Dad said nothing. He delivered the friends to their homes and bypassed our house.

"Where we going?" I asked.

"Going to find him," my dad answered. "No Sypult gets his ass kicked. You'll fight him again."

As a matter of pride, we went looking for Ronnie. I prayed so hard that night to the good Lord to save me. Not in a thousand years could I defeat this hoodlum. My prayers were answered, but I was humiliated, and I had embarrassed my dad.

He gave me a hard whipping with his belt when we got home. And he didn't speak to me for weeks. Hard love was the mode of the time. I suppose my dad would have been arrested today like football pro Adrian Peterson for beating his child as punishment. That was family discipline then. I didn't like it, and I still remember it. And I adopted other forms of discipline because of it. Dad loved me very much, and I have no hard feelings toward him. He probably was drunk. I took my licking and swore revenge — not on my dad but on Ronnie Masters.

On Saturdays, everybody went to the Eastland theatre for double-feature movies: cowboy flicks with Gene Autry and Roy Rogers, comedies with Jerry Lewis and Dean Martin and Abbott and Lou Costello, and romantic comedies with Rock Hudson and Doris Day. Little did I know that some girls referred to me as *Rock*. Why? I don't know, but I liked it.

Anyway, one afternoon as I was exiting the matinee, I saw Ronnie Masters enter the theatre with my ex. As he was getting seated, I took a run at him from behind and sucker-punched him in the back of the head. He didn't see me coming. Pride came before his fall.

He tumbled over the seat in front of him, and I bolted from the theatre at full throttle! I ran all the way home and announced to my dad that revenge had been delivered on that SOB. From then on, I was for sure on constant alert for Ronnie Masters. I boasted to my dad, but revenge left a bitter taste.

In writing about my childhood, I realize I had a wonderful eight years in Jordan, a perfect childhood. I had good and bad experiences with teachers in grade school and good experiences establishing myself as an athlete. Girls played a role as well — some with favorable outcomes, and some, not so favorable.

I learned many lessons along the way: respect for everyone, effects of positive and negative motivation, rejection of labels and society's standards when wrong, pride in doing what was right, and a heavy heart in doing what wasn't.

My Opie Childhood

Until the third grade, I lived a life like Opie's. Not in Andy Griffith's Mayberry, but in a tiny coal mining village in West Virginia.

Gary, Sonny, Kenny, and I — rowdy, rugged little guys — shared everything. We rode bicycles on a cinder-covered dirt road, the only road in our community, hoping the potholes had rainwater puddles to pedal through. We walked on the forbidden railroad tracks and pressed our ears to the rails listening for trains. We ran headlong like the wind when we heard one coming, pumping our arms up and down for the engineer to sound his whistle.

We skipped rocks on the Monongahela River and proved our arm strength based on who could throw the farthest. Gary had the strongest arm and could throw a curve ball when he came out of the womb.

We shot marbles in a circle drawn on a smooth spot in the dirt road. We had fistfights over some marble games and ran home to tell our moms, who invariably made us return to stand up for ourselves.

And, of course, we shot hoops on homemade basketball rims, nets long gone, pretending to be Hot Rod Hundley of the WVU basketball team.

We listened to Bob Prince announce the Pittsburgh Pirates games on the radio. We were engrossed in Jack Fleming's play-by-play account of West Virginia Mountaineer football. We imagined every punch Joe Lewis threw in his heavyweight boxing matches.

We traded favorite baseball cards, spreading our collections on the floor, sprawled around the radio, haggling over every trade. For five cents, we could buy one card that came with bubble gum from the company store. Scratch that. We actually bought the gum and the card was a bonus.

We were outside from daylight to twilight together, unrestrained, screaming and hollering, randomly playing, disorderly, struggling, and at times violent.

We all went to the same schoolhouse that held three grades in two rooms. Mrs. Reed was our only teacher. We attended Sunday school at the only church (Presbyterian). We played any and every sport, church-league basketball, and tackle football on the slate dump. At seven, I was the best tackler, not afraid of anyone, including sixteen-year-old Jimmy Frank.

Once during a rock battle, I hurled a rock into Jimmy Frank's fort (a ditch beneath a dirt mound). Caterwauling the likes of which I never heard before, some cursing, and commotion followed. Jimmy, his head split open, ran home like a wounded wildcat. Blood was everywhere. And we got in trouble — lots of trouble.

One day we decided to play cowboys and Indians — the name offended no one then. We shouted, "Bang, bang, bang" and pretended to shoot arrows from bows, dying dramatically, arms flailing, our bodies writhing on the ground.

War paint, we needed war paint. Sonny's family had a black house-maid named Lucy. Lucy had lipstick in her purse. We decided to steal the lipstick and paint our faces.

When I came home with my lipstick-painted face, my father asked me where I got the lipstick.

"Lucy," I answered.

"Tomorrow you'll turn into a black boy," he said. I stayed up all night worried about the transformation.

On another occasion, we got curious about sex. Kenny stole one of his dad's girlie magazines. We didn't know what we were looking at. But we poured over the nude pictures and decided it was time to have sex.

Lucy was our chosen target because she was there. Sonny was

"Gary Tinder and I remain the closest of friends. When we get together, we yap and yap and sound like two grown-up Opies, still at play."

chosen to ask Lucy the question because it was his house and his maid.

"Lucy, will you have sex with us?" Sonny asked with all the courage a five-year-old could muster. We all watched and waited and hoped.

I can still see Lucy's black face turn red. We just stood there. She grabbed us and one by one delivered a vigorous spanking. No more sex for me!

The coal company shut down, and we all moved away. I lost track of Sonny and Kenny. Gary and I relocated to a nearby city and were neighbors and best friends all through high school. We even roomed together in college before our lives took different directions.

Gary and I remain the closest of friends today even though we live in different states. When we get together, we yap and yap and sound like two grown-up Opies, still at play, controlled to some extent only by our wives.

Grandpap's Cards and Coal Mine

Did Grandpap Sypult lose a coal mine in a card game?

When the Sypult clan gathers, invariably this question about Grandpap surfaces. I for one think he lost a coal mine in a poker game with his cronies. I want to believe Grandpap was a maverick and gambler like Nick the Greek, Wild Bill Hickok, and Doc Holliday. I like the romantic and glamorous image of an undaunted daredevil with a coal mine and an eye for a pretty woman.

My Aunt Mary Belle said Grandpap never owned a coal mine. She was most protective of his reputation as a respected man in the community with many friends. He also had a reputation of never backing down from a fight. This much I know for sure: Grandpap started working in the mines at twelve years old and rose to superintendent in two different mines. He also was part owner of a trucking company that delivered coal to homes in Fairmont, West Virginia. Pictures of Grandpap sitting in one of many Sypult Brothers Coal Company trucks remove any doubt about ownership of one coal business.

By day, Grandpap worked in the mines; by night, he gambled at the card table, mostly at the Elks Club, and he was a regular at the racetrack. After work, he donned a white, starched shirt, smart suit and tie, and pocket watch and chain. I remember him as a manly man, immaculate in dress, commanding, and handsome.

He was also a member of the Ku Klux Klan, something Aunt Mary Belle would be mortified to hear me say. But my father recognized Grandpap by his snazzy shoes under a white robe whenever the Klan marched the streets.

Grandpap played baseball as a youngster. He was a catcher. When I joined Little League at age ten, I wanted to be just like Grandpap. He taught me the basics: good, comfortable crouch behind the plate and a strong target with my glove for the pitcher, the opposite hand making a fist.

"Why a fist, Grandpap?" I asked.

"So that foul balls hit toward you don't break your fingers," he answered.

Wait a minute, I thought. *The catcher has a mask to protect his face, shin guards to protect his legs, and a chest protector. Who said anything about foul balls breaking fingers?*

As luck would have it and much to my chagrin, I was a disaster as a catcher and a sorry baseball player. I couldn't hit a curve ball; I actually had trouble hitting a straight ball. I was injury prone: I split my lip misjudging a ball thrown to me at first base and got a nasty cut above my eye on a foul ball. While standing in the on-deck circle, I got hit in the ear by a foul ball; my ear rang for a week. And I severely pulled a groin muscle and hamstring running the bases. I got more injuries playing Little League than I did playing major college football. Baseball and I were not a good fit, so I quit to avoid more indignity and pain.

Grandpap was one of the founders and financial supporters of the Fairmont Black Diamonds, a minor league affiliated with the Pittsburgh Pirates. He certainly lost money in this baseball venture. But there were other rewards: He served on the board of directors, enriched the community with professional entertainment, and enjoyed his association with the team.

One day, a man approached me and asked if I was Pete Sypult's grandson.

"Yes Sir!" I answered with pride.

"Toughest man I ever knew," he said. I beamed. "One night, I saw your grandfather in a fight over another man's wife."

Another man's wife? Grandpap? I hadn't heard this story!

"Guy hit him over the head with a brick," he said. "Brick broke in half. Pete whipped his butt good though." So Grandpap was back in good standing in my eyes.

"Did I tell you he lost a coal mine in a card game?"

Perhaps Grandpap's womanizing and in-your-face behavior stem from a lack of positive male role models. His father, fittingly known as Jake, left his wife Betty for another woman. Betty was pregnant with their eleventh child at the time. She raised those children by herself, her sons working at a very young age to help their mother. Most worked at a glass factory preparing liquid gas for the blowers. All those children never forgave their cheating dad for the hardship he caused.

Other than being a low-down cheat, Great Grandpap Jake was the son of William Henry who fought for the Union during the Civil War. William Henry married Elizabeth Jane Fredrick, and they brought thirteen children into this world. Elizabeth was probably a full-blooded Cherokee or Shawnee. In those days, families hid Native American roots and took American names. All the Sypults, I must admit, have Native American traits: dark complexions, high cheekbones, and hairless chests. And the men never lost their hair. I carry these same traits — except for the dwindling hair on my head.

My Great Grandma Betty, the wife of the low-down, good-for-nothing cheater Jake, arrived in America in 1882 along with her parents and nine brothers and sisters. Six of her siblings had already died in Switzerland. Her father, Alphonse Girod, wanted to see New York City before departing to find work in West Virginia. He feared he would lose his children while sightseeing, so he tied all ten to a rope and led them around the city. In time, he and his wife Marie produced six more children for a grand total of twenty-two.

I do not know why Alphonse and Marie migrated to America except to find work and live the American dream. I wonder, among other things, where they got the money to sail with ten children?

Alphonse and Marie produced twenty-two children. Grandma Betty and that low-down, good-for-nothing, cheating scoundrel Jake had eleven children. Jake's parents, the Civil War hero and Native American wife, produced thirteen children. That's a total of forty-six children I know of! That's a whole lot of fruitful collaboration.

One last thing: Who made Aunt Mary Belle the sole authority on Grandpap regarding the coal mine and card game?

In my recounting of events, Grandpap lost that coal mine in a card game. His opponent cheated and broke a brick over Grandpap's head.

Grandpap whipped his butt and stole his wife. The woman he stole is my Grandma Minnie!

Did I ever tell you about Grandma Minnie's tobacco chewing?

"Sixteen Tons"

"Sixteen Tons," a song made famous by Tennessee Ernie Ford, focuses on the plight of coal miners so indebted to the company store, they can't afford to die.

For the first eight years of my life, I lived in Jordan, West Virginia, a coal-mining community. Jordan had a population of roughly one hundred people and was located nineteen miles from the state university. My father was the manager of the company store. He was also the butcher, postmaster, Boy Scout leader, and deacon in the Presbyterian Church. We had the *only* house with an indoor toilet. We pumped fresh water from a spring since our running water was undrinkable.

Jim with his father: "The day I was born, my dad declared, 'It's another quarterback,' a moniker that would become my destiny."

The miners were paid scrip, credit vouchers exchanged for goods at the company store — no cash. The coal company owned the miners' homes and deducted rent from their pay.

Explosions were common. Every day wives and children waited for the ferry to cross the Monongahela River bringing the miners home from work. Everyone waited to see if husbands or fathers or brothers or grandfathers were safe.

Coal dust coated the miners, their white eyes peering from black faces. Their fingernails rimmed in black, a black that defied soap and water. Most miners chewed tobacco to keep the coal dust out of their mouths.

The miners had a shower room at Drummand's, a local bar with a poolroom. They drank beer and moonshine, shot pool, and sometimes fought about women or words.

When I ate at a friend's house, the father had meat, and the wife and children had potatoes and gravy. The father, after all, brought home the pay.

There were a few African Americans in the community. They lived far up the hill. The men would occasionally come to our house to ask my dad for an extension on their scrip. Dad invited them in for a beer. He trusted these men and would always grant their requests. If they had children, I never saw them. They were bused thirty miles each day to a segregated school.

The Jordan mine died a slow death, and eventually the whole area was strip-mined. All that remains are a few foundations and chimneys amid the weeds.

My Grandfather Pete started working in the mines at age eight carrying buckets of coal to support the family. He eventually retired as a respected supervisor. Rumor has it Pete once owned a wildcat mine but lost it in a card game. Two of my uncles were also supervisors in the mines.

Coal mining runs deep in my family. They were rough, tough people with strong family values and very, very proud as are most West Virginians. I was lucky to know these people and be a part of this life.

In 1907, Monongah experienced the first great mining disaster. Three-hundred and twenty-eight men were killed in an underground explosion. My maternal grandmother, Ollie, lived there at the time. My mother, Virginia, was born there. Monongah is also the hometown of Nick Saban, the head football coach at the University of Alabama.

After my first semester in college, I brought home academic marks that were less than stellar. Dad took me deep into the mines and showed me where my grandfather and uncles worked. They saw daylight only on their days off.

"If you don't get your grades up, this is where you'll end up," my dad said. Those words and that drop into the blackest of black scared me straight.

After graduating from WVU, I entered graduate school. That year, the second great mining disaster occurred in Farmington; seventy-eight men died. Farmington was only a few miles from my home. It's the hometown of Senator Joe Manchin, my friend and teammate at WVU. His uncle died in the accident.

Sam Huff, also from Farmington, was the best professional football player to come out of West Virginia. When my WVU head coach said, "That kid Sypult hits like Huff," I felt highly complimented.

After the Farmington disaster, Congress passed the Coal Act providing increased inspections of mines, more safety regulations, and a concentration on health standards like black lung and clean air. The government needed experts to execute the plan. The University created a master's program in this field. I decided this direction would be an excellent alternative if my teaching and coaching profession didn't work out. I was in the first class to earn a master's in Industrial and Systems Management Engineering.

Like Jordan, the coal industry in West Virginia is dying a slow death. Coal production is in decline as coal is depleted and mines are played out. Machines replaced miners, and 90 percent of the jobs are gone. Strip mining is also in decline as it is very costly. Natural gas, fracking, solar and wind energy are less expensive. The demand for coal in China, the leading consumer, is weak. Today it only takes a dozen men to work a mine. Today there are fifteen thousand miners or less.

Jobs are always in jeopardy because of Wall Street and investors who buy failing mines at a low price and flip them for profit.

When miners are jobless, their health care can end. Pensions are in danger as miners accept lower pensions because they have no choice. While working, they earn $60-$75,000 a year. When they are laid off, unemployment skyrockets. Most miners have little to no education and aren't trained for another profession.

Finally, politics: West Virginians love Trump. Why? He campaigned against the war on coal. He signed an executive order to deregulate the mining industry to create jobs. Consequently, safety and pollution regulations are ignored. Like Trump, the miners are skeptical of the government.

Trump selected Wilbur Ross as Secretary of Commerce. Ross bought a mine in West Virginia that had over two hundred safety violations. He severed pensions and benefits to make a profit and kept the mine running. Then there was an underground explosion that killed twelve men. Ross flipped the mine and made no contribution to support the families of the deceased miners. People were not happy with Wilbur Ross.

Jim Justice, the governor of West Virginia, also ran his campaign by promising to open four new mines and create new jobs. Governor Justice owed the state $4.5 million for unpaid safety violations from previously owned mines [and agreed to pay $5 million delinquent safety fines in 2020]. West Virginia had the highest death rate among miners in the country in 2016.

Hillary Clinton is hated in West Virginia. Hillary wanted to shut down every mine, create different sources of energy production, and retrain miners to do the work.

Despite the danger, these wonderful people of my home state will work in the unsafe environment and breathe the polluted air that destroys their lungs. It's what they know. It's what they do.

My background is coal, my family is coal, and my education is coal. Even so, I never returned to coal.

PH and His Heroic Dance with Life

"I'm Paul Lewis," a man approaching me made known as I exited the practice field. His work boots and pants were caked with mud. His biceps and triceps bulged from his sleeveless T-shirt. His dark, leathered face, prominent ears, buzz flat-top, and uneven teeth interspersed with gold cut an imposing figure.

He grabbed my hand; his grip felt like a steel vise. The muscle under his thumb was the size of a light bulb. He squeezed my hand and shot pain through my arm. He recognized my discomfort.

"Would you like to have strong hands like these?" he asked, showing me his flexed thumb muscle.

"Come to work for me, and you'll develop your whole body," he said in earnest.

"Seriously, Jim, one day you can play for the Mountaineers."

Paul Lewis had me hooked — thumb and all.

I was a high school sophomore, somewhat tall but very skinny. I was the team's backup quarterback and sometimes starting defensive back. I may have dreamed of playing for West Virginia University, but Paul Lewis was the first person to articulate my dream.

Everyone knew him as *PH*, but no one knew what the *H* stood for, and he would never tell. He had been a homebuilder before World War II. When war was declared, he was the first man in our city to enlist even though he had three young children and was a millionaire. He joined the United States Marine Corps. He wanted to be in the toughest unit defending our country.

PH believed in four things: the United States of America, family, helping others, and West Virginia football. His brother, Art *Pappy* Lewis, was the head football coach at WVU from 1950 to 1959. The highlight of Pappy's coaching career was playing in the Sugar Bowl in 1954. He coached Sam Huff, who is in the NFL Hall of Fame, and Chuck Howley, the MVP of Super Bowl V.

In the Pacific Theater at the Battle of Tarawa in the Gilbert Islands, a Japanese soldier jumped into PH's foxhole and stabbed him in the mouth with a bayonet. PH shot and killed the enemy soldier, but not before the Japanese soldier shot PH in the knee, shattering it.

PH underwent reconstructive surgery on his mouth. His knee, however, was beyond repair. He was sent home and told he would never walk again.

Determined and undeterred, PH sat on the ground,

"I dreamed of playing for West Virginia University, but Paul Lewis was the first person to articulate my dream."

grabbed a shovel, and dug a foundation for his new house. He grew stronger and stronger and was soon walking. He re-established his business and earned another million dollars. In 1958, while Eisenhower was president, a recession forced PH to abandon his building business. He and his oldest son, Bobby, started a stone business to recover previous losses.

I went to work in the summer of 1962 for PH, mixing mud (cement, sand, and water) for a dollar an hour. It was strenuous work. Besides mixing and carrying mud and stone to the masons, I worked in the quarry where we split rock by hand using picks, wedges, and sledge-hammers. In one year, I became twice as strong.

PH lived life on his own terms and was very independent. When we finished a job, we got paid. When PH had money in his pocket, we spent long hours at breakfast and lunch telling stories, joking, greeting friends, flirting with waitresses, and enjoying each other's company.

When his pockets were empty, we worked long hours and didn't get paid until the job was finished. This irregular payday was frustrating to many of the employees who depended on a regular salary, but it was the way PH lived his life.

PH knew how to handle people. He encouraged me daily and spent time talking with me about every facet of life. No topic was off-limits. I saw how he cared for people, especially those who were on hard times. He helped anyone willing to work and gave many second chances. He was kind and generous. He was funny and interesting. He taught me to believe in myself and be positive no matter the circumstances. Many of his life lessons, I carried into my coaching career and influenced hundreds and hundreds of players.

One particular day, I experienced another side of my boss. A man drove up to the job site and asked to speak with PH. The conversation got heated. The man was a tax collector and demanded that PH pay his overdue taxes. PH said he would pay when he was "damn good and ready."

He had fought for his country and paid a very dear price for it. He told the man to "get in line."

The taxman then accused PH of avoiding his taxes by filing for bankruptcy. PH exploded. He reached into the car, grabbed the man's ear, and tried to pull the taxman through the window — by his ear. If PH's grip was anything like his handshake, this man's ear was in agony. I saw the situation and was able to get behind PH and lift him off the ground. I was yelling at the man who was having trouble starting his car to hightail it, as I couldn't hold PH forever. Thankfully, the taxman left, and we never saw him again.

Yes, I grew stronger every summer, and, yes, I played for West Virginia University just as PH had predicted. He took much pride in my football career and me. He never missed a home game and always waited outside the locker room to greet me and offer encouragement, along with a story or two.

As a graduate assistant at WVU, I was assigned to drive to Ohio and bring a prized recruit back to Morgantown. I invited PH to accompany me on this trip as he was a powerful conversationalist and took much pride in West Virginia football. Before arriving on campus, PH had convinced the recruit to attend WVU. The coaches were amazed the young man was ready to sign when he stepped out of the car. In 1969, this recruit, Eddie Williams, rushed for 208 yards and was voted the MVP Peach Bowl player in a 14-3 win over South Carolina.

I worked for PH throughout high school and college and in my early coaching career. I always had a job during the summer and any break in the school year. I also learned a valuable trade and earned my stonemason card.

Most importantly, I met a man who significantly influenced and shaped my life. He was my mentor and friend. To this day, I hear his hearty laugh, see his beloved truck named Old Red, remember the nicknames he loved giving each employee, practice his napping techniques he learned in the Marines, and share my memories with others as I recall this man and his heroic dance with life.

Untold Stories

Harry Bower had a story. He didn't tell his story. He didn't write about his story. I don't know Harry's story. I don't know because I didn't bother to ask.

Harry was a friend of our family. His wife, Pearl, was a large woman who drank too much. She was loud and flirted with male friends without mercy. Dad didn't like her tongue in his mouth when she planted a hello or goodbye kiss. Harry worked as a salesman in the men's clothing department at Hartley's department store in Fairmont, West Virginia. My mom worked in the accounting department.

Harry was a handsome man: lean, well-dressed, quiet, gentle, and unassuming. He played football at West Virginia University in the '40s. That's all I know about Harry.

In the mid-'60s, I was a high school student-athlete and headed to West Virginia on a football scholarship. I paid little attention to Harry and asked no questions. In my youthful exuberance, ego, and belief that college football in the 1940s was inferior to the modern-day game, I neglected Harry.

I regret I didn't ask Harry to share his experiences with me which I'm sure were of note and interest. He likely had tales and lessons of value. I regret never inquiring into the background of my grandparents and aunts and uncles. I regret I didn't record their stories and experiences. They are so valuable in revealing our personal identities.

I, too, am a Harry Bower. I have stories to tell, but unlike Harry, I have a platform.

In 2014, for example, my alma mater played in the 50th anniversary of the Liberty Bowl against Texas A&M. I played in the very first Liberty Bowl fifty years back. To my surprise, many senior teammates voted against accepting the bowl bid altogether. Playing in this game meant long, brutal practices, and many key players did get hurt.

As it were, my brother, Robert, got married on the same day and afternoon as the Liberty Bowl. I had rented my first tux to serve as best man before the opportunity to play in a bowl game came about.

When I bowed out of the wedding, I displeased many family members. My dad displeased more than a few as he kept a watchful eye on the game before and after the wedding ceremony — probably during as well.

Utah, our opponent, arrived a week earlier with wives and new sports coats. During the week, they went to New York to see a Broadway show. The WVU players arrived two days before the game and were given a stipend of ten dollars to spend while the University received tens of thousands of dollars. I did receive a watch presented to me by Ed McMahon, Johnny Carson's sidekick on *The Tonight Show*. And I rode on an elevator with two beautiful and famous women at the time: sisters Eva and Zsa Zsa Gabor.

"Hello, boys," Zsa Zsa said. She never called us *darling*, but she smelled great.

The game was played at the Convention Hall in Atlantic City, New Jersey, home of the Miss America pageant. It was the first bowl game ever played indoors. The playing field had to be shortened because a regulation field would not fit in the building. Sod was brought in to cover the cement-based floor. No one had heard of AstroTurf yet. Hitting that field was like colliding with a paved street.

It was the first college game televised nationally. There was concern the cameras would overheat because Convention Hall had no air-conditioning. There was far less concern for the players. Little air was circulated, and some players needed oxygen. It was difficult to breathe. There was no room to position cameras on the sidelines to televise the game, so cameras were mounted in the rafters and shot the entire game from the end zones.

Utah won the day. They had a faster, well-rested, and happier team. I did defend against a future All-American and All-Pro receiver — Roy Jefferson. He won some battles; I won some battles. I tackled him and separated his shoulder, an injury that put him out of the game. At the time, I felt a sense of pride in that hit — but not the hurt.

I still hear about missing my brother's wedding **for a football game!** But I cherish the winning season that led to our Liberty Bowl invitation. My playing experience and teammate camaraderie are memorable in so many ways: the excitement, intense physicality, commitment, competition, strategy, and sacrifice. I love the game of football, a game I was able to coach for forty-five years.

All of us like Harry Bower have valuable stories waiting to be told. Storytelling is an opportunity to recount our lives on this planet, capturing the time, place, and personal history. Our stories record who we are and what.

2
WVU Captain/High School Head Coach
1963-1972

Quitting Was Never an Option

H E WOULD BECOME ONE OF THE MOST FAMOUS football coaches in history. I was a rising senior on the team: denigrated, disheartened, and disgruntled.

He told me and four other players to meet him in the wrestling room. The temperature was hot — sweltering hot. Garbage cans were strategically placed around the mat — for vomiting. The room was polluted with stale human sweat. The atmosphere did not bode well. I sensed pain — maybe torture — even terror.

"My mission today is to get your scholarships," he said. "Run in place, and when I blow the whistle, hit the mat with your chest, and repeat the exercise when the whistle blows again. You can quit at any time."

He blew the whistle. I started running in place and asked myself, "Why is this happening? How did I get to this point?"

Out of high school, I was recruited and signed to play quarterback at West Virginia University. It was a dream realized.

I became the starting quarterback on the freshmen team. After a rocky start, I performed impressively at season's end, completing several passes to win the final game.

In the spring, however, I developed a sore arm, probably from throwing too many passes in practice, and was subsequently moved to free safety on defense. There, I gained a reputation as a very aggressive player, along with the nickname *Bwana* which meant *headhunter*. As a sophomore, I earned the starting job. We had a great season and were invited to play in the Liberty Bowl.

As a junior, I was an established veteran, and we won our first three games. Then we had a disappointing 41-0 loss to Virginia.

"Why did the defense play so poorly?" a teammate asked me later that week.

"Too slow, I guess" was my witty response.

That answer was the beginning of my spiral downward as it ended up in the local newspaper. "Sypult Puts Foot in Mouth" screamed the headline. That offhand remark also landed my butt on the bench.

I felt as if I got a raw deal. I had no communication with the coaches. I became bitter and angry.

During the off-season, the coaches suggested I was better suited to play linebacker, but I needed to gain weight. I had new life and with much gusto gained thirty pounds. In two months, I got fat.

Then the current coaching staff got fired, and new coaches arrived. I had visions of playing quarterback again, but now I was overweight, out of shape, and worse, labeled a malcontent.

So I ended up in the weight room doing up-downs to a whistle until I quit. Only I remained as my four teammates opted to give up.

"You can't beat the whistle, Sypult. Just quit."

"I'll die before I quit!"

Somewhere in my DNA or background, quitting was never an option.

"Keep blowing the whistle!" I bellowed.

Finally, it was the coach who quit. He walked out disgusted.

In the spring, I was a player without a position. I was told I would not play quarterback. I was told I would not play free safety. I wasn't listed on the depth chart ... anywhere. I was on a team, unlisted, with no purpose and no identity.

Every day, I stood alone. Hoping I would get discouraged, the coaches didn't coach me. I simply put on my uniform and watched practice. Finally, an opportunity occurred. Coach Marshall Taylor asked if I ever played tight end. At this point, I would have played anywhere.

I earned a starting job. Then I was moved to wide receiver. Again, I earned the starting role. During the season, I was thrown the ball only five times, and I caught every pass. My job was to block, so I led the team in blocking.

At season's end, I was elected team captain.

My college career was a difficult and painful experience, but I not only survived, I excelled. In the end, it was a priceless period of personal growth. I suffered, I was humbled, but I grew.

The next year, I entered the coaching profession and coached for forty-five years. My playing career and experience afforded me the character, strength, and insight to make intelligent decisions affecting others' lives.

I understood what it was like to compete and win. I knew how it felt to be fired and benched. I knew injustice, disappointment, bitterness, and humility. I knew, most importantly, how to go head-to-head, never quit, overcome unfair circumstances, and endure the pain that occurs in life.

As a coach, I was sensitive to my players when their goals and ambitions fell short of expectations. I could also guide them to an avenue of success because of my personal journey and experience. Life can nullify a touchdown, and often you will be blindsided. It is your fighting spirit, however, that endures and extraordinary determination that allows you to overcome and conquer.

"I was recruited and signed to play quarterback at WVU—a dream realized. My senior year, I was elected team captain. Football lives inside me. It's in my blood."

I have no bitterness toward West Virginia University or any coach. In fact, I am most appreciative of my experience and opportunity. I learned many valuable lessons that have served me well. I will always be a proud Mountaineer.

Sometimes, I still hear that whistle in my head. It calls to me: *Don't quit, Sypult. Don't quit. Die before you quit.*

WVU Helmets and Head Injury

At WVU, I either had a headache going into a game or knew I would get one. My head and helmet were my weapons. My nickname was *Bwana* which meant *headhunter*. When I was a safety on defense, any opponent crossing the middle of the field entered my territory. It was my land, and I had his head by using my head.

In the '60s, our coaches taught us to tackle low. Hit 'em at the knees. Better yet, the ankles, they said. Umm. That meant my head went straight down, and I would make contact with the top of my helmet. The helmet had no padding save for the ears and suspension strap that held the head in place. So theoretically, the head would not slam into the top of the helmet upon contact.

Fifty years ago, we were not worried about improper hitting with the head. Nothing much was said about long-term consequences of head trauma. What was once acceptable belongs in *Grimm's Fairy Tales*.

The trainers asked these questions before a player could return to action after being knocked senseless: *How many fingers am I holding up? What is your name? What day of the week is it?* Their scientific appraisal was archaic and rudimentary.

Vince Lombardi, noted for his iron discipline, cleared his players out of the training room by saying, "You can't make the club if you're in the tub."

The game is inherently dangerous and violent. It is an extreme contact sport. Helmets have greatly improved, coaching philosophies have evolved, and the game is fortunately much safer.

When I Became Somebody

When I finished my playing career in college football, I dreamed of being somebody.

Not my wife's *somebody* who tracked mud on the rug or ate the cookies or broke a dish. What didn't I break! I was *that* somebody, I cannot deny ... even though I tried over the years.

I wanted to be *somebody* in the NFL, but I was too slow. My 40-yard-dash time at the Buffalo Bills tryout ended my professional football career — in 4.8 seconds.

And so, I began my coaching career as a graduate assistant at WVU, my alma mater. That's when I became a different *somebody*.

- Somebody needs to pick up lunch.
- Somebody needs to walk that recruit to class every day.
- Somebody needs to drive that player's wife to the grocery store.
- Somebody needs to take that recruit home to Charleston on Sunday (a four-hour drive each way)
- Somebody needs to pick up a recruit in Ohio (a six-hour drive one way).
- Somebody needs to break down the plays on film and prepare a report.

I was *that* somebody: babysitting spoiled players, delivering lunches, and pouring over game tapes. When the *somebody* jobs came up, I felt the coaches' eyes on me. I began to answer to the name *Somebody*.

A graduate assistant is at the bottom rung of the coaching ladder in college, but this bottom bar launched me toward my brass ring to be a head football coach in college. With great enthusiasm, I performed all my duties. I was being taught and influenced by some great mentors like Bobby Bowden who was an assistant coach, and I appreciated the opportunity.

Soon I was given more responsibility and rewarded with a coaching position on the field. My value to the staff was enhanced when I substituted for a coach to speak at a booster club. I gave a passionate, powerful speech (to my way of thinking) and discovered I had a gift as a speaker. Afterwards, my speaking skills were recognized, and I was sent to all parts of the state to deliver talks to various groups.

When I completed course work for my master's degree in industrial engineering, Jim Carlen, the head coach, called me into his office to discuss my future.

"Jim, what do you want to do? What are your goals?" Carlen asked.

"To be a head coach in college," I answered.

"Stay here with me," Coach Carlen said. "I can hire you as a part-time coach and give you more responsibility. With experience and in a couple of years, you'll have a full-time coaching job in college."

Part-time, I thought. My family situation had changed. I was married and had a young daughter. Our means were modest, meaning *downright poor*. My wife worked as a secretary in the English department to buy food and pay bills. Eating at McDonald's was a special night out. We had no car and walked everywhere. We were

Mountaineers through and through, hiking a mammoth hill to and from campus every day. I couldn't even buy my wife shoes to replace the ones with holes.

"Coach Carlen," I said, "I need a full-time job now. I am ready to coach. Get me a head football coaching position in high school."

Coach Carlen seemed bowled over. "You're not ready for that kind of job. I won't help you or recommend you," he blurted out. At the time, Carlen was thirty-five and quite young for a major college head football coach.

"Fine," I brazenly answered. "Don't help me. I'll get my own job."

The next day Carlen called me into his office again. He told me the superintendent of the Randolph County school system wanted to interview me for the head coaching position at Elkins High School — a school in the largest football division in West Virginia.

"Let's see if the superintendent of schools thinks you are ready for that kind of job," Carlen said with a knowing smile and some sarcasm.

I interviewed successfully. I was offered and accepted the job. My speaking engagements were not for naught.

As a high school football coach, I soon discovered somebody had to wash the uniforms and clean the toilets. Sometimes I was *that* somebody. But I was teaching fundamentals, designing strategy, and mentoring young men. I was the *somebody* giving orders and making decisions. I was the *somebody* meeting and loving the challenges that come with the title.

I was twenty-one years old and, at the time, the youngest high school head coach in the country. That's when I became the *somebody* I wanted to be.

Ah, Reality

As a college senior, I took a class that should have been called "The Reality of Public School Teaching." It was one of those required education classes supposed to teach how to teach but never did.

A burned-out former high school phys ed instructor I'll call Leo Nutz taught the class. Nutz sucked on cigarettes and hated teaching. He had bad breath, a perpetual three-day-old beard, and white hair that stood up like Bernie Sanders'. A glint of joy appeared in his eyes as he described the classroom horrors awaiting us. We tolerated him while he related how students would be inattentive and crude in behavior. Nutz said we would likely drop out of teaching, and our public schools were going to hell. He spoke a truth we did not want to hear.

Nutz railed about the absurd demands of administrators and ridiculous responsibilities of teachers. He told us we would have demeaning duties such as checking toilets to make certain they were flushed. I remember saying to my buddy and teammate Larry Canterbury, "Rest assured, I will never flush student toilets!"

In 1915, Elkins High School in West Virginia was built. Photographs of the school displayed two steps leading *up* to the main doors. In 1968, when I arrived as a coach, the steps led *down* to the main doors. The school was sinking.

One of my first duties was making sure the toilets were flushed. It was called "Hall Duty" or "Hall-and-Flush Duty."

I also washed the uniforms, mopped the bathroom, repaired and cleaned the lockers, and painted the locker room. Before every game, I lined the fields and cleaned the locker-room toilets. In passing, one urinal, installed circa 1915, was not fastened to the wall properly. It was a disgusting green, yellow, and brown. While trying to clean it one day, I kicked it out of frustration, and it fell off the wall. The principal chose to reattach the urinal instead of buying a new one.

In addition, I mowed the grass on the practice and game fields, taught five classes of American history, and coached basketball and track.

In the off-season, I planted bushes and trees, weeded the grass surrounding the stadium, repaired the fences, and painted the press box and concession stand. I also drew bus duty after school to ensure no fights took place in the parking lot. Did I mention I flushed the toilets during class breaks?

From 1920 to 1953, Elkins High achieved exceptional success on the football field under Head Coach Frank Wimer. Three imposing life-size photos of alumni from this era dominated the school's main entrance: Marshall *Biggie* Goldberg, an All-American at the University of Pittsburgh and NFL Hall of Famer; Albert *Big Sleepy* Glenn, national record holder for most touchdowns scored in a season — 49; and his brother, Marshall *Little Sleepy* Glenn, the head coach in both basketball and football at West Virginia University.

Wimer became an icon in the community. After retiring, he was also selected to the West Virginia Hall of Fame. Whenever he appeared at a game, the announcer proclaimed, "The *great* Frank Wimer has entered the building." The crowd rose and gave him a standing ovation.

From 1954 to 1967, under *greasy* Bob Erwin, the football program gradually began to sink like the school building. Amid great expectations, I was hired as only the fourth head football coach since 1915. I was twenty-one years old, a fresh-faced, first-year coach.

I signed a contract in the poorest county of West Virginia for $4,300 — that's right, $4,300 a year. Unbeknownst to me, the county had a pending bond issue for teacher raises in October. The bond had been defeated in a prior vote. This time if the bond failed, the teachers would resign in mass, another thunderbolt. So we started the season uncertain if there would even be a season or school the next month.

Another surprise was the off-putting tradition of scheduling the previous state champion as our opening opponent. That meant we opened with Bluefield High School, a powerhouse program loaded with outstanding players. I took twenty-nine players on a six-hour school-bus ride to the southern part of the state to play Bluefield. Bluefield dressed eighty players including six Division I prospects. The game was, putting it mildly, disastrous. They blocked almost every punt we attempted. Opening the season with the state champions was one tradition I quickly ended.

When I got home, I got a call from Coach Wimer, *the* Coach Wimer. "Meet me in the alley behind your house," he said. "I don't want to be seen with you." With that unexpected invitation, the *great* Frank Wimer entered my life.

In an alley amid old cars, junk, barking dogs, and feral cats, Coach Wimer eyeballed me like my KKK grandfather when learning I was dating an Italian.

"Son," Wimer said, "I'm going to teach you how to punt a football without getting blocked." He called it "the one-step punt." It was an invaluable lesson. Subsequently, I had only two punts blocked in forty-five years of coaching football. I eventually became known as a punting guru of sorts.

"Don't ever tell anybody about this meeting," Wimer said. "I don't want anyone to think I'm meddling." I have never told this story to anyone ... until now.

That week, I also learned another talent I didn't know I had:

impromptu storytelling. I was scheduled to do a radio show with the local sports announcer each week. I arrived at the studio not knowing what to expect and was informed the announcer had unexpectedly died. After that shocking revelation, I had another rude awakening: I had to do the show by myself. Just a mic and me!

"Hello, sports fans," I began. I don't know why I used that opening, but my buddies never let me forget it. I started talking about the game, players, anecdotes, whatever came to mind. The words poured out of me. I spent the entire program talking into the mic, telling story after story, making our opening loss sound like a win. I made that butt-kicking Bluefield game sound like a victory for Elkins. I soon learned the value of humor, emphasizing the positive, and providing good copy for the media.

In October, the bond issue passed. Our schools remained open, and I got a 50 percent pay raise. I went from extreme poverty to mere poverty.

It took three years, but we finally got our team on the winning track. By the way, I never scheduled Bluefield again.

Later, as a college head coach, I taught a class called "Coaching Football." On the first day, I brought rags, brushes, and mops to class and taught my students how to clean toilets.

Ah, reality!

Shoot, Leichlighter, Before the Lights Go Out!

In 1967, I started my head football coaching career at Elkins High School. My responsibilities included coaching track, wrestling, and junior varsity basketball. I also taught five classes of the same American history class every day ... to many students who would likely quit school when they turned sixteen.

My junior varsity team played a regular schedule against varsity teams of smaller schools in Randolph County, the largest county east of the Mississippi (1,040 square miles). Travel to play schools in other counties was impractical and costly for the smaller schools. So my junior varsity team became one of their opponents.

One of those small schools was Pickens High School, population sixty-six, and nearly three hours via school bus while still within the county borders. The school's enrollment was twenty-two; the graduating senior class, four; and the basketball team had only six players. My principal made it very clear that Elkins had never lost to Pickens. *Never*!

The stage was set for what became one memorable game. A tiny bathroom with a toilet, sink, and urinal served as our dressing quarters. We changed into our uniforms one player at a time. The gymnasium was likewise tiny. There were no bleachers for the fans. Only one row of benches ringed the playing floor. The entire population of Perkins attended the game and crammed into the seats — all sixty-six of them. They were hungry to make history.

Natt Jackson coached the Pickens team. Natt, a former football player and Purdue graduate, weighed over 300 pounds. He belonged to the Jackson clan, the only black family in Randolph County.

Jackson's star player was Leichlighter. I don't remember his first name, but he could shoot as accurately as Steph Curry — at least, on that night. The other five players could not shoot; they couldn't dribble or pass either. In a word, the rest of the squad was *terrible*.

The game started, and Leichlighter got hot. In fact, he got *white* hot. Everything he threw up went into the basket. He couldn't miss. The home crowd got excited, and I got concerned. *Elkins never lost to Pickens. Never!* resounded in my head.

We were down ten points when the unimaginable happened: The lights went out. We sat stock-still, blinking in the dark, unable to see, rooted to our benches. A quiet settled on the room, a room that moments before had been charged with cheers and shouts. Someone called the janitor and his flashlight into action. He promptly placed pennies behind the fuses in the electrical box. His *high-tech* solution brought the lights back on, much to the delight of the crowd.

The game resumed. Shortly thereafter, the lights flickered and went out again. The fans groaned. The janitor, toting his flashlight, was summoned again. He performed his magic-pennies trick, and the lights returned. The fans cheered loudly. The game resumed. But the lights went out again and again and yet again, each time returning briefly after the janitor resorted to the earlier penny remedy.

Seizing the opportunity and hoping to prevent an embarrassing loss, I called timeout and pled with the local and lone official to cancel the game. Coach Jackson also seized the opportunity and argued to continue the game. The official, a resident of Pickens, decided the game would continue and any basket would count as long as the lights stayed on.

With the lights on, the frenzied fans cheered with abandon. Above the uproar and unbridled enthusiasm for a possible win, I heard Coach Jackson shout as clear as if he stood beside me, "Shoot, Leichlighter, before the lights go out."

I can still hear those words. At half-time, we remained down ten points. I instructed all of my players to guard Leichlighter, *only* Leichlighter, and to leave the other four Pickens players unguarded. As I said, they couldn't shoot, dribble, or pass! Leichlighter couldn't get the ball, and his teammates were helpless. The strategy worked. We recaptured the lead. Then the lights went out again.

Coach Jackson called timeout. Then and there, he took the other side of the argument. He said the game should be canceled because of the uncertainty of the lights. His official, who it turns out was Jackson's next-door neighbor, agreed, and straightaway the game was cancelled.

Later in the season, Pickens came to Elkins to play on our home court. Our home court was the gymnasium of Davis and Elkins College. The court was huge, three times the size of the Pickens' court, and even Leichlighter was fatigued after only a few minutes. We won by forty points. My reputation remained solid.

I coached basketball for one season *only*. All these years later, I remember Pickens High School, Coach Nat Jackson, the dark gym, and the words "Shoot, Leichlighter, before the lights go out!"

Oh, Doo-Dah-Day!

In 1971, I accepted the head football job at Liberty High School in Bedford, Virginia, a small town in the southwestern corner of the state. Sharron, my wife, and I visited the school and were impressed by the facilities and manners of the students. The *suh, ma'am,* and very real hospitality won us over.

Liberty was a school newly built for the newly integrated students of the area. I was a newbie in racial relations and conflicts. I grew up in an ultra-white community, and my first job had only *one* black family. I did play football at West Virginia University when the team was first integrated. We had a few black teammates, but WVU was not the Deep South.

Virginia was. *The War of Nawthun Aggression* was still being fought in Bedford. The principal, Mr. Lee (not Robert E., but *Lee*) was a Southerner; and the assistant principal, Mr. Sherman (not William T., but *Sherman*), was a Northerner. Unlike their courageous Civil War monikers, Lee and Sherman avoided sticky situations by being conveniently absent during any conflict.

Liberty's football program had won twice in two years, and Principal Lee wanted to win but was uncertain how. He also feared criticism that would jeopardize his position.

"Mr. Sypult," Lee said early on, "if it comes down to thee or me, it will be thee." Mr. Lee was betting on me to win like a bobtail nag in a horse race. No doubt, he would deliberately shorten my tail if I didn't win. How long that race would be was not clear. *Doo-dah! Doo-dah!*

Mr. Lee associated *black* with cheating and *white* with honesty and integrity.

"Mr. Sypult, you need to wear a black hat," Lee said, insinuating I break the rules to win. At other times, Lee said I needed to wear a white hat. When to wear which hat was not clear.

Preseason, my assistant coaches made me aware of many talented black athletes who did *not* play football. I visited them and sat on their porches and in their living rooms, listening to their concerns and complaints: Namely, white coaches were not fair to black players. I assured them I would be fair and asked them to give me a chance. Several joined the team.

We struggled that first season. Although we had talent, the players were accustomed to losing. If we fell behind, they gave up. Also, my white leaders fueled the flames of dissension. My quarterback Mac was a tall, strong-armed, white athlete. He consistently refused to pass to black receivers. He did not like black players, did not like playing with them, and certainly would not befriend them. Even though Mac was my best quarterback, I made the decision to start Bill, the second-team quarterback. Bill was 5 foot 7, rather pudgy, slow, and hampered by two arthritic knees. Bill, also white, was a strong leader and a winner. By and by, Mac quit the team, and many of our problems disappeared.

The school had severe racial and discipline problems and was a hotbed of tension and strife. These good ol' boys and Southern belles had another side. Every day there was a fight on campus. I soon learned the art of breaking up a fight without getting punched. *Doo-dah! Doo-dah-day!*

One lunch hour, I saw students rushing towards an obvious squabble. A circle formed around two plus-sized black girls, the crowd encouraging them to fight. I ran toward the fray, but the students made every attempt to prevent me from interfering. I finally worked my way inside the circle. The girls were punching, scratching, and kicking each other. I got between them and held them at arm's length. One girl reached across my body and grabbed the other girl's blouse. In a jerk worthy of athletic praise, the girl with an impressive range of motion ripped the blouse and bra off the other girl. The crowd cheered.

Nude from the waist up, the mortified girl grabbed my arm and held it in front of her humongous breasts. The crowd roared. I stood between them, my arms outstretched, holding the girls apart but baffled as to how to proceed. I decided to remove my coat to cover the half-naked girl. The crowd loved the show: the girls struggling to get free and do harm, me wiggling out of my jacket, my awkward maneuvering to drape said jacket over the exposed heaving breasts — not to mention *my* embarrassment. Somehow and finally, I managed to march the young *ladies* to the principal who, of course, had locked himself in his office.

Early in the season, I noticed several cars coming down our winding dirt driveway to our house. About thirty blacks emerged from the cars, carrying signs that conveyed their purpose: "Fire Sypult."

Two black fathers, madder than two wet hens, knocked on my door. I invited them in. Bob King, the new basketball coach forewarned about the visit, arrived soon after. I invited him in as well. Bob, a 7-foot-something white man, had played basketball at Virginia Tech. He had been known to carry a revolver inside his coat and was at the ready.

Meanwhile, I looked outside, and my wife was serving freshly baked chocolate-chip cookies to the crowd amassed in our front yard. Never underestimate the power of chocolate-chip cookies.

We had two running backs on the team — one white and one black. The white running back had more ball carries than the black one, according to the fathers. They said I was unfair. I explained I was unaware of the count and certainly didn't care who ran the ball. I called plays designed to defeat the opponent. Further, I was the coach, and I was fair. The parents' role was to support the team and serve as good examples to their sons. I stood up, ending the meeting.

I'm pretty sure they saw Bob's revolver when he stood with his coat unbuttoned. The fathers stood, shook my hand, and left. The crowd dispersed and disappeared in a trail of dust.

I survived the first year of daily confrontations, hatred, and racial tensions. My second year, we racked up seven wins. Winning promoted school spirit and alleviated the barriers of mistrust and violence that dozed like a dormant volcano.

At the end of year two, the seniors and faculty advisors were practicing graduation exercises inside the gym. I was teaching American history in a classroom attached to the gym. I heard a loud commotion and opened the door to investigate.

Something *funny,* as in *frightful,* was going on all right. Some white students had unfolded a huge Confederate flag during the rehearsal. A disturbing, hair-raising race riot and mayhem ensued. State and local police surrounded the campus. Fire trucks and ambulances arrived to treat the wounded. Helicopters hovered overhead. Several students and teachers were carried out on stretchers, many seriously injured.

Clearly, it was time to move on. *Oh, doo-dah-day!*

3

ASSISTANT COACH IN COLLEGE
1973-1991

Wah, Wah, Wah

THERE'S A SAYING IN COACHING: "You might lose them all. You might win them all. And in all probability, you will be fired."

In 1974, Coach Bill Peck offered me an opportunity to coach college football at Middle Tennessee State University in Murfreesboro, Tennessee. Coach Peck was an ex-paratrooper in World War II. He dropped out of high school to serve his country. After the war, he graduated from college, entered the coaching ranks, and became the head coach at MTSU. A native of New Jersey, Peck smoked a big cigar and was tough. He spoke with a strong Jersey accent, and Southerners viewed him as a *Yankee*.

My coaching friends warned me: "You'll be stepping into the frying pan." Coach Peck was not popular, they said, and would soon be fired.

During my interview, I asked Coach Peck about the firing rumors. "Good question, Jim," he growled in his scratchy voice. "Let's ask the president of the university that question." Peck wanted to hear the top dog's answer. I did too.

The president of MTSU was a tall man with a flattop, a daring hairdo for a university president. His hair was red, and his name was Scarlett, Mel Scarlett. I dared to ask him about being fired.

"Young man," Scarlett said, "there are two people at this university who will *never* be fired: Coach Peck and me."

I trusted the president's words and signed up as the defensive back coach. Did I say I was young?

Our opening game was against Tennessee State University in Nashville. The Tigers had won the Black College National Championship the previous year. It was their fifth straight championship.

The contest was played at Vanderbilt University in Nashville. TSU was a predominantly black school, and it seemed every black in

Nashville attended the game to see their homeboys put a beating on our mostly white guys.

During our warmups, the Tennessee State players emerged from their tunnel in single file. They walked completely around our team, trying to intimidate us, while pointing their index fingers skyward, chanting: *AP! UPI! No.1!*

The high-stepping Tiger marching band, touted as the "Aristocrat of Bands," started a drumbeat: *Boom, boom, boom! Boom, boom, boom!* Their majorettes shimmered in tiny, shiny outfits. Band members swayed and danced in unison in the stands. The huge horn section blared. *Oom-pah!* The music was funky, and the beat, strong. *Pow-chicka-wow-wow!*

Their players walked from our end zone to theirs and formed two lines from the goal to the fifty-yard line. Each player faced a partner five yards apart. The smallest players, small by comparison, stood in the end zone. As the lines extended to midfield, the players grew in size and weight. The lines ended with two ginormous players: 6 feet 9 inches or more and 300-plus pounds.

Rat-a-tat-tat, rat-a-tat-tat! beat the snare drums. *Boom, boom, boom! Boom, boom, boom!* resounded the base drums. *Swish, swish, swish!* went the cymbals.

After a well-planned pause, their two smallest but not-small players retreated five yards. Another pause. *Rat-a-tat-tat! Rat-a-tat-tat!* Then they sprinted directly at one another. *Boom, boom, boom!* In reckless abandon, they met head on, smashing into each other. *Kaboom! Oom-pah!*

The next two players in line took their turn. They slowly retreated five yards, paused, and then charged headlong toward each other. *Kaboom! Oom-pah!* These head-on collisions continued up the line to the next two and the next and next. *Kaboom, kaboom, kaboom! Oom-pah!*

The drums continued to beat. *Boom, boom, boom!* The crowd rose to their feet. *Rat-a-tat-tat!* Our players stopped stretching and started watching the spectacle unfold.

As the smashing sequence continued, the players got bigger, the retreat further, the collisions more violent, and the drums louder. *Boom-chicka, boom-chicka, boom-chicka, boom, boom!*

The crowd hooted, hollered, and whooped, the noise

deafening: *aahhhhh*!

Finally, at midfield, their two largest players stood facing each other. They retreated to the opposite sides of the field, fifty-three and one-third yards apart. They paused, poised for the final hit. The crowd roared and danced in the aisles, crazy in anticipation of a humongous collision in the middle of the field.

Finally, after a spellbinding minute pause, these two huge players sprinted toward each other, picking up speed and running full force. *Boom, boom, boom*! pounded the drums. *Rat-a-tat-tat! Swish, swish! Boom, bang, boom!*

All of a sudden, these two massive forces barreling toward each like two snorting, charging bulls came to an abrupt *stop* ... stopping *inches* from each other. *Inches*. The fans fell silent as if in a trance — breathless, waiting, watching, hushed.

Slowly, ever so slowly, one of the giants raised his arm, and with his index finger, he poked the other in the chest. *Pause*. The other, a huge lineman, fell to his knees and collapsed on his back, subdued by a one-finger tap.

Wah, wah! wailed the trombone. *Wah, wah, wah*!

The crowd erupted into uncontrolled excitement and wild behavior. And the funk band broke into the Tiger fight song. It was a spectacle, circus, and Hollywood production rolled into one. Even I wanted to cheer and join the party.

Much to my surprise, our opponent's pregame show not only energized the TSU contingency, but our players as well! We were not intimidated. We played an outstanding game that night, and we upset the No. 1 team in the country: 20 to 10.

Jim with his wife and daughter at MTSU: "As an assistant, I learned how not to act as a head coach and what is important: faith, family, and football—in that order."

At this point, we might win them all; we couldn't lose them all; and our chances of getting fired diminished. The frying pan cooled considerably.

Alack and alas! We lost eight of our next ten games. The frying pan got hotter with each loss. At season's end, Coach Peck and the entire football staff got fired. Some time later, President Scarlett with the red hair got fired.

Wah, wah, wah!

Ben and *Mad Dog* Melvin

I worked for seven very different head coaches. Some were smart, experienced, and professional; others, not so much. Almost all had enormous egos. One was an alcoholic; one, a bully; and one, a womanizer. The womanizer was a Harvard graduate, and among other misdeeds, he invited his wife *and* his girlfriend to the same staff party.

As an assistant, I learned to follow orders of the head coach who in some cases qualified as a genuine idiot. I also learned how to be me and no one else — even though I always wanted to be like Vince Lombardi and Bear Bryant. Most importantly, I learned how *not* to act when I became a head coach.

In 1974, I was hired at Middle Tennessee State University and fired at season's end, along with the entire football staff. When a head coach is fired, usually the entire staff is fired.

The athletic director hired Ben Hurt, one of his former MTSU players, as the new head coach. Ben had coached at the University of Houston and Texas A&M. He referenced every play, decision, and conversation with "When I was at Houston and Texas A&M ...." It was a reference made so often, we assistants referred to our school as *Middle Houston A&M.*

Ben had coached with Melvin *Mad Dog* Robertson, his best friend, who was considered one of the finest defensive minds in college football. Ben's proof of anything began with "Well, Melvin said ...." With that opening, the argument ended. Ben never experienced an original thought in his life and only knew what Melvin knew.

My head was on the chopping block. Members of the previous staff competed for the two open coaching positions. It was dog-eat-dog and uncomfortable competing with my coworkers and friends. It was also demeaning. Ben made me carry his briefcase to his car every night after work, his unwritten rule and head-coach perk — probably learned from Melvin.

"I had to do this for the head coach when I was an assistant," Ben said, "and now you'll have to do this for me." For the record, I never asked any of my assistants to carry my briefcase ... even though they always offered to do something for me.

I became a holdover from the previous staff and was not fully trusted by Ben. On the practice field, I could never please him. He never told me how to coach my position, but at the end of every practice, he would say, "If Melvin knew you were coaching like that, he would turn over in his grave." Melvin hadn't died yet. Would I ever say as much? Not a dog's chance in hell.

It was a dog's life. To rid my frustrations, I pounded a heavyweight punching bag or ran around the track after practice until I was exhausted.

Who the hell was this Melvin? I didn't even know what he looked like, but he was dogging my life.

The best cure of what ailed me was to have more of the same: *the hair of the dog that bit me.* I told Ben if he wanted me to coach like Melvin, he should send me to Texas A&M so I could learn from Melvin.

So he did. I flew to Dallas and then took a twin-engine propeller plane across the desert and rolling tumbleweed to College Station, Texas. I landed in lush greenery, an oasis and home of Texas A&M and *Mad Dog* Robertson.

Melvin was scheduled to meet me at the airport. I departed the plane and saw no one except a janitor: a short, skinny, one-eyed man with a shirt open to his belly button. A huge medallion with the state of Texas hung around his neck, and a gigantic Aggie-steer belt buckle clinched his baggy man jeans. Turns out, he wasn't a janitor after all; he was Melvin!

Melvin silently drove me to the football facility housed in a high-rise. The elevators opened into a huge room with no furniture, but the floors, walls, and ceiling were covered with plush white carpet. At the end of the room sat a tall, beautiful blonde secretary dressed in white at a white desk. Behind her on the wall was the maroon Texas A&M logo. It seemed an Aggie heaven.

We entered the offices, and Melvin introduced me to no one. He locked the door to his office and spoke for the first time. "Don't talk to any of those coaches you just saw. They don't know *shit.*"

Melvin went straight to work. He started diagramming and draw-ing defenses on the whiteboard. I sat facing him writing everything down at a feverish pace. Melvin cursed at least once in every sentence. His favorite word was *fuck*. His second favorite was *goddamn*. He used these words as interjections and nouns, verbs, adverbs, and adjectives.

He pounded the whiteboard with his fists. Forearmed it. Pelted it with chalk. Spit formed on his lips. His good eye opened wide; his glass eye too. Suffice to say, he was animated.

I had just traveled two thousand miles to meet with this man. I hadn't eaten in a dog's age and didn't eat for another five hours. Finally, at the hotel, I ate something, but I did not sleep as Melvin left me with a projector and an armload of game tapes. I stayed up all night taking notes and writing down questions.

The next day, Melvin lectured another six hours on his techniques and defensive strategy. Remember, this was one-on-one teaching with one of the finest defensive minds in the country. Melvin was an exceptional football strategist giving me, a pup, individual instruction.

We met with the players first and then went to practice. Melvin stormed into the room and demanded every player's attention. He bared his teeth, growled, and barked his commands. They sat straight in their chairs, doglike, with both feet on the floor. Melvin looked like Willie Nelson, but he commanded like General George Patton.

On the field, it was more of the same. Melvin coached every player. He saw everything. He stayed on the move for three hours. Incidentally, he had ordered all of his *don't-know-shit* assistants to the sideline. Apparently, he did not trust or respect the coaches he hired to help him. The only coach on the field was Melvin. He invited me to join him. I felt privileged.

"Have the courage to ask, the courage to be refused, and the courage to be grateful."

Before I departed for home, Melvin took me into his office and again locked the door. He got out his keys and unlocked his desk. "Don't tell anyone what you are about to see," he said. He opened a drawer that held the defensive playbooks of every NFL team. Melvin apparently did not share information, and he was paranoid that others would reveal his secrets.

Mad Dog Melvin was also consumed with a single passion: defensive football. "I don't fish. I don't play golf. I don't go out with my wife," Melvin said. "I stay home and study every one of these books."

I returned to Middle Tennessee State with the power of Melvin's knowledge. Ben did whatever he did because Melvin did it — no other reason. Whenever Ben asked me why I was coaching something on the field, my answer began with a standard, "Melvin said ...." *The hair of the dog!*

Soon thereafter, Ben promoted me to defensive coordinator. Why? Because "Melvin said."

Off-kilter

It was the inaugural meeting of the new head coach with our staff. We sat in the room anticipating his opening remarks and vision for the football program. His name: Dave Fagg. His definitive name: a cross to bear.

"Let me tell you about my Lord and Savior" were Fagg's opening words. He began a witness for his newfound faith in Christianity. "How would you like to have goddamn rusty nails driven into your hands and feet?"

"This is gonna be different!" one of my coaching buddies whispered to me.

Minutes later in the same speech, Fagg suddenly blurted, "All women are sluts!" He paused before adding, "Hell, my wife is a slut!"

Off-kilter, I thought. I wondered what he thought of Mary, mother of Jesus.

This *devout* guy was a bully and an intimidator. When he was challenged (often by me), he exploded, threw a chair against the wall, and stormed out of the room. He never apologized or showed remorse. The next meeting, he acted as if nothing had happened and continued with business. No trace of religious leanings.

After one loss, Fagg put the game tape on the conference table. He then threatened the staff by saying we were going to view the tape and explain to him why the team played so poorly. It sat on the table for an entire week. The Friday before the game with the next opponent, Fagg played the tape and demanded we explain ourselves. It was nerve-racking and demeaning. Each week, I wasn't sure who the enemy was — our next opponent or our head coach.

Time to pray.

We worked ungodly hours. Fagg demanded we stay late and into the early morning working on the game plan. It was *not* unusual to prepare until 3 a.m. Even if the game plan was completed and finalized, he kept us in the football offices. He wanted to give the impression of a hardworking staff. Most people were asleep and oblivious to our after-midnight vigils. Generally, Fagg left the office early and never returned. We couldn't be sure if he would come back, so we stayed.

One of my associates bet even Lou Holtz, the head coach of Notre Dame at the time, wasn't working at that hour of the morning. I said, "Why don't you call and find out?"

Fagg made the call. "Lou Holtz, Notre Dame football" was the response. So working in the wee hours became our norm.

Based on experience and observation, I concluded the bizarre behavior of some of these head coaches was due to the circumstances of their previous employment. I investigated the coaching tree of my boss. He had been an assistant in a big-time program that was somewhat successful. His boss was very demanding and also a bully. His boss's boss was a very successful coach in the NFL and a Super Bowl winner. He too was a bully and had a reputation for working ridiculous hours. We learn from our leaders and often become whatever we experience. It's like an abused child becoming an abusive parent.

I worked for a head coach by the name of Ben Hurt who on occasion referred to himself as *Ben-Hur,* the Jewish character in the movie. Ben was not a Jew. He had never been a head coach before, but he held the golden ticket: He played college football for the athletic director who was choosing the new head coach. Holy Moses!

Hurt was a perfect example of the Peter Principle. He had been a loyal and good, if not great, assistant. Then he became a head coach and was terrible. He now had to make decisions that affected the entire team. He did not have the intellect or skill to perform these duties.

He relied on poor advice from his friends who had little knowledge of our situation.

Hurt wanted to have a reputation as a disciplinarian. His approach, however, was preposterous. For example, he banned all facial hair. Braids were popular with our black players, but Hurt set limitations as to the length of the braids. Assistant coaches were even required to measure the length from time to time. Awkward. No such rule was applied to Caucasian players with long hair. Racist.

In addition, Hurt banned cursing in the locker room and on the field. On the first day of camp and installation of the *no-cursing* rule, John Pyle, an imposing player, walked into the team meeting. John was 6 foot 9 and easily spotted. He sported a trim and very thin mustache. It caught the eye of the head coach.

"*Fuck*, John Pyle," Hurt said. "You chap my *ass*." The cursing rule ended before it began.

On another occasion, one of our better players, George, kicked in the team cafeteria door because it was locked; he then physically assaulted a graduate-assistant coach. I recommended the player be suspended from the team. Hurt was furious with me for making such a suggestion. No matter. The school expelled the student-athlete. The heartbroken head coach tearfully presented George a game ball before he left. Crazy!

Hurt wanted to win ASAP. He was advised to cut scholarships of players who were recruited by the previous staff and failed to help our team win immediately. Hurt cut fifteen scholarships. Most of these players were local. The papers slammed us. The high schools banned us from recruiting at their schools. We were forced to recruit out-of-state and junior college players. The decision to withdraw these scholarships hurt us greatly and prevented us from building a solid program. We all got fired after four years. No surprise there.

At Davidson College, I worked for a head coach named Vic Gatto. Gatto, a Harvard grad, was hired by a rookie athletic director and Yale grad who tried to impress everyone with Ivy League ties. Harvard and Yale backgrounds added prestige to our school's reputation. Supposedly.

When the Harvard man arrived on campus, he held our first staff meeting. His very first order of business was to organize a book club. *A book club!* We had the longest losing streak in the country, and we were forming a book club! Welcome to the Ivy Leagues.

This guy was a brazen womanizer. He brought his mistress with him to his new job while his wife stayed home in Boston. Unorthodox. He even slept with his mistress in a house he rented to current players. Unseemly. The players were confused. I was confused. When his wife arrived on campus, it got more confusing. When Gatto brought his wife *and* girlfriend to the same staff party, it was uncomfortable! So much for ethics.

Davidson is a prestigious school with high academic standards, strict rules of conduct, and religious affiliation. Nonetheless, Gatto provided kegs of beer for the players and even brought strippers into the locker room to celebrate birthdays. Not my idea of prestige or seemly behavior.

Gatto required players and coaches to be on a first-name basis. That's one order I refused to follow. I earned and was proud of the title *Coach*. The players did not call me *Jim*. I was *Coach Sy* then, and I'm *Coach Sy* now.

Gatto's undoing, *termination*, was his 4-47 record, not his conduct. Hard to believe.

Over my career, I've come to know some excellent coaches as well as some real oddballs. But, as my father always said, "Some people aren't completely worthless; they can always serve as a bad example." How right he was.

The Land of Gunfighters

"Come in," a disembodied voice said. "The door is unlocked." I entered the hotel room, prepared for the meeting but not the *greeting*.

"Pull up a chair, and sit down." So I did.

I looked down at Jim Tait, the head coach of the University of Richmond, lying on a king-size bed. He was *au naturel*, in his altogether — to be blunt, *butt naked!* His body was hairless and pink, nothing to brag about, with a bulging ... belly. It was not my call to ask about his birthday suit, and he never brought it up. The situation was strange and disturbing, and his nakedness, an image I can't unsee.

My interview began.

College football coaching is a perilous and insecure profession. A coach can be fired at a moment's notice. If a team is not satisfying administrators or alumni, a coach can be on the firing block. Often circumstances beyond the coach's control, such as injuries to key players, can determine his fate. It has been said, "It's not *if* you're going to be fired, but *when*." It's also been said coaches are the last gunfighters of the Wild West because of the danger, risks, and nature of the profession.

Job hunting is a constant pursuit. Some coaches start hunting for another job the moment they are hired for a new one. There's even a website called *footballscoop.com* devoted to hirings, firings, openings, and rumors about changes in the coaching ranks. College coaches check this site religiously.

As for interviews, coaches are completely exposed: their careers, examined; knowledge, scrutinized; and body of work, laid bare. They're naked before an athletic director, coach, or committee deciding their fate.

Speaking of which, the naked-coach encounter took place in San Francisco at the American Football Coaches Association Convention. Coach Tait had a position open. I secured an interview with him late in the night — actually early, early morning — as he was preoccupied until then. I can only imagine how. Despite the weird situation, the interview went well, and Coach Tait invited me to visit his campus.

A few days later, I interviewed before the whole football staff. They were all fully clothed as was I. I talked at length about coaching the defensive backs — the open position and my expertise. Coach Tait seemed pleased and asked me to discuss the entire defense. I felt negative vibes from the staff as I continued to talk.

After an hour and more of my coaching gems, Coach Tait asked Boots, one of his assistant coaches, to show me around campus. We jumped in Boots' new-smelling courtesy car with deep, leather seats — a perk supplied by some devoted car dealer.

"If you get the job as defensive coordinator," Boots said, "I'm quitting!"

I was taken aback by the comment and lost all confidence in getting the job.

After the campus tour, Boots delivered me to Coach Tait. There and then, Coach Tait offered me the job!

I thought, *Well, goodbye Boots.*

Then, Coach Tait got very serious and proceeded to give me the lowdown. "The job is yours, Jim, but I have to be honest with you ...

I'm getting fired next year."

I didn't take that job, and Boots didn't have to quit after all.

Later, I secured an interview with Bob Talman, head coach at Virginia Military Institute. I flew to Roanoke, Virginia, in bad weather. As we were about to touch down, the plane suddenly aborted the landing due to fog and low visibility. We were rerouted to Charleston, West Virginia, and then I was sent back home. Was this rerouting an omen? Was I superstitious? Do I live and breathe football?

The following week my interview was rescheduled. I arrived in Lexington, Virginia, and had a positive interview with Coach Talman and his staff. I was housed with an assistant coach's family on campus — probably to save VMI money.

My sleeping arrangement was less than desirable as I shared a room with his two-year-old child in a crib. Unable to sleep, I decided to take a walk on campus. As I approached the cadet dorm, a sentry greeted me with rifle at the ready!

"Halt! Who goes there?" he asked.

My feet stopped dead in my shoes.

"Identify yourself!"

At that very moment, I decided I would not be joining the school Robert E. Lee and Stonewall Jackson made famous. A strict military school with young people carrying guns was not for me.

I had other interviews with equally bizarre twists. One time I was offered a job that required me to bend the rules; I'm not a rule-bender. I was offered another job *three* times by the same head coach who withdrew each offer a few days later. And I interviewed for a head coaching position at three different Baptist colleges. The selection committee at each posed classic Baptist questions: *Could I preach in the pulpit? Could I raise money? Do I drink whiskey?*

I learned a lot while hunting for jobs and undergoing interviews. I was on display, in the line of fire, and stripped of human dignity at times. Sure, peculiar personalities, perils, and oddities came my way. But the values and football programs of various coaches — good and bad — helped me hone my own. Along the way, I gathered sound football strategies (ammunition), sharpened my problem-solving (six-shooter skills), and mustered a mountain of courage to confront the inevitable exposures and instabilities that come in the untamed territory of coaching.

That's how I survived in the land of gunfighters.

4

AMERICAN FOOTBALL IN ITALY/PRO HEAD COACH
1986 and 1988

The Italian Way

I N 1985, AN ENVELOPE addressed *Davidson College Football* appeared on my desk. That envelope that came to me by chance changed my trajectory dramatically and thrust me toward two enriching years abroad.

The letter was from Fabio, a young coach in Bologna, Italy, with a professional football team called the Towers. Fabio was requesting permission to visit our preseason camp to learn more about the American game. I thought his request intriguing and extended an invitation.

In Italy, soccer is called *football*, and, on occasion and in jest, I had called soccer *a communist sport*. Let me be clear here: Most of the Towers were communists, communists playing American football. Seriously!

Despite a language barrier, Fabio and I communicated about football on a whiteboard. I learned about American football in Italy, and he learned some English. At the end of camp, I expressed my interest in coaching in Italy. Its art, architecture, and food called to me.

The next summer, Fabio contacted me and offered me the head football coaching position of the Bologna Towers — with one condition: I hire him as my assistant. I agreed.

I got a six-month leave of absence from Davidson College and secured a contract from the Bologna Towers. Two days after our final college game, I left the United States with my wife and daughter for a remarkable experience. *Experience* is a word I give my adventures, the awesome and the awful.

We flew Yugoslavia Air to Belgrade, Serbia, to catch a flight to Milan. Very young customs officials armed with M-14 automatic rifles greeted us. With steely eyes, they inspected our passports and luggage in a brisk, unnerving manner. Finally, time inching forward, they escorted us to our plane and allowed us to leave. We barely made our connection to Milan but felt relief as if released by the Gestapo.

Fabio and Massimo (our public relations director) met us at the airport. What should have been a four-hour drive to San Lazzaro took only two as Massimo drove like Mario Andretti. Lightning speed on open highways and in cities, danger at every curve, seemed the mode of the Italians we came to know.

Silvia Bentivoglio, the team owner, and Coach Sy, touring the landmark Towers of Bologna, Italy.

San Lazzaro, a suburb not far from central Bologna, held our new home, a furnished apartment and tiny refrigerator with a freezer that iced up weekly. Tired and weary after twenty or so hours of travel, we were whisked to dinner at an elegant restaurant named Elle 70 Bar. A seven-course meal with the team's administration followed, fruit being the last course. The meal ended with a disagreeable *grappa* which Italians sip but I knocked back quickly like medicine. Day became night became day, and we finally got to sleep until we woke. Time lost all meaning.

Bologna has three nicknames: the *Learned One* for the University of Bologna, the oldest university in the world; the *Red One* for its red-tile roofs and now 60 percent communist population; and the *Fat*

One or *la grassa* for its famous cuisine featuring *ragu alla Bolognese* and tortellini and tortelloni. I ate all of Bologna's signature pasta that first night and earned a nickname: *la grande forchetta.* Translation: *the great fork.*

At the meal was the team's owner, Silvia Bentivoglio. Silvia was an attractive woman in her early twenties who wore red, purple, and blue fur coats — whatever fashion was fashionable. I couldn't tell how attractive she really was as her heavy makeup covered blemishes, imperfections, and her real face. Silvia and most Italian women looked glamorous from a distance because of excessive makeup and stylish clothes.

Silvia's family ruled Bologna for centuries. It was reported her bedroom ceilings contained paintings from the Renaissance. To me, she was notorious for walking into the team's locker room unannounced. She served as the team trainer as well. I can still see her massaging a player's strained groin with his pants around his ankles.

The team president also suspended Silvia for two weeks when she provided whisky to the players on the team bus after a game. I later learned she and Fabio had once been lovers. That relationship had a nasty ending, and they were now mortal enemies. Fabio was probably the one who blabbed about the paintings on Silvia's bedroom ceilings.

A word about Fabio: We soon learned he lied a lot and was incompetent. He had a terrible relationship with Silvia who refused to raise his salary. He threatened to quit; I convinced him to stay. He had made a commitment to me, and he was my only contact with the team. He stayed but was not happy.

When Fabio lied, he stuttered badly and forgot English. I dealt with his quirks because I had no recourse. I couldn't believe a word he said. He reminded me of the Italian version of Pinocchio — a Venetian mask with the long nose worn at *Carnevale.* When we Americans heard any stretch of truth, we called it *a Fabio.*

Fabio was our translator in a city where few spoke English. Whenever he interpreted my words to the team, organization, or press, I wondered if he even understood what I said. I suspected his translations were often more what he thought than what I said.

Any request we made to the team for assistance most often received the same response: *subito* which means *immediately.* To the Italians, *subito* meant *in a month or so.* They would also shrug their shoulders and dismiss the most inexplicable behavior with "That's the Italian way."

At my first practice, my new team presented me an armful of long-stemmed gladioli and called me *Coach Grande*. I was pleased with the name though uneasy about earning such a title, considering. They applauded my effort to speak to them with the few Italian words I knew and hand motions that came naturally and spontaneously. Italians usually speak with their hands as much as with words. As if by osmosis, I became one of them. I knew some Italian curse words and hand motions that I couldn't use, of course.

My players were eager but decidedly bad football players. This group of young men, ranging in age from sixteen to thirty-seven, had suffered through a 2-12 record the previous season. And one team, the Grizzlies of Rome, had trounced them 82-0. Remember, that's a football score, not basketball.

I studied tapes of previous games and concluded we needed to develop fundamentals and eliminate mistakes to give our team any chance to win. I drew up a two-hour practice plan that would address our problems. I was determined to execute each segment perfectly before moving to the next. At our first practice, it took two hours to get my team in a straight line for calisthenics.

Italians have no concept of a line. When arriving at a stoplight in a single lane, four or more cars would crowd side by side waiting for a green light.

I also learned a stoplight in Italy didn't mean *stop*; it meant *slow down*.

Could I, by chance, turn this team around and win?

Emboldened by many bottles of Chianti, I could ... and I did.

Pioneer in Football

Few American football coaches go to Italy to coach foot-ball — *American football,* not soccer. In 1986, I did. In 1988, I did it again, this time leaving my American coaching job permanently ... and so I thought.

Italian football began in 1979 in Bologna, Italy, and had grown in popularity. The skill of the Italians had improved gradually because of the influence of American players and coaches in the young Ital-ian League.

I was *Coach Grande, the great one,* to my Italian players and a *master strategist* to the Italian press. Newspaper, radio, and television coverage was heavy. In truth, I felt like a pioneer in football.

The entire experience was paradoxical. While my dream to travel became a reality, I struggled with the language barrier and longed for conversation beyond *Good day!* and *How are you?*

I enjoyed the long meals and what the Italians called *midday rests* and contended with the no-lane, hectic traffic and explosive tempers. I loved the inexperienced but eager players, traditional family gatherings, and warm friendships but suffered with the team's disorganization and absurdities of League decisions.

One year we won and went to the playoffs; another, we lost and went to the play-outs. It was the best and worst of times admittedly, and I'd do it all again.

Andrea Tugnoli: "Together with my family and great friends. There are no skinny people at my house." Note the jumbo portions of lasagna.

The Bologna Towers

Our Club, the Bologna Towers, was economizing and flew us from New York to communist Belgrade. In Belgrade, we stared into the barrels of machine guns, pled for our luggage to be sent with us on the connecting flight, not a later one, and hastily boarded our flight to Milan where we were greeted by more guards holding guns.

We were then transported to Bologna, a city of five hundred thousand, via a caravan of cars driven by animated players who spoke very little English but used hand signals quite well to convey their feelings.

At least they were unarmed.

We were given a modest apartment lacking only in modern conveniences — namely heat. Heat was centrally controlled by a landlord who begrudged every raised degree in temperature.

The Bolognese survive the cold by wearing multi-colored fur coats and by staying in bed in the winter. They survive the summers by wearing little clothing and staying in bed.

1986 was one of Europe's coldest winters of the century, and Bologna was as cold as Buffalo, New York. We adapted and survived the coughing, shivers, bedsores, and something the Italians called the *febber*.

We had a miniature refrigerator that barely chilled foods and after a lengthy search found ice cube trays in a *plasticeria* (plastic shop). In a mere fifteen hours, ice the size of sugar cubes in heart-and-star shapes could be had, but an entire tray scarcely filled a glass.

We also had a washing machine constructed during Mussolini's reign. It washed clothes in two hours flat and turned our white clothes gray. Our clothes dryer was typically Italian — plenty of balcony space for clotheslines. We had a commode without a lid and shower without

American players Kevin Johnson (Concord College) and Jeff Wiley (Holy Cross) with Coach Sy, walking the Cinque Terre.

a curtain. And we had a bidet; I washed my socks in it.

We settled into the lifestyle and prepared for the season.

Players

Our two American players — each team was allowed two — finally joined us. They were a welcome sight and sound. I had been without English-speaking male companions for two months, and I talked them into submission.

The League dictated the American positions with constant rule changes. First, American quarterbacks were not allowed; then they were but with only one American in the game. Finally, both Americans could play at the same time, but neither could be a quarterback.

The arrival of the American coach and players was critical to practice attendance. These were the *only* times *every* squad member attended practice. Curiosity was the motivation. Since lack of attendance was a major problem, I planned lengthy and arduous workouts for these two occasions.

Italians are not paid to play American football, and they quickly emphasized that football was a hobby, not a livelihood. On the other hand, the Italians were grateful for their paid American teammates who played both offense and defense and who often had to run and pass without blocking and tackle without assistance.

The Italians were highly critical of the American players as well. In fact, Americans were immortalized in victory and ostracized in defeat. When the team won, everyone partied. When the team lost, the Americans lost. Who said football was a team sport?

Practices

Practice was always eventful. Upon my introduction to the team, I was given a huge arrangement of long-stemmed gladioli. Six months later, I learned the Club had economized again. These flowers had originally been a gift from one owner's family to another in honor of a wedding anniversary. Well, needless to say, a huge argument between the two families ensued. Before I even began my coaching duties, there was dissension. I didn't even want the flowers.

Our first practice was a nightmare. We engaged in a demanding Oklahoma drill: run, block, and tackle. The Italians pushed, pulled, shoved, slid, stood up, fell down, crumbled, cried, cried, and died.

Okay, they lacked toughness and a few fundamentals.

The first lesson I taught was that contact might be painful. The players got hit and writhed on the ground and wailed to the heavens. They received immediate attention from teammates, coaches, and managers and got carried from battle with wounds unbeknownst to me or anyone. Then, within minutes, they pranced into action, miraculously healed.

The first lesson I learned was that this curious behavior was a cultural phenomenon and direct link to soccer. When a player appeared severely injured on the soccer field, a hush settled over the stadium. Doctors and trainers ran to the motionless or writhing-in-pain athlete. Eventually, the player rose, limped one way or other, and then burst like a deer toward the game action. I ridiculed my players for similar behavior. Nothing worked.

Finally, I made a rule: If a player got hurt and left the field, he could not return. This rule worked.

I was also very diplomatic when correcting and criticizing. In Italy, there was no simple *Yes, sir* or *No, sir*. The replay was a debate. The player explained his actions, drew conclusions, and philosophized. Had I attacked his family, heritage, culture, or manhood? Translations of the simplest kind took fifteen minutes. All this for stepping with the wrong foot?

We practiced at night on a hard, dirt field covered with gravel that ripped the flesh. We had one light for illumination. Drills started in safely spaced groups. However, the players eventually converged into a small area, blindsiding each other, coming closer and closer toward that single ray of light, creating one blind collision after another.

The field was located on church property, and when the priest went to bed, he turned off our light. Our practices began at 9 p.m. after a soccer team held practice, and the priest, an early riser, was anything but sympathetic to us or our odd-shaped ball and American game.

Fortunately, we later moved to a fully lit and grassed facility. Unfortunately, the sidelines were unmowed, and the grass was six feet tall. Every stray pass and shanked punt created long delays as players searched for lost balls.

On one occasion, our defensive end (an avid soccer fan named Andrea who organized pre-practice soccer matches) discovered that a teammate had playfully kicked his soccer ball into the tall grass. He left the field to hunt his ball during a defensive drill. We urged him to return. He cursed us. We told him there weren't enough players to continue without him. He cursed us some more. We promised to help him in his search after practice; he returned.

Imagine this, football fans: a football coach searching for a soccer ball at midnight in chest-high grass. I did some cursing of my own.

We never started practice promptly if a soccer match was televised, as our players trickled in only after the outcome had been safely determined. Even on game day, the players followed the play-by-play of soccer matches as radios blared on the sidelines and in the locker room.

Organizing practice frustrated me. It was a continuous improvisation. I would schedule a defensive drill but have only five defensive players in attendance. If we had a greater number of offensive players, we practiced offense. If the kicker appeared, we kicked.

I insisted on attendance and intensity. I developed one comprehensive practice plan: We began with every basic fundamental and advanced to all offensive plays, defensive schemes, and kicking situations and to every game tactic and strategy. In our two-hour time frame, we completed only one quarter of the plan. Gradually, we progressed to one-half and then three-fourths. At the season's end, we completed all in less than an hour! I sensed improvement.

Locker Room and Nudity

The locker room was like a scene in an X-rated movie. Players stripped before mom, wife, and sweetheart. Moreover, most players undressed in the hall or outside because the locker room was so small.

Seemingly oblivious to the various degrees of nakedness, our female owner, friends, and family strolled in and out patting backs and chatting nonchalantly. Players yelled for someone to *close the door* to curtail drafts but not the flowing tide of fans and not from any sense of decorum or modesty.

The two American players were very uncomfortable with this arrangement, to say the least. As a matter of good taste, however, the Italians always donned robes to walk to and from the shower.

I Had to Learn Italian

Teaching football in a foreign language was far from easy. Two assistants — an Italian and an American — served as translators.

Locating them for assistance wasn't easy either. They often engaged in gossip with uninvolved players or spectators or discussed team business with management. It was difficult to seize the moment.

What I said wasn't what was translated. I could depend on that. Something was always interpreted though ... regardless of comprehension. The Italian translator guessed the intent of my frequent colloquialisms, and the players generally received a different meaning. The American interpreted me verbatim, and the players understood nothing. I *had* to learn Italian.

I once gave a talk about courage and self-preservation. "It was time to make a circle with the wagons," I said. No one could clarify the word *circle*.

"Our opponents had us surrounded like Indians — the poor bastards," I said. The Americans' laughter subsided, but no one could translate *surrounded*, let alone the humor. The Italians were baffled; the Americans were laughing again. I disappeared and hoped someone had heard of John Wayne or seen the movie *Patton*.

Celebrating a win with Italian coaches Toni Manigiafico and Vincent Argondizzo.

Coaches and Fabio

As a matter of fact, my defensive coordinator, Toni Manigiafico, patterned his football philosophy after General Patton. If one of his defensive charges made a mistake or loafed, he would order endless, punishing laps or push-ups. He also had a vicious left hook that got their attention. Nevertheless, the players adored Tony, and we communicated easily with an odd mixture of English, Italian, diagrams, and sign language.

Our Achilles' heel was Fabio, assistant coach, translator, and liaison to the Americans. He spoke excellent English but stammered and stuttered when he lied ... which was often. He quit the team twice, failed at every chore, was negative about any new idea, questioned game decisions, doubted the abilities of the Americans, and was extremely secretive about the operations of the organization. It was his job to make our lives easier.

During my first year, courtesy of my Italian teacher who read the Italian sports pages, I learned my team was on the verge of financial ruin. Even though a collapse would have terminated my stay, Fabio never *mentioned* the situation to me.

When the Italian League finally allowed American quarterbacks to play, it was Fabio who advised me to recruit a linebacker and running back instead — disastrous advice if ever there was any.

After rebuilding the team and securing an adequate sponsor, I agreed to a third year with the Towers. The president and Fabio shook my hand and gave me their word of honor, a valued Italian tradition. Five days before our return to Europe, Fabio telephoned to cancel my contract. Remember that Machiavelli made his home in Italy.

Game Day

The players supplied the hoopla on game day. When we traveled, there was always the suspense of who would miss the autobus. If we played in Rome, an eight-hour ride, we left at four in the morning which increased the odds of losing players. And often players arrived for a game moments before kick-off.

On the trips, the Italians laughed, sang, and screamed. They bashed each other with empty plastic water bottles and played an Italian form of Trivial Pursuit. At rest stops, they threw water bombs, wrestled, and mooned the tourists. They smoked incessantly, and the kicker sipped vino. It was wild but refreshing. They treasured the friendships, camaraderie, and participation. It was the purest form of play. In the midst of it all, the Americans were typically quiet and intense.

We had a capable trainer named Luigi, but the Americans preferred my taping. When the Italians learned of my skill, I was in great demand. They provided me with adhesive and thin electrical tape — expensive and poor in quality — that tested my taping ability and made their limbs look like mended pipes.

The Italians, aged sixteen to thirty-five, played hard and played to win. Although the game was dominated by the Americans, there were some fine Italian players. When a team had a combination of both, it was sure to win.

Officiating often determined the outcome of a game and could have destroyed football in Italy. There were long delays — many games lasted four to five hours — and several times the officials arrived two hours late. Then they called a penalty almost every play and improperly enforced the infraction. In effect, the officials confused everyone, including me.

We had American and Italian crews. The Italian referees spoke little English but always gave a pregame speech emphasizing their intention not to cheat. This claim raised my suspicions slightly.

Women served as line judges on the Italian crews and were easily influenced. On one play, our receiver caught a pass on our sideline that was clearly four yards out-of-bounds. I signaled the pass good, and the uncertain female judge awarded us a successful catch. It was a first for me and served to increase my sideline calling.

I chose to befriend the Italian officials and felt it unsound to question many calls. They heard every criticism, saw every expression, and sensed an attack on their intelligence about our American game. They retaliated with unusual calls like defensive clips, offensive facemasks, and intimidation of opponents with laughter. No joke.

American crews were generally military men stationed in Italy. They communicated better and allowed the game to flow naturally. We still had problems with the enlisted men. Once, when I substituted for an American player, the referee called an illegal substitution infraction on us. He claimed our player had run onto the field with a play and returned to the sideline without participating. We contested his judgment without success, and he lashed back at us: "You college boys ain't going to get away with that."

The rivalry between Northern and Southern Italians was more bitter than anything in the States. When we played the Gladiators and Grizzlies of Rome, the contests resulted in vicious tactics and brawls. In one contest, a Roman linebacker aligned himself fifteen yards from the ball and sprinted full speed into our quarterback before the ball was snapped.

The action was deliberate, flagrant, and cause for expulsion from the game. I appealed to the referee.

"You throw him out," he said. "He'll do the same thing to me!"

The Romans threatened our players with knives and guns and promised to attack us after the game. After one contest, they stalked our players swinging their helmets at us. I gathered my team, retreated to safer ground, and refused to leave the field without a police escort.

It was a bit of a surprise when Fabio said, "They'll kill the police too."

At this point, *the violent world of football* took on a whole new meaning for me.

Absurdities

Meanwhile, absurdities abounded within the organization. For instance, our owner/manager Sylvia, age twenty-two, was grounded for a month by her parents. And Fabio informed me that Mauro, our best receiver, had a severed spine and couldn't play. *A severed spine? He'll never walk again!* I thought. *Probably a chipped disk or something.*

To my surprise, Mauro claimed he could play. Dr. Luigi Venterolli, our team doctor, said he couldn't. The player then signed a release that cleared the team of any liability. Renzo Bissoli, our team president, finally said, "No." The receiver didn't play, and we lost.

The very next day both Luigi and Renzo cleared this severed-spine receiver to play.

Even so, my greatest coaching challenges were ahead. The quarterback, Pierre Luigi, quit the team because another player called him a name. The captain, Claudio, accepted a job that coincided with practice and game time. And the outside linebacker went on vacation in Africa. Young players studied for exams instead of playing games, and others suddenly disappeared for military duty.

Our nose guard, Novello, pled insanity when drafted into the Italian army. He was placed in a military hospital for observation and released from duty just in time because the tests to determine his insanity were positive. Crazy or not, he started for us.

The starting tackle broke his collarbone in a motorcycle accident.

Both defensive corners broke their collarbones in the same game. The soccer buff broke his ankle in a pre-practice soccer match. The kicker kicked with a torn cartilage in his knee. The defensive tackle suffered from lactic acid. One starting guard was mentally depressed. Our star Italian running back bruised his ribs, and I developed kidney stones. At this point, I decided to *pass* more than run.

The Americans were also injured. Our tailback turned green after eating a prosciutto sandwich and missed a game. Then he bruised his hand which blew up like a balloon after every game. The doctors wanted to drain it like a bloodletting. We refused the treatment. Our linebacker twisted his knee and bruised his coccyx. He lifted weights to correct the problem.

Medical care for the Americans was a concern and always a question. "If the Americans were injured and required extensive treatment and rehabilitation," I asked Fabio, "what would the Club do for them?"

"We would send them home," he answered in his monotone Munchken voice. We played on baked dirt in Bologna, red clay in Rome, and coral in Ancona. In Bologna, it was literally three yards and a cloud of dust.

In Ancona, the field resembled cement pavement, so we asked the field management to water the surface. A groundskeeper appeared with a water hose, stood at the fifty-yard line, and created a huge mud hole in the middle of the field.

In Grosseto, we had plush, green grass! Unfortunately, the morning of our game, it drizzled, and we were refused access to the field because a soccer match was to be played there the next day.

We moved to another field — dirt, only eighty-seven yards long, and twenty miles from anything. Five players from the other team hastily lined the field with sawdust using only their eyesight for accuracy. The sidelines were crooked, and the end zones nonexistent. Yes, we played with some very creative field markings.

To complicate matters further, the League kept the teams in constant turmoil with incredible decisions. Although illegal players were discovered, games in which they participated weren't forfeited. Once, a team lodged a protest which allowed them to advance all the way to the Super Bowl final, even though they lost in the quarterfinal and never played another game. The League was young, and their leaders inexperienced.

Daily Frustrations

Other than all that and cigarette smoke everywhere, our cars wouldn't start, the heat was turned off in our apartments, and when the washing machine was on, the electricity went off. While defrosting the refrigerator, my wife stabbed the Freon line with a butcher knife, and I fell from the bathtub and broke the commode with my ribs. The Club suggested we use our balcony to keep the food cold, and a technician took a month to repair the frig.

Despite the mishaps and Fabio, we struggled and agonized over our situation until somehow satisfaction and success came our way.

David Turner, a running back from Davidson College, led the entire Italian League in rushing and was unstoppable. The Italians nicknamed him *Turbo, Turbo* Turner. Rob Younger, a 6 foot 5, 275-pound lineman from East Tennessee State, played linebacker for the first time and opened huge holes for Turner.

Kevin Johnson, an All-American from Concord College in West Virginia, was lionized by his teammates for his heroic efforts. Jeff Wiley, an All-American from Holy Cross, arrived late but made the

team exciting with precision passing.

The Italian players started to perform well too. The quarterback threw short, controlled passes to his receivers. The offensive line learned several blocking patterns and opened holes for the backs. The defense improved. We started to win,

Andrea Tugnoli's reaction to "The Scream" photo: "Coach Sy had the same face when I was trying to block a defensive end."

and then we couldn't lose. We finished second in the League and made the Super Bowl playoffs.

Perks

The Americans became a close family. We partied at incredibly lavish discos, drank strong European beers and excellent local wines, basked in the sun at sidewalk cafes, and stuffed ourselves with pizzas, octopus, squid, eel, tortellini, and foods hard to duplicate or find in the States.

We often traveled to Florence by train and marveled at the Duomo, Uffizi, and incredible art. We celebrated *Carnevale* in Venice, attended Christmas mass at the Vatican, revered St. Francis in Assisi, tread Mt. Etna (an active volcano) in Sicily, witnessed a mugging in Palermo, pondered the mosaics in Ravenna, dodged traffic in Naples, and followed Napoleon's exile to Elba.

We climbed the Acropolis in Athens, explored Knossos in Crete, hopped the Dalmatian Islands, skied the Alps in Kitzbühel, hiked the Cinque Terre on the Riviera, strolled the Champs-Élysées in Paris, felt the pain at Dachau, listened to Mozart in Salzburg, saw an opera in Vienna, and sunbathed in Capri, on Lake Lago, and on both sides of the Adriatic Sea.

We dined on goulash in Innsbruck, drank beer in Munich, picnicked beside the Leaning Tower in Pisa, and much much more.

I will never forget this Italian adventure. Despite the differences in culture and language and attitude, I discovered a sameness in the sport of football whether it's played in Italy or the United States. The Italians shared with me the things that are good and right and pure in sport and life. I hope I left them a little of the same.

Dirt and Night Practice

Dirt, dirt, and more dirt! Dirt was my introduction to American football in Italy. The practice and game fields were dirt with stones mixed in. I assumed the fields once had grass, but the heavy traffic of soccer teams of all ages from daybreak to dark took a toll. I didn't see one blade of grass — zero. My players walked the field before every practice collecting and discarding dangerous objects that could rip into their exposed body parts.

One week we played the Ancona Dolphins located on the Adriatic Sea. The field actually had coral in the dirt. Landing on that field resulted in cuts and gashes. Our American running back, David Turner, took one look at the field and refused to play on such a perilous surface.

So I asked the game officials to water the field to soften the turf. They laughed and said every field in Italy was hard and unsafe. I located a custodian and asked him to water the field. He agreed and took a garden hose to the playing area. He stood in one spot and created a huge mudhole, a hole the players had to sidestep to avoid injury.

Finally, I convinced David to play. I told him the Italian players had to play on that field and said he was whining like a baby. Ironically, that high-risk field worked to our advantage: David avoided tackles and scored nearly every time he touched the ball. Ironically, our defense was not happy because they got little rest between possessions.

The field conditions were consistent throughout the league, and few complained except the American players — naturally. When we traveled to different locations and on rare occasions saw actual grass, everyone cheered. It was like discovering water in the desert.

On one Sunday afternoon, our bus pulled up to our opponent's stadium. It was the city's official soccer site and had lush and greener-than-green grass. The excitement of my team was overwhelming. As we departed the bus, it began to rain. It rained and rained and rained some more.

Jeez-oh-Pete! Our game was moved to another field — dirt, of course — to protect the verdant field of green the likes of which we never saw again. I dreamed in green, and grass green became my favorite color.

During my first season, we had adequate lighting. However, on my return trip two years later, we were challenged in another way. The practice field was dirt as usual, but we had only one light, and that light was a single bulb mounted on a nine-foot pole. This limited lighting made for some creative planning for drills. In the early part of practice before dusk became totally dark, we could pass, catch, and kick. The vision/optics became problematic later as the entire team huddled around the single light.

One night the light bulb went out. After some investigation, we discovered a priest who lived at the school adjacent to the practice field had mistakenly turned the light off before retiring. Thereafter, I assigned a coach to police the priest. Jokingly, we referred to the sudden darkness as *an act of the Almighty*.

Because of the heavy demand for practice fields, Italian soccer teams practiced until 9 or 9:30 at night. Only then could our football team use the field. Before every practice, I'd take a long nap, eat dinner, and drink a bottle of Chianti to cope with the crazy-fast traffic — the Grand Prix of Bologna. The Chianti was also excellent.

Before leaving for practice, I kissed my wife goodbye and told her I would be home around 3 a.m. Not many wives would accept that routine. I then stopped at the corner bar for the best espresso in the world, espresso that gave me a needed boost for the night ahead.

I drove to practice, met with my coaches, taped the ankles of my two American players, and waited for the field to come open. My Italian players trickled in because of classes, work, and the certain wait. Some tossed soccer balls in a nearby basketball hoop. Some hooted and hollered and pranced about like young stallions. They all loved American football ... almost as much as I did.

When we finally got on the field of dirt, always dirt, I surveyed the ranks to see who was there or who was not. Players would occasionally miss practice for work or school-related issues ... or the *febber*. The *febber*, I learned, was not a disease. The *febber*, according to my Italian coach Vinnie, was a buildup of lactic acid in the muscles — commonly known as *soreness*. I saw the *febber* as a convenient way to skip practice.

After practice, the entire team piled into fast-moving vehicles and visited a local *trattoria*. We were rather boisterous, and the coaches and players relished the food, drink, fun, and camaraderie. Our dining broke up around 2 a.m.

Sometime thereafter, I crammed my body into an English-made, low-to-the-ground car called Mother Theresa, a name the manufacturer chose, not me. With gas at $4 a gallon, I asked for a small car, so the club got me the smallest it could find. It was small all right: My butt was inches above the road.

At that hour, the streets were somewhat deserted and traffic no longer daunting. At least, the roads were paved, not dirt, and I had headlights and streetlights to navigate my way — not a light bulb.

Jeez-oh-Pete! It was a good time!

When in Rome ...

At 3 a.m., we boarded a bus with airline-sized seats for an eight-hour drive to Rome. Remarkably, we were playing the Gladiators in

Rome! We felt like Christians in the Coliseum about to be fed to lions. After the game, we boarded the same bus for our return to Bologna. Down and back, no overnight accommodations.

At daybreak, one player started strumming his guitar. Others began to wake and move about. Soon, a spirited tune sparked an Italian songfest. The players sang and laughed and danced in the aisles. When the sun peered over the horizon, the bus was rocking with music.

In America, such festive behavior before a football game would be unimaginable. Players and coaches, intent on their thoughts and opponent, put on serious game faces. At most, they wear headphones to listen to music, never disturbing others.

This Italian pregame frivolity was different. My two American players wore customary game faces and looked at me to put an end to the festivity.

"Coach, aren't you going to stop this silliness?" they asked point-blank. "We have a game to play!"

"I'm not going to change a thousand years of culture," I said.

My Italian players had a different approach to sport. First, they genuinely enjoyed their teammates. They greeted each other with enthusiasm and love. They hugged and laughed as if they hadn't seen each other in years. Sport was fun, and game day was a time for celebration. Initially, I thought them silly; but my thinking changed as they competed with toughness and utter seriousness when the game began.

At half-time, I was drawing plays and making adjustments. When I looked up from the whiteboard, half my team was smoking cigarettes. *This would make quite a photo opportunity*, I thought, *Coach talking to his team with most of them lit up!*

Many Italians smoke ... if not tobacco, hashish. Yes, *hashish*! *Culture.*

After our first game, I learned an important lesson about the team organization. We lost to a top-notch opponent and played really well. Despite the loss, I could see we were contenders and was pleased. At any rate, the team owners were not pleased, and they wouldn't talk to me.

I asked one of my Italian coaches why I was getting the silent treatment.

"You are the American coach," he answered. "You know the American game. We brought you here to win. The loss today was your fault."

If we lost, the Americans were blamed and shunned. If we won, everyone was happy, and the team won. The city won as well. Anything the city won — surfing, cycling, thumb wrestling — warranted a party. The Bologna flag was hoisted. Horns blared as the team headed to the piazza, and wine flowed more than usual in the streets. Incidentally, the players, the most macho among them, walked arm in arm and generally danced with each other at discos. *Culture.*

Before one game, I approached the locker room to give my team final instructions. Sitting outside the door was my place kicker, Massimillano Magnarella, sipping a glass of wine. "What the hell are you doing, Mag?" I asked.

"Just chilling and relaxing, Coach. Chilling and relaxing." *Culture.*

Before another game, I headed to the bathroom when one of my bilingual players stopped me at the door. "Coach, I wouldn't go in there if I were you."

"Why not?" I asked and walked in.

To my surprise, several players were huddled together taking pills of some sort. Later, I learned they were popping uppers. Apparently, these pregame uppers were common around the league as there was no drug testing. *Culture.*

After another game, an opponent with a heavy beard and black grease under his eyes walked into our locker room looking for Massimo Terracina. Massimo was a colorful, older player who didn't get much playing time. He worked as a journalist and freelanced as a reporter of American football in Italy. He also attended fifteen or more Super Bowls in the States as a journalist and was quite popular with the American press. To put this in perspective, I have yet to attend *one* Super Bowl.

Anyhow, Massimo had written some unkind words about this disgruntled player who now surveyed the room like a lion stalking his prey. He was wearing a bandana pirate-style and missing a few teeth. Without so much as a "Ciao, Bello," he advanced toward Massimo and punched him in the face. Not a single teammate came to Massimo's defense. Well, that's one way of handling the media and fake news.

In 1986, every young man in Italy had a one-year military obligation. One of my players, Carlo Novella, undersized but an excellent player, was exempt from service because he was considered mentally unfit. Every year he was required to return to the military to be retested for his condition. Carlo informed me he would miss a week's practice to be re-evaluated. If deemed sane, Carlo would become a soldier. I did not expect him to play that week or even that year.

The night before the game, I was driving to practice when a car with the horn blaring nearly drove up my exhaust pipe. I thought the person behind was angry about my relatively slow but safe driving. At a traffic light, the driver jumped out of his car, ran to my mini vehicle, and started pounding on my roof! It was Carlo.

"They said I was still crazy," he shouted with excitement. "I can play tomorrow." So this crazy Italian unfit for the military played the next day. And played very well, I might add. *Culture.*

My two American players cursed freely and often, partly because they thought no one could understand them. Actually, their Italian teammates listened carefully, hoping to pick up American slang.

"Jeez-oh-Pete! Coaching in Italy was a good time!" Jim, aka Coach Grande, with offensive tackles Andrea Tugnoli and Fausto Di Francesco.

One night before practice, Carlo walked past me and proudly tried out one of his newly acquired phrases. "Good evening, my favorite *fuck ing* American coach," he said with a broad smile. I laughed a deep laugh. Certainly, Carlo thought his greeting friendly and appropriate.

As for me, I found myself chilling and relaxing. Just chilling and relaxing. *Culture.*

Carnevale and Terrorist Police

In February of '86, we decided to attend *Carnevale* in Venice. *We* meaning my wife, Sharron; daughter, Jill; two American players, David and Rob; and Vinnie, my assistant coach and student at Bologna University — the oldest university in the world, by the way. Jill's boyfriend John, who was visiting for two weeks, also joined our merry group.

Venice is a two-hour train trip from Bologna, and we were fortunate to visit this marvelous, historic city many times. Obviously, we lived in a favorable location as Florence was only a one-hour train ride.

We arrived in Venice and boarded the water taxi at Piazzale Roma. Our destination: Saint Marco Square. The island, famous for its extraordinary masks and costumes during *Carnevale*, exploded in color, music, festive activity, and risqué behavior here and there. The celebration was in full force, and we were more than happy to join the masquerade, drink vino, and gawk at the revelers from around the world.

Jesters, jugglers, nuns, and an assortment of characters in vibrant colors and period costumes paraded in the square, singing and dancing — the setting, magical. There were kings and queens, noblemen and women from centuries past, their opulent costumes matching or similar in color. Think Marie Antoinette in a ball gown. They wore half masks and typical Venetian masks adorned with gold, pearls, crystal, and feathers, some with beaks and hooked noses, most with vibrant headdresses.

We bought bright wigs — yellow, blue, green, and purple — with loop-like ringlets and joined the merrymaking. We danced in the streets with strangers, drank Chianti from the bottle, ate burgers at McDonald's (yes, McDonald's), and marveled at the stunning costumes. It was a grand outdoor celebration, and we partied late into the night and early morning.

At some point, John, Jill's boyfriend, had a diabetic attack. His experiences in Italy from beginning to end were memorable but not in a good way. At the airport, he was strip-searched, authorities suspecting drug abuse after discovering his insulin needles. He also accidentally locked himself in a public bathroom and could not get out ... for some untold time. And Jill's interest in the hapless young man waned way before his flight home.

His misfortune did not dampen our spirits in the least ... well, maybe a little. John and Jill spent the night in Venice to recover, and the rest of our troop caught the train around 2 a.m., arriving in Bologna at 4. With our curly wigs still on our heads and the glow of the evening still in our hearts, we continued to dance gaily in the streets as we made our way to our car.

David, a black running back, took the driver's seat. Rob, a 6 foot 5, 275-pound tackle, rode shotgun. Sharron, Vinnie, and I piled into the backseat. Vinnie, an Italian American from Milwaukee, Wisconsin, was the only person in the car who spoke Italian.

All of a sudden, as David engaged the car, a black SUV zoomed past and sharply cut us off. Three men leaped from the vehicle adorned in black helmets with visors covering their faces. Their black uniforms were equipped with bulletproof vests, and, worse yet, each man carried a machine gun. These were *not Carnevale* costumes!

They swiftly surrounded our car. I was aghast and paralyzed. These men intended to do us harm. Doom and death pervaded the moment.

My first thought was *we are being robbed*. I reacted and yelled at David, "Go. Go!"

David responded, "You go!"

His hands shot upward. A gun outside the window was pointed directly at his head!

Instantly, all passengers in the car grew silent. We were filled with sudden fear, petrified, and immediately sober like a shot. In seconds, our lives could end. I personally had never been in such a dangerous situation, and I'm certain neither had any of the other Americans. This was life or death.

The doors opened, and we were ordered to exit the car. The gunmen demanded our passports and told us in no uncertain terms to put our hands behind our heads. I told Vinnie to explain who we were and what we were doing there. Unfortunately, Vinnie, who was only 5 feet, 2 inches, suddenly forgot all the Italian he ever knew. He stammered badly and was sweating bullets. It took a while, but he gradually regained his composure and explained our presence.

The gunmen examined our passports, and one of the three shoved mine into my chest. "Ciao," he said with a smirk. They were gone as suddenly as they had arrived.

Needless to say, the ride home was quiet and tense, as we each considered the possible outcome of that encounter. Later, members of our Italian football team told us that if David floored the gas pedal and tried to escape, all of us would have been shot with no questions asked.

What we didn't know was six years earlier on August 2, 1980, a group of neo-fascists had bombed the central train station in Bologna. Eighty-five people were killed and two hundred injured.

The Italian terrorist police had stopped us. They were alerted to five strange-looking characters dancing about in Harpo Marx wigs departing the train.

Carnevale was a great experience, but the ordeal with the terrorist police is one experience I could do without.

Passion in Bologna by Jill Sypult Marcus

My family took a year-long Italian detour to Bologna, Italy, soon after I graduated from college. I loved everything about this surreal place — the food, the art, the men ... at least until I learned most Italian men remain mama's boys for life.

Mom and I were there on my dad's coattails, and we watched him transform an unlikely American football troop of Italians into a winning team. Who knew there was such a thing as an Italian Super Bowl? As a bystander, I witnessed my dad, aka *Coach Grande*, swiftly become a sports celebrity. He took his Bologna Towers to the Super Bowl in Rome — a battle with the Gladiators no less.

While my dad was trying to break the team's smoking habits, I had the luxury of time to roam the markets, explore ingredients, and teach myself to cook and eat. Bologna is, of course, the food capital of Italy. This wonderful city is thankfully skipped by tourists and is full of porticos, food markets, and scores of communists playing bocce.

Most weekends were spent eating and celebrating at the players' homes with their families ... with their mamas and *nonnas* at the kitchen helm. These five-hour, multi-course celebrations started early with a lesson in folding tortelloni and always ended with too much grappa and limoncello.

Super Bowl Shindig
As a thank-you for their hospitality, we hosted a celebration at

our apartment during the American Super Bowl. I was in charge of the food for this shindig, and at twenty-one, what did I know about catering to this crowd?

So I cooked what I knew and threw together what I thought was a typical Italian dish that was loved by all. A little pasta, some roasted chicken, béchamel sauce, and sautéed porcini mushrooms. Ecco, we have chicken tetrazzini. Long story short: They had never heard of such a dish, loved it anyway, and my recipe and picture appeared in the Bologna newspaper the next day. It was there I found my passion for food.

Classic Chicken Tetrazzini

In your favorite skillet, with a glass of Brunello di Montalcino in hand, sauté a handful of chopped shallots in two tablespoons of butter. Forgive me: The more I enjoy the wine, the more nebulous my quantities become. If you use good ingredients, the quantities matter less, and your dish becomes like a John Coltrane jazz riff.

Jill Marcus: "While my dad was trying to break the team's smoking habits, I had time to roam the markets. Bologna is the food capital of Italy."

Back to the recipe. On medium heat, add a half pound of your favorite chopped mushrooms. You can use button or cremini mushrooms ... but porcini mushrooms are special if you can find them. Sauté mushrooms and shallots in butter until golden — about four to five minutes. Dust with salt and pepper. If you have fresh thyme in your garden, add a few sprigs to your sauce. You can pull these out later after the flavors have evolved.

Transfer the shallots and mushrooms to a bowl. Add another four tablespoons of butter to the pan. When the butter is melted, add a third cup of flour, and stir until mixed thoroughly. Add two cups of chicken stock, and stir until it begins to thicken. Add one cup of heavy cream, and simmer for two to three minutes. Remove from the heat and stir in three-fourths cup of shredded Parmigiano-Reggiano cheese and one cup of chopped green onions or peas. I don't like peas, so I use green onions. If you like peas, add fresh, uncooked hard peas. You can also add raw chopped asparagus pieces. *Buon appetito!*

Editor's note: Jill, Coach Sy's daughter, found her passion for food in Bologna, Italy, and now owns restaurants, cafes, and a catering company in Charlotte. Of interest, Jill also led the Italian football team in dance workouts to improve their flexibility, muscle development, balance, and athleticism — her father's objectives. How did the Italian and American football players respond? They never complained ... despite sore, seldom-used muscles. In fact, Jill and her leotard were quite a hit.

5

METHODIST COLLEGE/UNIVERSITY HEAD COACH
1992-2010

Signature Stories

I COACHED FOOTBALL FOR FORTY-FIVE YEARS, twenty-six as head coach. I have been known to tell a story now and then to motivate, illustrate, and entertain. Some stories I repeated every year.

My players looked forward to two most especially: my sex talk and "The Wild-Horse Rider" story. These stories have colorful language. Remember, I was speaking to a group of young men who hear and use profanity frequently, and they were not offended.

Story No. 1: I was sitting in an athletic staff meeting at Methodist College when the dean of students, George Blanc, walked in and asked to speak to all the coaches, men and women, about a very serious matter.

"People," the dean began, "we have a major problem on campus, and the president is very concerned about it."

Major prob-lem? Probably eligibility or money, I thought.

"I love the demands, sacrifices, and glitter of this great American sport and the young men attracted to it."

Anything but sex.

"Sex among students is rampant and out of control," he said. "They are having sex in the dorms, the forest, the closets, and down near the river. It's male on male, gal on gal, threesomes, and you name it."

Silence. Eyes rolled, mouths opened, and expressions of disbelief to near laughter spread through the ranks.

Really? Sex on a college campus? Our students having sex? Unbelievable.

"I need your help," pled the dean. "The president wants to put a stop to it. You coaches have a powerful voice. Please help me. Talk to your student-athletes. Help me control this behavior."

Now I ask you: Has any outside party ever controlled the raging hormones of healthy young men and women? Coming between a couple in lust is ill-advised and possibly dangerous. Nevertheless, my assistants asked what I was going to do.

"Give them a sex talk," I answered, knowing instantly what to say.

My father had a great sense of humor and offered useful advice, especially about sex. His advice to me as an often confused, inquisitive teenager was all the ammunition I needed.

I gathered the troops after practice and told them to listen carefully. "I'm going to talk to you about sex," I began.

Silence. Complete and total silence like a nunnery at night. There were a few smiles but no giggles or uncomfortable shuffling. They were riveted as I shared my father's gems, one by one, with embellishments when needed.

"This is what my father told me when I was your age:
- *No* is *no*!
- A *yes* may be a *no.*
- Violation of that rule is jail. It's called *rape.*
- Beware: You might spend a lot of time in court. And jail.
- A few seconds of pleasure can result in a lifetime of hell.
- You better be able to trust her.
- You better like her.
- Always use protection."

I remember thinking, *Jail. Court. Trust. Hell! Maybe, I need to rethink this sex thing.*

I did not address same-sex sex. That subject was above my pay grade. I left multiple-partner sex, animal sex, and deviation from the norm in whatever form for the dean of students.

Dad got his point across. By the quiet response of my players, I did too. Thereafter, that annual sex talk became a much anticipated and highly touted topic among the players. They repeated my words and expressions and often took to imitating my voice and gestures.

Story No. 2: "The Wild-Horse Rider" story began literally with a bang in 1992 during a lightning delay in the third quarter of a 0-2 season. We were slightly behind. I heard one player bitching. So I did what any good head coach would do: I shattered my clipboard over a dumbbell rack, shards hitting a backup quarterback in the face. Words then flew from my mouth.

One player described the moment in a group chat: "At the top of his lungs, Coach Sypult shouted, 'goddamn it! I'm sick and tired of the bitchers and complainers. It sounds like a bunch of *fucking* doctors and lawyers in here. We need some fighters and wild-horse riders to pin their ears back and fly down the field and hit somebody.'"

Timing was critical for this talk. I always told it when we were facing a crisis. By far, my "Wild-Horse Rider" story was the most repeated and remembered by my players.

I always began, "There are five types of people: doctors, lawyers, fighters, fuckers, and wild-horse riders.

"Doctors and lawyers are good people and serve the public honorably. But in a crisis, they can be deadly," I said. "A doctor can find an ailment and prescribe a cure even if the ailment is non-existent and prescription non-effective. A lawyer loves to debate and present his case. In a locker room, a doctor and lawyer discover problems and attempt to resolve them, thereby causing dissension and division.

"The fighter is the loyal base. His main goal is to make a positive impact and help the team win and reach goals. He follows the rules, works hard, stays positive, and performs tasks to the best of his ability. The fighter is essential to a successful team.

"The fucker is ... well, a fucker. He breaks the rules, is likely to give up quickly, embarrass the team with asinine actions, and influence others negatively. He is poison.

"And then there is the wild-horse rider. He is the intangible person. He is the winner. He may or may not be the best player on the team, but he finds a way to win. Whatever it takes, he will do. He performs. He leads. He runs toward danger and overcomes it.

"Not many are wild-horse riders, but a team needs a wild-horse rider to win. I always ended this talk with a question: "So doctors, lawyers, fighters, fuckers, or wild-horse riders ... which one are you?"

Invariably, after that story, every player approached me in private and asked, "Coach, which one am I?"

I would look each in the eye and tell him the truth.

Camp

A rite of passage takes place every August in the game of football: preseason camp. Quite simply, camp is stifling hot, humid, sweaty, and stinky — a real grind. For fifty-three years as a player and coach, I relished every minute of it. It was hell, and I adored it. It was always rigorous, exhausting, and stressful, and I always loved it. God help me, I loved it.

In high school, I would get up before daylight, pack a lunch, and walk to practice. The uniforms did not get washed for a week. After morning practice, I would take all my clothes to a sunny spot outside and dry them while I ate lunch. I would sleep in the shade until the afternoon practice and then don the dirty, stiff, but dry uniform. Each night, Mom washed the contents of my *ditty* for the next day. A *ditty* is a football term for jock, socks, and cut-off T-shirt, the T-shirt a fashion statement except for those players with chunky midriffs.

Also in high school, we were ironically not allowed to drink water! Drinking water was a sign of weakness. Yes, we *were* thirsty. So I secretly stored cut-up lemons inside my helmet and sucked on them to quench my thirst. I cannot remember anyone suffering from heat exhaustion or heat stroke.

In college, we held preseason camp at Jackson's Mill, the childhood home of Stonewall Jackson. The practice field defies description: an airport landing strip, hard as I-95 with as many potholes — dirt mixed with gravel, and dust as thick as chalk. We were allowed water in college, and the trainers fed us salt pills to hydrate us before and after practice. Again, no one died.

Eventually, trainers and coaches realized that players performed better if they drank more water. Now water is available all the time on the field, and water breaks are scheduled during practices. Players consume humongous amounts of water, sports drinks, Gatorade, and even pickle juice. Yes, pickle juice because it actually prevents cramps.

The grittiest affliction of camp was what we called *jungle rot*. Because most days were swelteringly hot and humid, sweat poured from us, soaking our underpants and shorts that rubbed against our inner thighs. After prolonged rubbing, this area got irritated, red, and sore. Everyone walked around like a cowboy after a long, grueling roundup. The only cure, and really only a short-lived cure at that, was to wash the area thoroughly in the shower and douse it with baby powder for the less daring or Gold's medicated powder that stung like the dickens. Before practice, players would slather heavy layers of Vaseline on the affected area that only relieved the situation, not cured.

Camp wasn't always hot. In Bologna, Italy, where I coached for two years, it was icy cold and snowy. Camp began in November and lasted four months. We had no indoor facility. On freezing evenings, I would utilize our tiny locker room with a short, narrow hall to coach two players at a time for fifteen minutes while the rest of the team watched tape and learned plays drawn on the white board. Then I would rotate another two into the hall for work on technique.

Every night, coaches were wary of a dreaded visitor we called the *Turk*. This phantom guest, it was rumored, would lurk around college football camps, seeking players who questioned their desire to play college ball. In the middle of the night, the Turk would send the player in question from the dorm to the nearest interstate highway.

When we suspected the Turk might be in camp, we sounded a warning whistle that was soft and had only two notes repeated over and over: *Whe-whill, whe-whill.* Players disappeared from camp for a variety of reasons — the most common being *I don't love the game anymore.* Translated, this means *I'm homesick, I miss my girlfriend, I'm never going to play,* or *This college game is not like high school.* When they got home, they told mommy and daddy, *The coaches were unfair and never gave me a chance.*

I've had much experience with players who *Turked* — a verb for those who lost to the Turk and disappeared. If a player came to me before breaking camp, he was 100 percent past hope, beyond saving, doomed. He had already met his double demons of doubt and dropping out. I could not change the decision ... though I often tried.

Players who remained were unfazed by players leaving. Those staying the course acted like scavengers at a yard sale. Helmets, shoulder pads, and shoes were exchanged for better quality and fit. Jersey numbers were seized like hot goods at a Black Friday sale. Chances of moving up on the depth chart also greatly increased.

Another unwelcome guest, *Scotty*, arrived every morning. In the beginning of most every practice, we were greeted by a misty breeze. Gradually, Scotty, the sun, would peek his head above the horizon. Why we called the sun *Scotty* I do not know. I do know when the players yelled *Scotty*, it was going to be another scorching day, hotter than August asphalt.

I conducted three practices a day before the NCAA changed the rules, limiting practices to two. Our practice field was a mile from the locker room. The players had to walk down the hill to practice and, of course, up the hill after. To me, this walk represented players in great physical condition, players who could get up after getting knocked to the ground by an opponent. Football is an aggressive contact sport, and physical and mental toughness are musts.

We held meetings before every practice and longer meetings at night. Our pre-practice meetings were short and emphasized technique. The players ate a pre-practice snack before morning practice and a whopping lunch and dinner after practice. I set simple goals: Meet, practice, eat, and sleep; then meet, practice, eat, and sleep again. We encouraged players to make it to the next *Meet, Eat, and Sleep*. If they stayed on course, they would survive camp. For some reason, when a player quit, he always waited until after he ate.

At night, we covered the vision of the program, goals, rules, expectations, and core values. Team discipline was crucial. I expected every player to follow the team rules. Every detail was covered: for example, which peg in the locker to hang the helmet, where to store shoulder pads and shoes, and where to hang the jersey and pants. Every player had to execute assignments correctly to make the team successful. We taught players how to start and end meetings. How to clap and sit up straight. How to put on socks, tie their shoes properly, and take care of their feet. We covered every detail. Camp was a time of no distractions: no students, no classes, and *especially* no girls.

Players have a slight advantage over coaches in camp: They sleep longer. While the players are in bed, coaches are in meetings evaluating players and analyzing tape. These meetings can last until 3 or 4 in the morning. Then it's up at 5 a.m. to start a new day. Sleep-deprived coaches can be downright irritable, mean, and crude — like ripping handles off doors to wake players up. A coach with a few hours' sleep at 5 a.m. can make a Marine drill sergeant blush.

We used every teaching method to train our players. First, we would draw and explain the rules of the play. Then we would show tape or film from previous games for visual learning, and, finally, we would walk the players through the play for physical learning. My mentors, who cared little about being politically correct, taught me to coach to the *dumbest* player. *Dumb it down* and *keep it simple, stupid* are coaching axioms. And then repeat, repeat, repeat. It was supremely important that everyone understood the plays as one player mistake, *one*, could lose a game.

Camp produced a collection of crazy memories as well. One coach set off a firecracker in a meeting room to illustrate the sound of a good tackle. Another brought an unloaded rifle to a meeting to emphasize a powerful, straight kick; the campus cops didn't appreciate his demonstration. I have been known to sleep in my car at the only campus entrance to deter players from slipping out after curfew. I saw freshmen follow their girlfriends home moments after checking into camp. Once I had to pry a player from his mother's arms; she had difficulty with her *baby* leaving home.

The results of preseason camps were on display every game of the season. Camp success was measured each week against opponents. Our grade as coaches was made public in the sports pages. Our methods and motivational techniques were fodder for fans and want-to-be coaches, no matter how informed or clueless. Our game strategies and play choices, criticized and debated by the masses. Yes, football camp in all its gore and glory fathered the season to come.

People get up every day and go to work. I got up every day and went to play. What fun! And they paid me too. Of course, it was a lot more fun when we won.

Kentucky Fried, At Your Service
November 6, 1993

In the third quarter of a game in Hampden-Sydney, Virginia, someone was tugging on my sleeve. I looked down at a woman on a mission. She was undaunted, unyielding, unfazed by the urgency of the game.

"You the head coach?"

"Yes, ma'am."

"Kentucky Fried, at your service. Delivering the postgame meal."

I had my arm around a player at the time, ready to send in a play.

"That will be $450." She thrust out her hand for payment.

I laughed out loud ... as did my players.

"OK," I said, "but let me call this play first."

I had to call a timeout to retrieve the money.

CoachSpeak: Notes in Journals

The Process: It's the process. Not the game. Not the wins. Not the trophies. It's the process. The passion. The grind. The players. The camaraderie. The competition. The organization. The breakdown of film. The grading. Putting the puzzle together. The off-season and in-season conditioning and weight training. Meetings, personnel decisions, and game planning. In coaching, it's the recruiting, practice, and organization of these activities. You must love the process more than the finished product.

Core Values: Evening meetings set the tone for the next day. Words like *accountability, effort,* and *team* emphasized the program's core values. *Enthusiasm*, for instance, was a key word. All day the coaches worked that word into practice and meetings. Players were asked to evaluate our team enthusiasm at practice and give examples of how they personally exhibited enthusiasm that day. One year, my assistants dressed like cheerleaders and performed before the team to demonstrate enthusiasm.

Game Day: The competition and adrenaline rush on game day are almost beyond words. It's *Christmas Day every Saturday.* The noise of the crowd, cheers, and band, anticipation of the next play, and afterglow of victory — even the heartbreak of failure. Captivating, exciting, intense, and almost astonishing.

Adversity: Every year I tell the players that adversity will strike. It will happen on the practice field. It will happen in games. It will happen during the year. And how they handle that adversity will determine their chances for success.

Work Ethic: How players prepare for adversity is important. How they physically prepare their bodies will be key. How hard they work. Their effort during practice. Taking no lazy steps. Not one. Making it a goal to give effort every play. *It takes no talent to give great effort.*

Attitude: Never give up — even when dead tired. The game is won when everyone else is tired, and players make the big plays. Their work ethic is their character. Their attitude is their spirit. Their character, spirit, and resolve will be tested.

Team: We can overcome mountainous challenges. When adversity hits, the team must pull together to weather the storm. The community must come together as one believing in each other, loving your brother regardless of his color, dialect, language, faith, or persuasion. And with patience, forgiveness, compassion, and unconditional love, trust each other's abilities, and don't care who gets credit for winning the game.

Communication: Play the game. Defend your turf. Know your audience. Know how they think. Learn how to speak to them. Words matter. Clarity matters. You can't be passive. You must see your idea. Be a brilliant communicator.

Leadership: Encourage initiative, skill development, and leadership. The leader can't worry whether everyone agrees with him. Real leaders are humble servants. I am here to serve, not be served. I am here to give, not get. We are nearest to greatness when we are great in humility.

Sypult and the Press

Editor's note: Jim Sypult, a former high school newspaper editor, gave smart interviews that resulted in good copy. In 1992, the student paper, *Small Talk,* published a story at the dawn of Sypult's days at Methodist. He sent a copy home, writing at the top, "Mom, they love me here, but we haven't played yet."

"I ask three questions of each player. Can I trust him? Is he committed? Does he care? When I am able to answer yes to all three of these questions about all of our players, I'll know we have the positive attitudes and proper mental discipline to win."

"Coaching is simple. You tell your players to do something, and they do it. If it's not their best effort, then they'll do it again. I won't cuss players or take away their personal dignity, but I will drive them, and I'll love them" (2/26/92 by R.T. Pope).

Fayetteville Observer

Editor's note: The *Fayetteville Observer* printed hundreds of stories about Coach Sypult over the years. The following are snippets of sports stories from 2006-2010 that reflect his wit and character.

In the fall of '92, the Monarchs were winless, and Chad Drake, Sypult's first recruit and starting guard, was about to quit. In crisis mode, Sypult convinced Drake to stay and averted one of many crises in the growth of MC football.

"Coach Sypult had inherited a legacy of guys that did not know how to win," said Drake, now a retired lieutenant colonel of the Marine Corps. "They should make a bronze bust of him and put it up. Because there was no program before he stepped in."

Sypult spotted Drake in a junior college program at Chowan College. At the time, Sypult was the assistant head coach at Davidson.

The walls of Sypult's office are lined with pictures of top players from over the years, and he is only too willing to tell stories about each. He discovered Quincy Malloy, a two-time All-American, in South Carolina at an all-star game. A inch or two taller, Malloy could have been a Gamecock or Tiger, Sypult said.

DeCarlos West, another All-American from the early days, told Sypult to stop recruiting him as he planned to go elsewhere. Sypult found Leon Ché Clark, an All-American and Marine, at Camp Lejeune (11/2/06 by Michael N. Graff).

In an apple-green shirt and dark-green tie, Jim Sypult looked as if he stepped out of *GQ* magazine. It was media day and the first webcast on the USA South conference website.

Staring into the video camera, Sypult talked directly to his *worldwide* audience, joking that a billion people were watching. He said hello to everyone in Turkey and his friends in Italy.

"Keeping his reputation as the comedian of the USA South coaching crew, Sypult turned media day into his personal comedy club, somehow including a vacation to Ireland, the mafia, soccer balls, and Frank Sinatra in his preseason prospectus of Methodist football."

He came with show-and-tell props: a basketball, soccer ball, golf ball, and football. He demonstrated how to hold a basketball and bend the knees before he bounced it in a straight line. He said a golf ball will go straight if it's hit square. Then Sypult held up a soccer ball, identifying it as a soccer ball, not a football, for his European friends. It bounced straight as well. Finally, he picked up a football and attempted to bounce it. It took a wobbly path. We never know which way a football will go, he quipped.

Sypult said he loved almost everyone in the room and the world before spotting a conference official in the crowd. "That ruins my day to see black and white striped shirts," he said.

Tony Lerulli, friend and head coach at Maryville, was his next target. Lerulli, Sypult said, tried to schedule Meredith, a women's college, that had recently joined the conference.

"Sypult was Richard Pryor in a row of football Ben Steins, offering a refreshing change up to the coachspeak that drags down most media events like this" (8/1/07 by Michael N. Graff).

In 2006, Chris Roncketti, Sypult's starting quarterback for four years, graduated. So Sypult was searching for a new dance partner: "I've had the same wife for a long time. Changing quarterbacks, that's like changing women, and I don't like change" (4/7/06 by Michael N. Graff).

Their practices are grueling, and camps, a matter of pride for those who survive. The number of recruits is staggering, and up to 30 percent of the players drop out before the first game. When one guy "goes down, the next Roman soldier stands up," said Sypult. "I'm a pit bull who gets cornered and goes for the jugular. I'm not going to lie in the corner and die" (9/9/06 by Michael N. Graff)

Ninety freshmen showed up for the first day of camp. Jim Sypult introduced each of his fifteen seniors who were also a class of ninety when they were freshmen. It wouldn't surprise Sypult if someone turned in his equipment after the first practice.

Sypult says he has ten thousand rules, but the seniors make "the real rules," and what they do, everyone follows. He told his seniors to look at the freshmen because "you were like them. And one day, they'll be like you. Remember when you were a freshman and you were scared and a pup and away from home" (8/15/07).

Sypult gets his players ready for battle through a tough conditioning program and practices in pads with full contact drills. "I don't believe in playing volleyball during the preseason, and then they get hit in a game and go 'What was that?'" (9/3/07 by Thomas Pope).

At times, Coach Sypult was a gambler. He attempted a two-point conversion instead of kicking an extra point in an overtime with Chowan College, losing 31-30. "I gambled and lost. I didn't play the odds. Don't send me to Las Vegas because I'd lose the house," he said (9/22/07 by Michael N. Graff).

Sypult contends with injuries and illness every week and every game. He never knows how many will be out until practice. When he asks for the injury report, he learns about hurt shoulders or a guy "over by a tree" who's sick.

"So we get who's next, and we get them in there to do it. I coach the guys out there who are healthy" (10/10/08 by Paul Shugar).

When Methodist lost to Maryville in four overtimes, Sypult said everyone played hard and was understandably heartbroken. "But my stance is that's life. It was a tough break. But you better get back up and remember how hard you fought to get back in that game" (10/8/09).

When Coach Sypult tore his Achilles' tendon in 2006, he slowed down in practices but sped up building relations with players, a positive in his book. It also caused him to contemplate retirement. He didn't win a game his first year at Methodist, but in four years, they were 9-1.

"A lot of it comes down to who you're able to retain in (NCAA) Division III football versus a scholarship situation," said Sypult, the league's Coach of the Year in 2000. "It's been up and down. Some tough times, some great times, but a heck of a ride" (4/17/10 by Thomas Pope).

The locker room at Methodist University is no longer in the back of the old heating plant, and the spacious new field house sometimes overwhelms Jim Sypult.

"Sometimes I'm like, 'What am I doing in here?'"

Sypult's old office was the size of a closet, and he not only gets lost in the new field house, but he can't find his stuff. He's used to hanging his jacket on a nail, grabbing his toothbrush, and heading out.

The new facility is "too clean" for him, he said. The old facility "had blood on the wall and sweat and spit" and was "his kind of place."

Sypult is not the only one taken aback. When some former players took a look at the new facility during Homecoming, he said "their mouths hit the floor" (4/30/10 by Paul Shugar).

"I've coached a lot of teams, and I've never had one quite like this," Sypult said. "Every time you think we should be left for dead, our kids come fighting back. Hey, don't blink" (10/23/10 by Don Wiederer).

Jim Sypult, "USA South's lead comedian," stole the show again at the annual media day although he wasn't even there because of a health issue.

"First of all, I'd like to say that I'm heavily medicated, so anything that I say can't be held against me," Sypult began in his videotaped message.

He avoided a trip to Maryville, home of friend and rival Tony Lerulli. "Tony, I would do anything not to come to Maryville," Sypult joked. "I didn't think cutting off my toe was going to be the answer to that, but that's what happened."

three up-downs, one backward roll, three more up-downs, and another forward roll ... in nine seconds.

There were the little-glory but exuberant second units: the GO-Team and Make-a-Difference Defense (MADD). There was the Pride Patrol, a rotating-position unit that left the locker room spotless after practice.

Sharron Sypult: "Jim always found a way to turn a negative into a positive. He joked about dragging me kicking and screaming to *Fayettenam*. He even found a positive in the 0-10 season: 'It is said losing builds character. The truth is losing reveals character.'"

The players had their own hand signal. Their own *Ready Ready Monarchs!* call to order and *Hey* response. They made eye contact, shook hands, and treated others with courtesy — winners in attitude and manner.

Uncertainty surrounded the first season's outcome, but the direction was certain, and expectation high, even among the faculty and school personnel.

The promise for Monarch football was sweet as only a young, enthusiastic group of inspired athletes can make it.

They expected some winning. Expected some losing. And expected to be heroes of their own stories with the promise of a daring tomorrow.

Conference champs? Not this year. A winning season? Hold that thought. A new era in Methodist football? A sure thing.

Coach Sy didn't win a single game his first year at Methodist. However, a national ranking, conference championship, and Coach of the Year award would follow.

One of a Kind
Ralph Isernia

Jim Sypult was truly one of a kind. A mentor, teacher, father figure, master motivator. He taught us the game and the right way to play. He cut through the BS to find what was truly important. There was never a task too small or unimportant that he wouldn't do himself. Back in the early years of the program, we had to do everything from line the field to wash the jerseys to (in his words) "clean the shitters." After a game, win or lose, you could see Coach Sy in the showers with trash cans filled with dirty uniforms, hot water, and detergent. He took a broomstick and stirred the uniforms in a presoak routine before he put them in the washer — "the proper way to do it."

Coach Sy was a stickler for details. To check the proper hand position for center-QB exchange, he would lie on his back, in the dirt, looking upside down between the center's legs to make sure the ball was hitting the QB's hands in the correct spot. I remember one camp we were having a heck of a time handling snaps for PATs. Frank Santora was snapping to Brian Turner, and the ball kept slipping through his hands. Now Brian was a pretty good athlete, and Frank was a very accurate snapper, so we couldn't figure out what was going on. As it turned out, we were using new footballs, and they were slick. Couple that with Brian's hands drenched with sweat from the 100-degree heat.

So Coach Sy crouched behind the snapper-holder combination to get a bird's-eye view of the operation. Frank snapped the ball, and sure enough, it slipped through Brian's hands and drilled Coach Sy across the bridge of his nose, opening a gash and splitting his glasses in two. He went to the trainer, not for medical attention, but for tape to hold his glasses together. Blood was still pouring out, but he never missed a beat.

In 1998, we were playing at Newport News Apprentice School.

It was always hot and steamy there, and we were playing "grown-ass men." In those days, we didn't travel with a purchase order for meals or a school credit card. Coach traveled with cash. And a lot of it. He had to pay for meals and hotel rooms. He also never left any of his personal belongings in the locker room. He kept everything on the sideline, including the cash which he kept on his person. Especially the early games, we would dress in shorts because of the sweltering heat. This was one of those games. As Coach would say, "95 and 95" ... 95-degree heat and 95 percent humidity.

Coach Sy always had his trusty water bottle with him in practice and games. When practices were going bad, he would kid with Jill Craig, the athletic trainer: "Hey, could you put some vodka in this [water bottle]? At least, I could enjoy something."

He sweated like a maniac. After the game which was a hard-fought victory, Bob Swank and I were responsible for getting the postgame meal from Burger King. We asked Coach Sy for the cash to pay for the meals. He sat down on the bench, took off his shoe, then his sock, to reveal a rolled-up wad of cash drenched in sweat and stuck to his foot. He proceeded to peel $100 bills off the wad and handed them to us. You should have seen the look of the Burger King cashier. We told her my wallet fell in a puddle. Yes, a puddle of sweat.

In the 1997 season, being nationally ranked for the entire season certainly gave us the confidence we could play with anyone. But the victory over Frostburg in the last game solidified that. All week long, Coach Sy talked about how we were going to get that team from the cold North down here into the heat of *Fayettenam*. "We're gonna suffocate and choke em," he would say with such fire, confidence, and certainty.

He had that way of pumping us up and making us believe in ourselves to the highest level. At Davidson, he would get the defense so fired up in his pregame speeches, they would be foaming at the mouth. I was on the offensive side of the ball and would sneak into the defensive-team room with a couple of other players just to hear him speak and "fire-up the troops." At Davidson, the speeches didn't result in a lot of wins, but we sure thought we could win.

In 1998, Frostburg was still smarting from our thumping the year before. They were out for revenge, and the elements were on their side. The boys from the South traveled to Frostburg to find a bitter-cold day in November, certainly the antithesis of the year before. The temperature was in the 20s, and the windchill made it feel a whole lot worse. Knowing this was the season finale, with no shot at the playoffs, some of the players seemed content to mail this one in and go home. Some certainly didn't want to be in the cold in the middle of nowhere. So just after warmups, we went back to the locker room for some final instructions before taking the field. Well, that was a sight I will never forget. It was not *The Wild-Horse Rider Speech,* but it had a similar effect.

Guys were huddled together to stay warm. They were putting on extra sweatshirts and sweatpants. But Coach Sy would not have it. He slammed his clipboard down on the locker-room floor, and everything went silent. "What's the matter? A little cold?" he quipped. Then he challenged them. "You gotta get tough. I'll show you tough." He took off his jacket, took off his sweatshirt, and took off his pants until he was standing in a polo shirt and shorts. "This is how I'm coaching today." The team looked at each other and followed suit. The entire game, I never heard one guy complain about the cold. Maybe that was the edge we needed for that goal line stand to win the game.

Ralph Isernia: "Perhaps the relationship Coach Sy had with his wife was the greatest living tribute to his true character and what was most important to him." Wedding photo with Coaches Eric Westerfield, Bob Swank (the groom), Jim, and Dave Eavenson.

Coach Sy was a great teacher and mentor to all of us — players and coaches. A lot of us got married while coaching with him. He was a great resource for advice on a lot of subjects, not just football. He set a great example we all wanted to emulate. Perhaps it was the example of the relationship he had with his wife (*Dr. Sy* as we always called her) that was the greatest living tribute to his true character and what was most important to him.

I can still hear some of his sayings. I can still recap countless stories he would tell — *war stories* he called them — which we were banned from telling past midnight on game nights. To this day, with my team and staff, I "coach the coaches." We do "pride patrol" with my team. I tell them the story about the wild-horse rider and ask which one are you? We do a senior walk and a burning of regrets. If a job is worth doing, it's worth doing right … including cleaning the shitters.

We don't get into the coaching profession to make a lot of money. We do it to impact the lives of the people we are fortunate to coach and work with. In my thirty years of coaching, I am blessed to have coached some remarkable players and coached with some extraordinary men. Coach Sy will stay with me forever.

Recruiting
Bob Swank

Coach Sy was one of the toughest people I ever met. I'm guessing it was his West Virginia upbringing. Our practices were tough. Our meeting schedules were tough. Our workouts were tough. I know a lot of coaches who would not make it through our camp or season … and several who didn't.

At the same time, Coach Sy was one of the most caring people I ever met. Every day, our coaching staff met for hours, and many of those hours were spent talking about players — how they were doing and what they needed to succeed. He truly cared about every kid in the program regardless of playing status.

For many years, Coach Sy and I traveled to Florida to recruit, and we recruited some *great* players and some *great* kids. We attended two-day recruiting fairs held in cafeterias and gyms at five or six different high schools over a two-week period. Coach Sy took considerable pride in being the first coaching staff at the fair and the last to leave. Sometimes close to a hundred coaches attended, but we were always the hardest working group there, and it paid off: No college in the country recruited as many players from Florida as we did.

Sometimes it would be 90 degrees at these fairs, so Coach Sy packed a cooler, a towel to wipe away the sweat, and a fresh shirt or two. We talked to kids all day, straight through, 7 a.m. to 5 p.m.

Fifty to seventy colleges set up tables, hoping players would stop and get acquainted. Many coaches only talked to kids who stopped at their tables. Many coaches were hung over from the night before and wanted to talk to as few recruits as possible — in order to regroup and party again that night.

Hundreds of kids came to each fair, and Coach Sy was adamant that we talk to every single one. Usually, we had a line fifty deep waiting to talk to us. There were times we had so many kids that Coach Sy actually *stood* on a table or a chair so people could see and hear him. The other coaches thought he was crazy. But that *crazy* took us to winning seasons and a 9-1 team.

On many evenings, Coach Sy, Joe Mayo, and I, three generations of football coaches, sat in our hotels talking about football, the world, and life. To this day, I feel blessed to have had that time and experience.

Remembering Coach Sy
Fred Van Steen

I came for my recruiting visit in early February of '92, and the name of the former head coach was still on the office door. I remember Coach Sy sitting in that metal chair behind his desk. When he spoke, he had a booming voice, and I knew I wanted to play football for him.

Camp in August was hot and humid and an all-day, all-night affair. I swear we were up at the field house at 6:30 a.m., ready for thirty to forty-five minutes of PT every day. We had a light snack, juice, and a piece of fruit, and then it was full pads on the practice field from 7:45 to 11. Lunch followed, a break until 2, another meeting, another practice from 3-6, dinner, and meetings from 7:15 to 10:30 or 11. We repeated this routine for ten days. Camp started with one hundred and twenty players and finished with ninety at best.

Coach Sy did a great job of coaching that year. In the opener, we lost to Charleston Southern by one point in a hurricane, and it got worse from there. The highlight was a lightning delay during game three against Salisbury State. Coach gave a good half-time speech, but we went out flat. Lighting struck during the third quarter, so back to the field house we go. Coach was talking to the offense when someone started bitching and complaining. BAM! His clipboard shattered over the dumbbell rack, and out came *The Wild-Horse Rider Speech.* Coach Sy was fired up! Unfortunately, we lost that game too.

He never lost hope that season — at least never showed it. Every week, he came up with some new motivation. We had the Super Bowl in week seven; World Bowl, week eight; and All-Universe Bowl in week ten.

I became very sick after the Davidson game with an upper respiratory infection and mono on top of it. The doctor said flying me home would do more harm than good, so they quarantined me for a week. The first person to call and come to see me was Coach Sy. He called every day to see how I was doing and if I needed anything.

In '93, we lost to Davidson. Always hated losing to the uppity Biffs and Tanyas. Well, a few select upperclassman decided Monday practices were easy — just film and a light jog. About thirty of us decided to drink a little before practice. Coach Sy caught wind of it, and that was the first time the sixteen 110-yard sprints were run at MC. Needless to say, those who had been drinking were throwing up and dying after the second or third sprints. Coach Sy just kept blowing the whistle to start the next cycle. "I think this will solve the drinking before practice!" he said.

When we played Gallaudet, we were hammering them — I'm guessing 42-0. I returned a punt — almost for a touchdown. A few plays later, Coach Sy says to me, "Great return, but I want you to remember how it felt your freshman year when we were getting stomped by teams and losing big." He paused. "I need you to fair catch it every time you're in there from now on." He was all about winning with class and not running up the score.

In '94, we had accomplished a lot, going from 0-10 to 4-6 and 5-5. We could have been 7-3 with a little luck. Coach had the program in a great direction. I was a golf management student and offered a job in Pinehurst to start working full-time while still going to school, but I'd have to quit football my senior year. I called and asked for a sit-down. I said, "Coach, I'm 5 foot 8, 150 pounds, and have made it this far with no serious injuries. I have an opportunity to get a jump on my chosen career path, and I can't pass it up."

He said, "Fred, I can respect you have thought this out."

In 2002, I saw on ESPN that Methodist College football was being investigated for a hazing incident and that Coach was reportedly encouraging this kind of behavior. I was shocked and livid. I followed the story, and when the college tried to blame Coach Sy, I went on a letter-writing campaign to say how such behavior is not anything Coach Sypult would condone, let alone promote. I was so relieved when all charges were cleared. I said, "Coach, I am sorry you had to go through that."

He said, "I'm going to put this behind me, Fred." He showed he was a bigger man than most when the bullets were flying all around him.

In March of 2006, I had been through the lowest of lows in my life. I had just been fired from my dream job, my wife was divorcing me, and the hole just seemed to get deeper every day. Coach Sy was working late when he saw me standing outside. "Hey, Fred," he said, "come down here for a minute." As soon as I sat down, he asked, "What's wrong? I can see it in your eyes that life has kicked you."

"Coach, you don't need to hear my troubles."

"No, son, I want to know what's wrong." It meant a lot that he was concerned and sought me out. Like my freshman year, he called to see how I was.

When I took my son to games, Coach Sy always made time to talk after, win or lose, and he always had some words of encouragement for my son.

Coach had a great influence on all of us who played for him. I am truly thankful for him being in my life and for the lessons he taught us. I can still hear his voice saying go to class, sit up front, call your mom.

The other story I loved hearing was how he got married after WVU played Pitt. He would always tell us that story the week of his anniversary. When he told it, we could tell in his voice how much he loved his wife.

Monarchs Remain Kings
Published Spring 1998 in *Bigger, Stronger, Faster*
Kim Goss

When Coach Jim Sypult took the job at Methodist College, there was no place to go but up.

Don't even think about inferring that the Methodist Monarchs, a Division III football team in North Carolina, are a bunch of delicate butterflies. The Monarchs are kings, and the lion is their mighty mascot. Those who question the team's sovereign position have only to look at the record books and the team's regal 9-1 season last year.

Of course, there was a time. In 1992 when Jim Sypult took over the position as head football coach at the college, he inherited a 2-28 record. While not a bunch of flighty insects, the team was playing more like a den of cubs than the king of beasts.

A college coach for twenty-six years, Sypult saw his path clearly delineated. The team had only been formed in 1989, so growing pains were to be expected. After finishing his first year at 0-10, it was obvious that his team needed to grow up fast. And they did. The following season they improved to 4-6, then 5-5, 6-4, and now 9-1 with a national ranking of No. 20. Although their 9-1 record didn't get them into the playoffs, it's obvious that the Methodist Monarchs are finally living up to their mascot's image as king of the jungle.

How did Coach Sypult turn things around? With a solid and systematic approach, one step at a time, as he explains to BFS readers in this insightful interview.

BFS: Did you have a difficult time motivating your players when you took over the program at Methodist College?

JS: When I came aboard, the team had an unfortunate image on campus and in the community as being a doormat. We steadily overcame it through a lot of hard work and a positive attitude.

BFS: Was it difficult to recruit good athletes when you took over?

JS: The year I took the job I got in late, so I didn't have a great recruiting class. When I had a full year to recruit, I was able to bring in a group that ultimately gave us our first winning season.

BFS: What goals did you establish for the team when you began?

JS: At first it was a numbers game — winning two games in a row was an objective, and winning a game on the road was an objective. When we got to the point where we were 6-4, we were just points away from being 9-1. That's when we got away from the numbers and our goal was to play the best football possible and take it one game at a time.

BFS: How would you sum up this year in terms of accomplishing your objectives?

JS: We had a magical year being 9-1. I say that because in six of those victories, we came from behind to win, and two of them were overtime games. So it was obvious that our players believed in themselves and proved that they could go the distance in the fourth quarter and win.

BFS: Your one loss was to Ferrum College, 31-12. What happened?

JS: We just had a bad day. The next week Ferrum played Frostburg State University and lost 30-0, and the following week we played our last game of the season against Frostburg. This was a team we had never beaten, and we ended up winning 40-12, so we felt we had rectified that loss.

BFS: Since your school doesn't offer scholarships, how do you attract good athletes?

JS: We make our living off the guy who might be an inch or two too short, or a step or two too slow, to get a scholarship. Also, it should be recognized that there are a lot of good football players who want to play college ball but who are not offered scholarships. We try to contact every high school and every prospect in the entire state, even if they are going to be offered scholarships. Because, the fact is, some of those guys are overlooked on national letter days, and we're the school that's been talking to them.

At Methodist College, we go out to meet the clientele, and a lot

Coaching D-III ball with Dave Eavenson and Ralph Isernia: No scholarships. No perks. No special treatment. Playing for the joy of playing — athletics at its purest.

of them are people just like me. I'm from the coal mines of West Virginia, and these guys are from the cotton mills and the tobacco farms, and most of them are first-generation students. Here, our first priority is to get a degree, and then to play football at its highest level.

Coach Sy: "Football is a great sport. I love the game. It teaches teamwork, toughness, overcoming adversity, getting off the ground and fighting again."

Sypult Coaching Policy Book

Team is everything. Be one with the team.

Keep going forward when everything seems to be pulling back.

Work for respect. Win hearts and minds. No one gets anywhere alone.

Listening is a skill. Listen with an open mind.

When someone wants to do something because of you, that's leadership.

We must lead by example. We must be the energy. We must be the courage. We must be the difference.

7

THE WILD-HORSE RIDER SPEECH AND CLASSIC STORIES

The Speech
Fred Van Steen

HOW DID *THE WILD-HORSE RIDER SPEECH* come to be? Here is a little backstory about Coach Sypult's motivation and the spark that made the words fly from his mouth.

The fall of 1992 was Coach Sy's first year at the Methodist helm and only the program's fourth year with a record of 2-28 going into that season. We lost our first game 19-20 in Charleston in a monsoon and then got blown out by Guilford at home in game two, 7-37, and it wasn't even that close.

So in game three against Salisbury State, we felt this could be a chance for the Monarchs to get a W. At half-time, it was close, 12-18. We were down but had some momentum just before the half. We made our adjustments and came out flat in the third quarter. Then a lightning delay came along, so we went up to the field house. We are in position groups, and Coach Sy is talking to the offense. Some teammate, who I'm guessing didn't finish the season, started bitching we suck or coaching sucks and the like. Those comments sent Coach Sy off into the greatest tirade ever uttered at Methodist.

It literally started with a BANG as he shattered his clipboard over the dumbbell rack, and shards of it hit Billy Hughes in the face. Then, at the top of his lungs, he shouted, "GODDAMN IT! I'M SICK AND TIRED OF THE BITCHERS AND COMPLAINERS. IT SOUNDS LIKE A BUNCH OF FUCKING DOCTORS AND LAWYERS IN HERE. WE NEED SOME FIGHTERS AND FUCKERS AND WILD-HORSE RIDERS TO PIN THEIR EARS BACK AND FLY DOWN THE FIELD AND HIT SOMEBODY!"

He was HOT, to say the least. Unfortunately, it didn't do the trick. We went out and shit the bed. It was a very trying first year for Coach Sy and that team. He and his staff tried to motivate us every day in one way or another.

The following fall at the start of camp, he gave *The Speech* again, only he was much calmer. He explained who those five people are in life and who he wanted to go to war with — fighters and wild-horse riders, not fuckers (fuckups). To this day, I can hear the sound of that clipboard being smashed and the sheer THUNDER in his voice as those words came out ... as if it just happened.

Coach Sypult may beg to differ as to how this went down. My memory is not as good as it used to be. Cheap helmets in '92.

"There's no better feeling than walking on the field from the *Methodome* before a game. Nothing like it!" Coach Sy leading the troops: Devontre Pearson #90, Jonathan Stutts #65, and Adam Mont de Oca #74.

Being a Wild-Horse Rider
Jonathan Byrd

Now, being called a *wild-horse rider* was the biggest compliment you could get from Coach Sypult, and I really think that to be a long-term successful lifter, you need to be one! A wild-horse rider is there to get the job done. He comes in ready to work, ready to help, and always ready to put forth his best effort.

Sometimes it can't be about you. It has to be about your training partners. Either way, the wild-horse rider has the wild-man streak but enough sense to calm it down when need be. The wild-horse rider is the guy at big meets all over the country who shows up and completes the job in any circumstance. He is ready to win and trains that way day in and day out.

Editor's note: Byrd is a national-ranked, competitive powerlifter.

Stripping in the Bushes
Jeremy McSwain

It was scorching, 100-plus degrees. We were going against the defense, and I didn't cover a botched toss and missed a block. As I *walked* back to the huddle, I saw him coming from a mile away! He looked like a bull to a matador, and I was the red cape fluttering at the hip. And then it happened. It seemed as though everything and everyone got silent. Even the mild wind quit blowing. I didn't know what to do, but the leaders on offense told me to take it in stride; so I tried to prepare. But NOTHING could prepare me for this.

I guess Coach Sy had been eyeing me secretly since the start of camp, so the potential in me was there. All I saw was spit flying and a whistle wagging, as he began to drill me straight into the bush. Before I knew it, he dropped his shorts to his ankles, letting me have it. I couldn't say a WORD! I couldn't move or think. All I wanted to do was hit *restart* because this guy was nuts — literally! Lol. He said I wasn't coachable, was undisciplined, not built for the next level, and if I couldn't get my act together, I could go. He pointed to the road leading back to campus.

It was in that moment I turned into a monster on the field. I heard those words, saw that image, and felt his passion for the entire year. Most players would have given up, and I almost did, but I had to prove him wrong. I didn't know how, but I had a year to get it right. Before the season began, I was starting on offense and special teams. I ended up the leading rusher on the team as a freshman. I was the leading kick returner, and he made me a gunner on the kick-off team — that was special to me. To end the season as the leading rusher, leading kick returner, and special teams Player of the Year tells the story of a young man evolving with true tutelage. I need to fact-check, but I may be the only player in Methodist history to rush for a TD, catch a TD, kick return a TD, and score a kickoff TD.

I remember being in my first film session, and I was the example. Coach Sy said who's this guy getting *waffooed*? The clip shows me flying through the air in slow motion. He replayed it for three minutes, and everyone was laughing until the punchline: "Now watch this. Look who tracks the runner down and makes a spectacular tackle — McSwain! Great job, McSwain," he said. "That's commitment!" It was then I realized he valued me, and I valued and still value that lesson.

I was still a work in progress throughout each year, but our bond was unmatched. I still hear his voice saying my name *McSwain*! He had a special twang when he said it! When my grandfather died, Coach Sy stepped right into that role. He was just a smooth, cool dude. He held us to the fire, but deep down, he was a softie.

Editor's note: McSwain said Coach Sy's disrobing meant commitment, being all in — one for all and NEVER for self. That's the Monarch Way!

Jonathan Willis recalls the occasion: "I still remember that day. I forget who Coach Sy was calling out for being lazy, but he pulled everything off and just sat down in the middle of the practice field. Lol. Good man!"

Never Give Up
Brandon Iseman

As players, we always felt lucky when we got to spend time with Coach Sy, especially on away trips because he would sit down with us and tell stories. He told us a story from his playing days at West Virginia when a new coaching staff came in and was trying to run off players from the old team. Coach said they tried everything to run him off to get his scholarship.

Nothing was working, so one day they went to the extreme and made him do up-downs, but backwards. Up-downs are a normal practice in football. You just chop your feet, and on command, you drop to the ground on your chest and pop back up — nothing crazy. But that day, they made him do it backwards, so on command, he had to drop on his back and hop back up. If you don't know, up-downs are extremely painful and hard. But he did them and never gave in. Honestly, there are a lot of good memories I'm thankful to have now.

Laundry Duty
Leon Ché Clark

Coach Sy had this weird thing about laundry. The angriest I can recall ever seeing him is when the laundry didn't get done one day, and some of us had wet gear. He fired the work-study crew, don't know who, and moved me from study-hall monitor to laundry duty. He said something like "You are a leader on this team and will be a captain one day. Part of that is helping take care of the team. If a guy comes to practice and his clothes are wet, we have already lost the day. He can't focus and is feeling sorry for himself. The first thing we have to do is get dressed. If we can't do that, nothing else matters. Get it right."

I guess Coach Sy's philosophy was "If you're going to be a leader, you're going to wash jockstraps." It is the crescendo of small things that makes the ultimate goal more likely to be achieved. So his *point* was not about laundry. It was about making sure little things are taken care of — things taken for granted or never noticed until they're not right.

Take Care of Your Feet
Lance Wilkie

The trick to making athletes compete all-out is keeping it fun ... or should I say interesting? One year, the team gathered in a large classroom during camp to review and discuss the day. It was a rough camp, and people were going down left and right. I expected Coach Sy to tear into us about bad practices or some other matter. To my surprise, he walked in with a bag and said he was going to do something different that evening.

He sat in a chair in the middle of the room with well over a hundred players and coaches staring at him. We had no idea what he was about to say. He proceeded to pull Vaseline, lotion, and tube socks slowly out of the bag — which generated some pretty big laughs. They had NOTHING and EVERYTHING to do with football. He told us he was disappointed in how many were getting foot blisters and not able to practice.

His demonstration baffled some because we could be learning plays, and Coach Sy was teaching life lessons. He took off his shoes and socks and began rubbing his feet with products from the bag.

Then he slid on his sock and stressed the importance of pulling our socks taut with no wrinkles because they could cause blisters as well. He finished by telling us to tie our shoes tightly so our feet weren't sliding around in them.

Why did Coach teach us to take care of our feet? Well, it could have been to lighten the mood as he did on many occasions. It could have been to teach us to pay attention to details. It could have been to ensure we were taking care of ourselves so we stayed on the field. It could have been he cared about our futures and didn't want us to experience foot problems. I tend to think it was all of the above. Coach Sy was a legend, and he impacted every person he came in contact with in one way or another.

Semper Fi
Mike McDermott

My plan was always to play college football after serving in the Marine Corps. My best friend, Leon Ché Clark who also served, told me to come and meet his coach and check out the campus. Three months later, I was playing college football at Methodist for Coach Jim Sypult.

I knew I liked him, but I didn't know what kind of man he was. We were on our third practice of the day, in the heat of a Carolina August, in humidity so thick we were practically swimming. Coach Sy blew his whistle to indicate the next stage of the session. Players ran about the field to their designated areas.

Coach Sy called out to the coaches that he needed more players for the drill he was running. One coach promptly screamed, "We need more bodies over here. Get moving. More bodies over here now."

Coach Sypult blew his whistle and jogged over to the coach in the middle of the practice field, amidst a hundred and forty to a hundred and sixty players, and did something he rarely did. He raised his voice to a coach: "They are *not* bodies. They are football players. They are *not* bodies; they are *men*."

That was everything I needed to know about his character.

Over the years, he became a mentor and friend. Ché and I were a bit older than our teammates as we'd spent four years in the Marines. As such, Coach would periodically pull us into his office to chat.

Sometimes just to shoot the bull and, at times, to get a pulse on the team. In one such discussion, he addressed the fact he'd recently been ill and had quickly lost a lot of weight. He told us of the medical ramifications and dietary restrictions.

Then he turned to me and said, "Mike, if I knew when I was drinking my last beer that it was my last, I'd savor it."

I said, "Coach, from now on, I'll drink every beer as if it's my last."

He was an honest and earnest man who told us the truth when it needed telling and gave us encouragement whether needed or not.

His passion for football was equaled only by his love for life. A masterful and funny storyteller, Coach Sy wove his experiences into lessons he'd deliver at the end of each practice to an audience that was completely captivated every single day. These weren't lectures he delivered. He spoke to us, almost as if individually, and what he said resonated with each.

We were the Wild-Horse Riders, and he was our lead Ranger.

Coach Sypult spawned countless coaching careers with a legacy of success all over the world from North Carolina to Hong Kong. He rightfully took pride in their careers and followed his former players, continuing to coach and encourage.

He loved football, he loved his teams, he loved his players. And we loved him. *Semper fi,* Coach Sypult!

The Fight Song
Leon Ché Clark

I started college in the spring after finishing my enlistment in the Marines in December 1992. I often stopped by Coach Sy's office for help not only with the adjustment to college life but also the transition from military to civilian life. In one of these conversations, I asked about a fight song. As the program was only in the fourth year, we did not have one. Coach Sy said, "If you want one, write one. I think it is a good idea."

I wrote what I thought was a traditional-sounding fight song. The original version was to "76 Trombones" from the *Music Man*, but it sounded too jokey, so I went with "Washington and Lee Swing" as the music. I submitted the lyrics to Coach; he corrected some grammar and said it was good to go. At the next team meeting, he introduced it to the team. During camp that next summer, he started the tradition of having each class sing the song after evening meetings ... which I believe is still carried on to this day. He also introduced the rule that we would only sing the song if we won.

The very first game of the 1993 season was a win at home, the first win in two years for Methodist, and the first win for Coach at Methodist. As the team ran to the end zone after the game, I yelled to Coach, "We are going to sing the song!"

He replied as he put his arm around my shoulder, "And you wrote it!" I did not play a single down that game, but "The Fight Song" was my contribution to the team. Coach told me a few years later that without a song, we would have had nothing to do in the end zone but put our thumbs in our asses.

Editor's note: Singing "The Fight Song" became a *spirited* tradition.

"The Fight Song"

It's time to take a stand for Methodist,
And we will show them all who is the best.
For when we face that college team today,
We will kick their ass and send them on their way.
And we will fight, fight, fight for every yard,
Crash the ends and hit that line right hard.
We'll drive ol' college off the sod, off the sod for old MC/MU.

The Coal Miner Story
Fred Van Steen

One story Coach Sy told often and with great passion was the coal miner story. He started off saying how important it was to go to class and do well in school. Then he described his freshman year at WVU when he starred on the football field but not in the classroom. He said things like "Hey, I was a big-time football player. I didn't need to go to class."

When he went home at the end of the semester, his dad saw his grades and was *not* happy. He made Coach get up at 5 a.m. and ride a coal car to the bottom of the mine. That would be his life, his dad said, if he didn't go to class.

Editor's note: Coach Sy became a good student thereafter. He said West Virginians were tough, proud people with strong family values, and he was lucky to be a part of that life.

RINGIN, DINGIN, SINGIN, and PINGIN!
Andrew Mullis

I will never forget camp my senior year. We didn't talk about anything to do with football ... just about life and what I wanted to do with the rest of mine. We sat in the lobby of Sanford dorm till like three in the morning! He was a great man who taught so many others how to be great men!

Later on, after graduation, I hadn't seen Coach Sy in years, and I came down for a game. I knew where to find him. I walked over to the chapel, and he met me coming out the door.

As he said it: "Mullis, looking good! RINGIN, DINGIN, SINGIN, and PINGIN!"

My response was nothing other than "Love you, Coach!"

We shook hands. I may have given him a bro hug, and again, we talked about life on our way back to the field house.

Then, as usual, Coach Sy was off to the field for specialist teams.

Coach Sy: "Coaching is taking players to places they have not been ... and getting the team to play with one heartbeat."

8

WE ARE THE WILD-HORSE RIDERS

KENNETH ASHLEY, #52, Defensive End
Because of Coach Sy, I knew there were good white men in this world. He was a positive influence in my life at a young age. He showed me patience, understanding, love, and discipline. I've seen the good, bad, and ugly, and I thank him for being part of the good. He was a great coach and even better mentor and man.

Rhyan Breen, #61, Offensive Guard

The first time I ever met Coach Sy was in the basement of Riddle Center during my campus visit in 2004. We had a good talk about football, and he asked if I was dating anyone and if she was a good woman.

I said yes. Turns out I was wrong as hell. But I remember him spending a couple of moments telling me how important it is to have love in my life. He and Dr. Sy are the couple I hope my wife and I one day grow up to be.

I also remember seeing *Football for Dummies* among a collection of books in his office. I knew this is the kind of guy I wanted to play for, one who looked at the whole picture but didn't take himself too seriously.

Mikey Brumbles, #37, Fullback

Let me tell you how Coach Sy helped me and so many others. In the four years I played under Coach, he gave me confidence and a great knowledge of life. He was not only a mentor, but he was like a father to me. He will never know how much he helped me. Thank you, Coach.

Jonathan Byrd, #55, Offensive Guard

Coach Sypult was much more than a football coach. He was a father figure to many of us. He helped mold and shape both my drive and work ethic. He was a very fiery coach and at times pretty intimidating. My freshman year, he once used all the timeouts in a row — in the first half of a game — just to yell at us! Funny thing is, it worked!

I was never a great player, but that didn't matter. He loved us all anyway. This is why we do the things we do now as men. This man was a hero to countless young men no matter if they were starters or strugglers. Called *awesome* by his players, he built a program at Methodist and raised more men than I dare to count! His legacy lives on with many former players coaching all across the nation.

Anthony Cassone, #40, Defensive Line

You've taught me so much more than just football. You taught me to … well, grow up. Words cannot express my gratitude. You shared so much with me and my fellow Methodist brothers. I can share my fondest memories I will cherish the rest of my life:

- Adversity — always learn to deal with it.
- Socks and cleats, yes, there is a checklist for properly putting them on.
- Pappa Sy, you got big balls.
- Doctors, lawyers, fuckers, wild-horse riders, and fighters — he put me in the *fighter* category which I took with pride.
- The best breakfast before conditioning — Gatorade, Nutri-Grain bar, and a banana.
- The best way to finish a long, tough day of practice — singing "The Fight Song" and eating ice cream with brothers.
- "Your wife is everything because she may be your only fan in the stands, cheering you on," Coach Sy said.

I remembered my freshman year when I was a fullback, and my position coach wasn't going to put me on the bus. At the last second, Coach Sy stepped in with his Wild-Horse Rider demeanor and said, "Cassone is fucking traveling."

When I got switched my sophomore year to defense, I was angry, I was selfish, I retaliated against my position coaches. Coach Sy pulled me into his office and chewed my ass. He showed me to think more about others, the team, and my brothers. To accept reality, fight adversity, and become a better person.

One of the best times in my life! Basically, Coach Sy is a part of me more than he knows, and one day, I plan on sharing what I learned from him with my two little boys. May he run field and dance on the beach happy for eternity.

Leon Ché Clark, #64, Defensive End

Contrary to rumor, I was Coach Sy's FIRST recruit at Methodist. My old roommate, Chad Drake, has tried to claim that title on a technicality over the years, but he was a JUCO transfer, so it does not count. Coach ventured into the Marine Corps Base, walked a gauntlet of MP K-9s, to introduce himself and shake my hand. Nine months later, we hugged in the end zone, celebrating his first victory at Methodist. It was the same after the first road win. Then the first Homecoming victory. We did the same after the tenth win, twentieth win, and first winning season. I was there for all of that.

Torre Crockett, #68, Defensive End

Good dude, good coach, definition of a team builder. We all left Methodist bonded to each other. All across the country, guys from Methodist are still close to each other! I learned a lot from Coach Sy. Great memories.

Patrick Doleman, #8, Wide Receiver

It's a great day to be a Wild-Horse Rider. It was an experience for us all. Coach Sypult was THE EXAMPLE of how coaching should be. I'm truly blessed to have played my favorite game in the world with a WILD-HORSE RIDER like him.

One thing I've observed over the years is the importance of having the right people around you. The importance of choosing the PERFECT WIFE! It's so pivotal in a man's life. If Coach Sy's wife wasn't the lovely person she is, it's pretty safe to say the EXPERIENCE we had with Coach wouldn't have been the same.

So I THANK God for placing you two together at the right time and right place. A single flower in a field can produce an entire field of flowers. We are just thankful you bloomed the way you did.

I know the entire Lord's Prayer by heart because of how we prayed together as a team before the games. I'm truly blown away by this experience. Coach Sypult is a LEGEND!

Jamaal M. Doran, #32, Fullback

Man, Coach was awesome. Nobody could give a speech like Coach Sy. He could motivate an ant to drink Raid.

If you met Coach Sy, you met a giant. Not in stature, but in spirit!

This man was a hero to countless young men. He knew how to spot potential and saw the best in individuals when we didn't see it ourselves. He was fair and had a way of bringing out the best in us. But make no mistake, he wasn't soft. He would dig into you if needed, only to follow up with compassion and love. He was more about building character and men.

Coach Sy was a true man of FAITH, FAMILY, and FOOTBALL. I believe his works will continue to live on through many generations. He planted seeds in younger players to work hard and do the right thing. I have seen it firsthand many times over the years ... and it leads back to Coach Jim Sypult somehow. The leader. The storyteller. The motivator.

Chad Drake, #68, Offensive Line

Coach, if it hadn't been for you, I would have left. I will never forget you picking me up when I was brokenhearted. I will never forget you encouraging me to play to the best of my ability. You live in the truth. Your savior is Jesus. You have touched many men. You are first class to take care of your coaches and families.

I am proud to be your first recruit on your first Methodist team. We wore *mint-green* practice uniforms for a year; I call it *character-building*. Without you, Methodist football was a train wreck.

I used *The Wild-Horse Rider Speech* from platoon commander to regimental commander. Of the five types of people, which one are you? My Marines loved it, and I always attributed it to you.

Andrew Farris, #84, Defensive Line

I just keep hearing all the things Coach Sy used to say. His voice is so loud in my head. I wasn't as close to him as the offensive guys, but he influenced me in so many ways. I learned so much under him that affects how I coach now.

David Foster, #32, Tight End

Coach Sypult loved each and every one of his players. He took care of us and taught us how to be men and how to love. Always had our backs. Never let us fall or fail. Taught us good morals, ethics, and character.

He was a father to us all. He led us, guided us, fought with us, taught us how to be men and love our families and God. He was the lion that protected his pride. He will forever be in our hearts and minds. He was a true Wild-Horse Rider. We love you, Coach!

Chris Gauntlett, #33, Free Safety

The man taught more than X's and O's. He raised many boys to be great men! Second father for most of us. Only father figure for a lot. Always did it the right way. My news feed is constantly flooded with very successful Monarchs. No way I would be the person I am today without him being in my life. Love you, Coach Sy. You are the original Wild-Horse Rider.

Andrew Geddie, #14, Quarterback

Coach Sy fired every bullet in the chamber. After a subpar freshmen camp in 2010, I played great in our first scrimmage and led the game-winning drive. Coach Sy walked up to me afterwards, shook my hand, and said, "Geddie, that was some good shit." He then got in his golf cart and drove off. Lol! I didn't hear him cuss much, so that was special. I'll never forget that day.

Justin Howard, #45, Linebacker

When Coach Sy took over the defense in '04, he brought back the passion, unity, and physicalness it needed. Totally transformed the defense into a brotherhood and togetherness I had not seen. We played as one unit, and we never lost our confidence on the field. It was the greatest experience playing under him on defense.

Tavares Hunter, #70, Defensive Tackle

Coach was our inspiration and will forever live in all of us. "The Wild-Horse Rider" story plus many others molded and changed us. He taught life, fatherhood, brotherhood, marriage, family, team, and so many more lessons. He gave me my chance, and every day I give back to someone what Jim Sypult gave to me. His legacy will live forever through the many lives he so greatly changed. I have Sypult blood in my veins! The Wild-Horse Riders love you.

Greg Hyslop, #59, Linebacker

Coach Sy was more than just a football coach. He was our mentor, our friend, and a father figure to all of us.

I was a member of the '05 championship season, and all we could think about in the moment was the great football we played. Now as I think back to that season and all the seasons I had with Coach Sy, the most vivid memories I have are the times he spent with me off the field, talking about everything but football — getting good grades, doing the right things, and just being a good human being.

The game is great but making an impact on young men is greater. Coach Sy will live forever through all of us.

Brandon Iseman, #63, Guard

Coach Sy called the team up one practice and started telling a story about seeing sea lions on the wharf in San Francisco. So he had the players lie on the field and act like sea lions and called it "Walrus Wednesday."

He was a great guy. Always believing in his players and looking out for us. I'm blessed to share my time with him.

Editor's note: Walrus or sea lion? Didn't matter. Coach Sy fancied a colorful phrase and fun practice.

Jesse James Iversen, #80, Wide Receiver

We can all attest to the impact this great man, coach, and mentor had on our lives. Let us honor his legacy and support each other. Let's show Coach Sy how even now, many years after our playing years have passed, we still have each other's backs. Many of us have never met, but we are forever linked because of the blood, sweat, and tears we shed with the same coach on the same field.

Mickey Jordan, #41, Linebacker

Wow! Where do I start about this great man? God put Coach Sy in my life for a reason. My freshman year of college, my father passed away unexpectedly. I was not performing well academically and had broken my ankle in practice. I decided this college thing wasn't for me, so I didn't return after my father's funeral. I started working and didn't plan on going back.

Jim Sypult did not let that happen. He called me every week to see how I was doing and to encourage me to return to school. I still remember the day he called and said, "Mick, what would your father want you to do?"

I replied, "I'll see you in August for camp."

This man became my father figure for the next four years, teaching as much and more about life as he did about football. God has a plan for us even when not-so-good things happen. I am so blessed God put Jim Sypult in my life. He taught us about life, football, and how to be Wild-Horse Riders.

Nathan Kindley, #88, Tight End

Coach Sypult has been a mentor and father figure to me. He looks you in the eye on your very first day, tells you you're not getting preferential treatment but he'll love you sincerely. What you get in this program is what you earn. And from the very start, you see how much you can grow and learn.

Koby King, #21, Free Safety

I was a running back my whole life, but my sophomore year coming into camp, Coach Sypult said I could play for him at safety. He believed in my athleticism. I could start right away or play behind senior running back Mike Hill. I won the starting job, and it was the best year of football I've ever played. It was all because Coach coached me HARD and believed in me. I took that same mindset with me to the army. Coach Sypult was a great coach and an even better person.

I was in Afghanistan in 2011. It was my third tour, twice to Iraq, and my first in Afghanistan. I was telling some people about playing college football, and a day later, Coach Sy friend-requested me, and I'm glad he did.

I wish I could tell him this face-to-face, but I honestly, truly appreciate everything he did for me my two years at Methodist. He tried to help when my grades were bad. He did everything possible. Even when I had a lot of family issues, he was there and checked on me every day.

Leaving the team, the school, and all my friends is something I'll always regret. The day I heard Methodist beat Campbell, I broke down and cried because I knew I should have been there battling it out with the team. I've grown up a lot since then and realized my mistakes, and that was one of my biggest. I've learned so much from Coach Sy, and I'm here to say he actually cared more about me as an individual than just one of his football players.

Quincy Malloy, #50, Defensive Tackle

Coach Jim Sypult was not just a coach or mentor, he was a father figure to me, and I considered him a hero. One of the most well-respected men I have ever had the pleasure of meeting.

He recruited me to play football for Methodist and was an intricate part in my employment at Methodist University. He will always have a special part not only in my heart, but my mother's and father's hearts for what he has done for me personally.

He is truly a hero in my eyes and will never be forgotten. I learned about honor and legacy from him. Honor the ones who came before us, and leave a legacy for the ones who follow.

Mike Maraschiello, #69, Offensive Tackle

When Coach Sy lost his toe and drove a golf cart, there was never a time he didn't pick up a player or two on the way to the practice field.

Tardy Rule for Coaches: Coach Sy started every staff meeting with a joke, and the only acceptable excuse for a coach being late to a meeting or practice was if he got lucky — the tardy rule.

Jason McCarty, #40, Defensive Back

The bond that was made and shared on the gridiron is just as strong today as it was then. It's hard to explain, but it's as if time stopped, and the bond is the same. I remember Coach Sy's stories about the West Virginia coal mines. Coal is needed to forge steel, and with great pressure and the right materials, things become stronger. Coach Sy had a sixth sense for picking players he could forge into men capable of great things. That's why he's the Blacksmith of Brotherhood. I miss all the guys and look forward to the next time we sing "The Fight Song." Coach Sy is the reason for the bond we all share.

Greg McDonald, #33, Running Back

Like so many others, Coach gave me the chance to continue my football career after high school when no one else did, helping to make me a better person.

No words can justify what he meant to all the young teens he helped turn into men. I myself will be forever grateful for the time I spent with him. He was loved and will be truly missed. Coach Sy will live on through all of his former student-athletes.

Corey McGuire, #21, Running Back

I was lying in bed thinking about Coach Sy. He was a heck of a man, and every day I use the life lessons he taught me. I was a tough kid when I got to Methodist, but Coach Sy turned me into a tough man. I consider myself lucky to have been coached by him.

One of our conversations that always sticks with me was when he would talk about family. He explained to me — and I'll never forget it — coaching is just a job he loves, and it means the world to him, but nothing comes before family.

As a young coach myself now, I try and keep this in mind when the school asks me to do things that would put my family second. I hope I can make my wife feel half the amount of love Coach Sy had for his wife.

Will McPhaul, #83, Tight End

Poppa Sy taught me so much and made me the man I am. My freshman year, we toured the National Mall before the Catholic University game. I was surrounded by seniors touring with Coach Sy's group. He looked around and reminded us that we were all his kids. And we should also be brothers on and off the field.

It wasn't the trip itself. It wasn't just football. It was knowing we are Coach Sy's children. He taught us to look after each other. He prepared us to be men and brothers.

Jeremy McSwain, #44, Running Back

Man, he truly walked me through the process of life and took the time to mold me. We were like a married couple, at each other's throats every year, but nothing could keep us apart. He gave me the Michael Vick sentence, had me in the stands like a bum for a few damn weeks, and then had my ass running laps at 5:45 a.m. But he wouldn't give up on me, and I'm forever grateful.

The realest legend. The only man to strip down in front of me ... with a whistle hanging from his neck in 105-degree heat behind the freaking bushes. The originator of the Wild-Horse Riders.

Jim Sypult may be gone in the flesh, but I can promise you this: His soul, wisdom, famous sayings, and leadership will last a lifetime, and that's the Monarch way.

Austin Money, #53, Center

Jim Sypult molded generations of boys into men and taught us how to be Wild-Horse Riders. I tell my boys stories about him all the time and appreciate all the lessons he passed on. It was an honor to have been at MU with him. I celebrate the man who has made this world a significantly better place.

Tyler Mosko, #27, Kicker

Coach Sy was a man of God, and we met regularly for Bible studies during lunch. We often sat in his golf cart or office and had talks about things unrelated to football—like his grandson Kyle. Coach was such a role model, and I considered him a second dad.

He genuinely cared about each of his players, even the freshmen and those who didn't play. I loved when he talked to me before an important field goal or onside kick; he always calmed my nerves. He gave excellent hugs and was a great coach and great friend. I really value our relationship.

When Brittany and I got married, Coach and his wife came to our wedding which I remember as if it were yesterday. It meant a lot to me, and Brittany and I always said, "Man, we want to be like them when we grow older—so in love."

Chris Nuta, #50, Linebacker

Jim Sypult unequivocally influenced hundreds, maybe thousands, of young men throughout his lifetime. Every single one of them was better for it. My life would not be the same today without him.

Matt Panza, #69, Linebacker

Without Coach, I would be nowhere near the man I am today. Coach taught me so much about what it takes to be a good man. I will be passing all of that to my son.

Alan Preston, #16, Quarterback

Coach Jim Sypult has imprinted on all of us. I know he imprinted on me. I see it every time I talk one-on-one with a player. Coach Sy would always give us his undivided attention for however long it took. If he saw a problem, he attacked it head-on. He was definitely one of the main reasons I stayed at Methodist instead of transferring.

He was a great man, and his memories and stories will be passed on through me and my fellow Horse Riders. I didn't know it then, but a lot of what Coach Sy said and did molded the way I coach today. From the way to build a coach-player relationship to his crazy stories to lying on the practice field like sea lions. Lol. It all makes sense now.

Jeremy Priebe, #85, Tight End

Jim Sypult was a great coach and a better man. I had a great time playing and coaching for him. It was always about more than football with him. Thankful for all the great memories.

J. Todd Purgason, #60, Offensive Center

I played football for Coach Sy at Methodist from 1994-1997. He taught us a lot. He believed in us when others didn't and provided guidance to go into the world to be productive citizens. Coach always talked about the importance of having a relationship with the Lord and caring for our families and friends. Now we lean on the Lord's strength, not our own, to get our families through this pandemic.

Rob Reimers, #53, Defensive Tackle

Coach Sy was a true leader. He was the first person I saw when I was told my best friend died, and he hugged me and told me everything was OK. And you know what? I felt safe, and I knew he was right. He's why I loved football. He's why I am who I am.

Irrington *Miami* Roberts, #97, Tight End

Coach Sy had to speak to the team about possible racial issues we would face playing Maryville College in Tennessee. I'm not sure how loud he said it, but I know he started off by saying he hated the fact he had to have this conversation in this day and age. That always stood out to me because no one in my life who was white ever spoke to me about racial issues, let alone LEAD with personal opinion. That meant a lot to me, not only as a player, but as a young black man.

Coach Sy was so much more than just a coach to me and all his players. He was a father figure who led by example with good old-fashioned values. And he was a man of his word. Coach may not have physically had a son, but God blessed him with hundreds of sons. Anyone who has ever played under Coach Sy is part of that family.

Chris Roncketti, #2, Quarterback

Jim Sypult, I would follow you into battle anywhere, anytime. I just hope you know how much you meant to so many and just how influential you were in our lives. You are the reason there are so many former Monarchs doing great things, and I will never forget those lessons you taught us. I hope I can make you proud. Until we meet again ... *Ready ready Monarchs!*

Andrew Rusk, #52, Linebacker

Coach Sy, the Father of Methodist football, gave many a chance at one last shot of our dreams to play college ball. It may have only been D-III, but it was the world to us and to him. He loved Methodist College and his boys.

He kept in touch with many of us. We could always count on a *Happy Birthday* from him. I remember a talk we had after my last game on the road at Shenandoah University. We had stopped at the usual I-95 rest area coming into the state of Virginia. He saw I was upset more at myself than anything. We had a nice talk that night. He really cared even though that same year he fired me mid-game from the Press Box at Monarch Stadium — true story.

He also made us Wilmington Boys take a picture with him, so he could put it in his favorite Kure Beach establishment. I learned so much from him, and he helped me meet many of my lifelong friends. The Monarch nation loves him and honors him. We had a great ride with the original.

Joshua Rusk, #58, Offensive Guard

I always enjoyed Picture Day because Coach Sy would gather all of us who lived near Carolina Beach for a picture to hang in a bar he frequented. But, really, I remember how we always knew he cared about us, and we loved him for that. He has shaped me so much in my coaching and teaching career from the things he taught that I could never repay. He was an amazing father figure and leader to us young men.

Frank Santora, #55, Linebacker

Coach was like a father to me. I dropped out for three years, and when I came back, he called me into the office, came out from around the desk, and gave me the biggest hug. He said how happy he was I was back. He asked me about my schedule. He got my classes back on track for what I needed.

Then he said, YOU are playing. I said I wasn't sure; he said I needed to. He was right. I needed him and the football family. He always made sure I was doing what I needed to in class. On the day of graduation, he was there as he was for all his players who graduated, smiling and happy that one of his boys got his degree.

He always said, "Those who stay will be champions." He wasn't talking about football. He was talking about what we start, we finish in life. He not only made me a better player, but he made me a better man and now father to my kids.

This man loved his players and pushed us on and off the field to become better men. I am forever grateful for what he did for me as a coach and friend. The original Wild-Horse Rider! I love him.

Scott Schwarzer, #13, Quarterback

Ready ready Monarchs! Hey! Bob Swank and Gary *Gunny* Cunningham joined our Chamblee, Georgia, coaching staff in 2019. I believe Coach Jim Sypult, the greatest head coach in Methodist history, is looking down with a huge smile on his face.

Long, long ago when I told Coach Sypult I wanted to coach, he told me to surround myself with good people. Fortunately, I get to relive my two years as a Monarch every day with Coach Swank. We often talk about our time at MC. Every day, I get to see the influence Coach Sy had on Coach Swank and me.

I almost quit playing football during my second season at MC because I was having trouble recovering from an ACL reconstruction. I sat in Coach Sy's office on a Monday after we defeated Guilford and told him I didn't think I could do it anymore. Coach Sy looked at me and told me I couldn't quit. I am so glad I didn't because I remember to this day the feeling of defeating Frostburg State to finish 9-1 and singing "The Fight Song" for the last time.

Coach Swank actually paraphrased *The Speech* to our kids this past season, and it really hit home. And our team motto was "Get It Done." There are so many quotes, phrases, and things about Coach Sy we all recall. From *The Speech* to hearing him tell our tailbacks (DeCarlos West and Dedrick Gaddy) to "stick it up in there" to my favorite story when he visited the coal mines his freshman year at WVU and realized he'd rather go to school than do that for a lifetime. Coach Sy will live on forever so positively in all of us.

Jon Sherman, #13, Wide Receiver/Tight End

When Coach Sy gave me a chance to chase my dream and coach college ball, I really didn't know what to say. The memories and lessons he taught me while I coached for him will always stick with me! Whether we won or lost, the bus rides coming back from the away games were the best because it was just the two of us talking. We sat next to each other and talked about everything from football to wine.

A day I will never forget was the day he asked me to ride with him to pick up his wife at the airport. We just hung out. Watching how he looked at and embraced her taught me a lot about balance. I could tell there was more to life.

Damon Sloan, #71, Offensive Line

He was not only a coach but also a mentor. I enjoyed playing for him at Methodist and still use a lot of his core values in my day-to-day life. To know him was to love him and to become part of his family. All these years later, we were still in contact. I loved him dearly.

Kyle Smith, #79, Defensive Tackle

First time I had Sunrise Services [aka discipline drills], Coach Sy showed up with a newspaper in hand. We ran only two laps when he honked the horn to stop. "Fellas," he said, "you're lucky the newspaper was a waste today."

I and another player were in the deer stand, filming practice. I was out due to a shoulder separation. It was 400 degrees in that deer stand. We were on the way down, and next thing you know, it broke, and down we went. Coach Sy walked over to check on us and yelled, "Riverside [Raleigh]. These boys are all right."

From the Sunrise Services to running pursuit drills and trying to get in front of his golf cart when he was the ball carrier. To the one-on-one meetings he and I would have just because. To him showing us how to take care of our feet. I could go on and on with stories that seem as if they were yesterday.

Coach Sy turned many of us from eighteen-year-old know-it-alls to young men. He taught us the game of life through something we all loved — football! The lessons I learned on the football field far outweigh anything I learned in the classroom. I'm thankful Coach Sy gave me a chance to live a childhood dream.

He means so much more to us than just *Coach*. He was a mentor, father, friend, and the wildest of Wild-Horse Riders. I will forever be grateful for the moments I got to spend with him.

Matthew Sposato, #63, Linebacker

I remember his speech about just how important your feet are and how to take care of them properly. He demonstrated the correct way to put on our socks, being ever so vigilant to make sure there were no wrinkles in them before putting on our shoes.

Editor's note: There's much to know about dry feet, sweaty feet, athlete's foot, and blisters.

Darrien Tucker, #12, Defensive Back

I came to Methodist as a transfer from a college in Tennessee. I spoke with Coach Sypult over that summer several times, and he spoke to me as if he had known me for years. When I finally came to Methodist in '95, I learned I didn't have the funds to stay. Coach Sy seemed as hurt to hear this as I was. I'll never forget his words to me as I left to go back home. He told me I'd be back and he would make sure of that. Just take care of my end, he said, and he would make sure I was taken care of when I came back.

Fast forward to '96. I'm back on campus ready to check in, and he comes up to me and gives me the biggest hug. It wasn't about the football player in me. It was the person he saw in me.

During my junior year, Coach thought it would be a good idea for me to run for Mr. Homecoming. With the help of the football team and Coach Sy, I became the '97 Homecoming King, representing the Monarch football team. Coach had a way of making things happen.

If someone asked me what I learned from this great man, coach, and mentor, it's to fight through adversity and to be a man and stand up for what I believe. The year we went 9-1, we went through adversity during a loss to Ferrum. Despite this loss, we finished undefeated the rest of that season. It's what he preached to us — fight through adversity.

I'm sure many of you have a story similar to mine because this is who

Coach Sypult was. He touched each and every one of us. He stayed by my side and believed in me. I love Coach Sypult and his family. I say love, not loved, because I truly believe he still lives through us. That story of the Wild-Horse Rider is true. And we knew where we stood. All of us will carry on the Sypult legacy. Many of his lessons will live on with us Wild-Horse Riders!

Fred Van Steen, #21, Wide Receiver

I loved hearing Coach Sy tell us to COMPETE on every play and in everything we do in life. I can still hear him and think of him often. I loved just sitting and listening to him tell stories. Didn't matter the subject. He was very entertaining and honest with all of us. He was always there to listen when we had a problem — one of the things I always respected.

Derek Webster, #43, Linebacker

My mentor! I'll always remember there being a birthday card in our mailbox. And if he saw us on our birthday while he was driving his Sebring convertible on campus, he would make sure to stop and say, "Happy Birthday!"

Antonio Wilkerson, #9, Wide Receiver

I had many options to attend different colleges, but the one college that stood out was Methodist. Jim Sypult saw the best in me and gave me that chance and opportunity to become a better person all-around. His legacy will live on throughout the entire Monarch nation. On behalf of the Monarch family, we love you, Coach.

Jonathan Willis, #51, Center

Jim Sypult always loved his players no matter what. Football was his life and the players — we were his men. In camp, when we were so tired and could barely keep our eyes open, it seemed he always knew how to make the room laugh with all his stories. Some of my brothers remember the foot-and-sock story — by far the best. But to know a man in the way he let us get to know him, we couldn't ask for a better role model. Papa Sypult, the Monarch nation loves and misses you.

9
CALL YOUR MOTHER EVERY DAY!

Celebrated Sayings of Coach Sy

DON'T BITCH OR COMPLAIN, LIE, CHEAT, OR STEAL, and call your mother every day. And don't make excuses! [Jon Sherman: "I will never forget Coach Sy calling me out in front of the whole team during camp because my mom had not heard from me in a couple of days or so. He made me leave the room and call her. It was always more than just football when he was coaching us."]

Ready ready Monarchs! Hey!

There are five types of people: doctors, lawyers, fighters, fuckers, and wild-horse riders.

Those who stay will be champions, not just on the field, but in life.

Every Snap. Every Play. Every Rep. Every Day. The Monarch Way!

We'll play them anywhere! Down back or in the parking lot!

You gotta PUSH-SH-SH yourselves.

GATA, GATA, GATA! [Get After Their Asses!]

The best fraternity is Phi GATA GATA.

Your work ethic determines your future.

It takes no talent to give great effort. [Matt Panza: "That's what my tombstone will read, but paraphrased: 'No talent, but great effort.'"]

Adversity. You've got to find a way to handle adversity.

Going through adversity causes us to grow stronger.

Don't show fatigue.

Just get it done!

Will we still be friends when I tell you the truth? [Sign over Coach Sy's desk]

Being early, you're on time. Being on time, you're late.

Monarch fed. Monarch bred!

The team is first. The team is everything.

One heartbeat, one soul.

Playing well, being worthy, and playing for the team, not as individuals, denote winning.

Individually, our fingers are not strong enough to get the job done, but when we bring them together [closed tightly], there is power and strength.

Our goal is to play the best football possible and take one game at a time.

If you believe, it is possible.

The challenge is what we play for.

Do it the right way, and trust in the Lord.

It's not *come on*. It's *let's go!*

It's not about right or left, but right and wrong.

Use common sense. Wrong is wrong from beginning, middle, and end.

Don't be that guy.

You're *not* a loser until you blame the refs.

You're either a gladiator, or you're not.

There is no preparation for some things in life.

It's not what happens. It's how you handle it.

It's not what you don't have. It's what you have.

It's not what you eat. It's how you chew it.

You can't poison the garden and expect it to grow.

No matter how you feel, get up, get dressed, and show up.

Do what you're supposed to do when you're supposed to do it. Be where you're supposed to be when you're supposed to be there. Every time.

We don't leave campus during camp. I sleep at the gate. Try to get off campus, I'll be there.

There's nothing better than to quiet a crowd that didn't expect you to perform.

It takes everyone! If I go down — Sypult down. [Bob] Swank up — here we go! [Coach Sy made it clear he didn't want to be "buried up 'ere at Guilford."]

What's a win? Your character is first ... your desire, discipline, dedication, persistence, and preparation.

It's not about our opponent. This opponent is just another opponent.

It's not about schemes. It's not about facilities. It's about players, and it's about people. We may have chicken wire for our lockers. But we're going to win with the right people.

It's not all about winning or losing. It's about helping and teaching players and coaches the right thing.

It's about building relationships and teaching the right thing.

It's about mental toughness, toughness needed to get the job done.

It's about spirit. It's about overcoming adversity, about presence like Daniel walking into a lions' den.

It's about the joy of football. Play for the love of competition, for the love of football. Good play is winning.

Play for the joy of playing because some day you'll be bald and fat with a snotty kid who wants to play the trombone. You'll look back on this day, this beautiful day God has given you, this gift, this opportunity to play football.

I have discovered that winning is secondary to influencing lives.

Memories have come from the people I've worked with — the players and the coaches.

"Let's fly around and hit somebody ... and stick it up in there!"

I had no sons of my own, but I had many sons as a coach. I have been truly blessed.

Go out, and have fun with your brothers.

Football lives inside me. It's in my blood.

What makes this such a great game? Take our spirit, our fire. We can do anything!

My heart will be in your heart. My spirit will be in your spirit.

Life can nullify a touchdown. Often you will be blindsided. It is your fighting spirit, however, that endures and extraordinary determination that allows you to overcome and conquer.

Life isn't tied with a bow, but it's still a gift.

When you're on the field, focus on football. When you're in the classroom, library, or study area, focus on academics. When you're with your girl, focus on your girl. Don't focus on the wrong thing at the wrong time.

Step on my track, and I'll cut your feet off [said to discourage players from walking on the track with cleats].

May God take my left testicle if I don't.

When you leave, it's better to lead the parade than let a posse run you out of town.

My father always told me all you have in the end is your integrity, character, and knowledge you did the right thing, and trust in God. I do trust in God.

Sypult Rule: "Players eat first and coaches last." Dessert was ice cream and sometimes cake. Chris Gauntlett's birthday cake was *sp-ay-cial*.

10
METHODIST ATHLETIC HALL OF FAME
November 2, 2019

Hall of Fame Introduction
Dave Eavenson

JIM SYPULT WAS BORN September 22, 1945, in Fairmont, West Virginia, the heart of coal-mining country. He was an All-State player at East Fairmont High School and three-year starter at West Virginia University for the Mountaineers. His senior year, he was the team captain, and he played under the legendary Bobby Bowden.

He loved his Mountaineers, and he loved the Monarchs. If he wasn't wearing green and gold, there was West Virginia on his shirt and socks.

He started his coaching career as a graduate assistant at West Virginia University and then went on to become a very successful high school coach at Elkins High and Liberty High.

He started his college career at Fairmont State and Middle Tennessee State and followed with a long tenure at Davidson College. I tell you, some of the best stories I have ever heard in my life occurred when he was the head coach of the Bologna Towers, a professional football team in Italy.

In 1992, he became the head football coach at Methodist. I'm going to refer to him as *Coach Sy* because that's just what we called him. He took over a program that was three years old, didn't have a lot of success, and he turned it into a winner.

He was DIAC Coach of the Year in 2000, head coach of our first conference title in 2005, and head coach of the 1997 team that was 9-1, a team that was nationally ranked. It is the best record in the history of the program.

He served nineteen seasons as our head coach and coached for forty-five years. Every program he went to, they won.

He was a perfect fit for Methodist. His blue-collar roots in West Virginia is exactly what our football program needed.

Some characteristics. Tremendous work ethic. I don't know another person who worked harder than he did. Fearless. There's a good story about a boat ride down the Cape Fear River I won't tell tonight in which he almost killed his wife, my wife, and me. But he was fearless that day. That's why we survived.

Demanding. Loyal. Detailed. Positive. Fair. And he cared.

He loved the game of football. I don't know anybody I ever met in my life who cherished the essence of the game like Jim Sypult. He loved his coaches, and he loved his players. Some of them are here tonight. Some I'd like to introduce: Quincy Malloy, Tavares Hunter, Mike Maraschiello, Rhyan Breen, Darian Tucker, DeCarlos West, and Trayfer Monroe. I learned from him to love your players.

Early on at Methodist, Coach was trying to establish a winning culture. I was fortunate to be here with him in the early years. I left for a short time and was very fortunate to come back and spend thirteen more quality years with him.

Early on, he had his challenges. First year, he never won a game. He said, "Eavenson, you never coached until you won them all, lost them all, and got fired. We just lost them all, and we're not getting fired."

He had this white pickup truck, a Mazda pickup truck, and in the back of the truck, he had a bed and a mattress. Players wanted to know what was going on.

He'd always give a speech at night: "We don't leave campus. In preseason camp, go to bed. You're not allowed off campus. I've got a mattress in the back of my truck. I sleep at the gate. Try to get off campus, I'll be there."

Not really sure if he ever did that. Nobody tested him and tried to sneak out at night. They thought he was sleeping in the back of that Mazda.

Football was different when Coach first got here because we were allowed to do very different things at practices. We would practice during the day, and there weren't many restrictions — some, but not many. Athletic training — a nightmare, I'm sure.

So we got up early in the morning, really early before the sun was up, and we'd go down to the practice field, and we'd have practice. After about an hour and a half, we'd take a break. On the practice plan, it was called *fruit and juice* — that was our definition of breakfast.

Stale bagels. Bananas. Apples. I don't think we even had anything to put on the bagels. And this *awful* substance called All Sport. I don't know if you ever had All Sport, but if you haven't, I wouldn't recommend the experience. So whatever the guys had for breakfast, it normally ended up back out of their system in thirty minutes. After fruit and juice, we'd go right back to practice. Then back to the cafeteria for fruit and juice. And practice two.

We also didn't have any resources back then. We did the best we could with what we had. When we travelled, we didn't take charter buses; we took one charter bus and a van. On the back of the charter bus was a sign I'll never forget as long as I live. It said, "Let the Good Times Roll." Old, silver, dilapidated. The driver was awesome. If you were driving behind — the smoke and oil that would come out of the back of the bus — you'd have to stay far enough back and have the windshield wipers on to see the road.

It would break down all the time. We'd get places late. Our meals would be cold. It didn't matter. Didn't matter to Coach.

Dave Eavenson: "On the back of the charter bus was a sign I'll never forget as long as I live. It said, 'Let the Good Times Roll!'"

One time we thought we had arrived. We were staying at the King James Hotel in Newport News, Virginia. King James! *This is going to be great,* players thought. King James in 1994. We arrived at King James. Whoa!

Checking in, and Coach Sy was in charge. We didn't have credit cards back then, so he would carry the cash in his sock. He'd reach down and start peeling out hundreds.

It wasn't a very secure hotel at all. "Just stand near me. We'll be fine," he said.

So I was walking around to scope things out. And there were *bullet holes* — right — *bullet holes* in the windows in the rooms. "Coach, we have a serious problem. We have bullet holes in a room."

"Where's the room?"

"It's in the front."

"All right, coaches stay in the front; players in the back."

We all slept on the floor that night.

Our locker room wasn't much to speak of. We had chicken wire for our lockers. None of that bothered him. Nothing. He always kept saying, "Adversity, you got to find a way to handle the adversity."

He used to say before games, "I don't care. We'll play the other team in the parking lot." And everybody believed that we would do that. He believed it in his heart. Doesn't matter if the bus breaks down. Doesn't matter if we had bullet holes. Doesn't matter if anything. We'll play them in the parking lot. And we'll show up. Hot, cold, rain, or shine.

We played at Frostburg State. It's up in the mountains, somewhere near Morgantown. And it's cold. So we're playing the last game of the year. We're starting to get the program going. It's freezing. Our players are not used to cold weather — a lot are from Florida, the South.

So pregame, they're walking around, and they're not happy. Players are not handling it very well. He walked in and peels off his jacket and throws it. He has on a short-sleeve shirt. He starts talking about cold and toughness. He rolls out of there to the game in a short-sleeve shirt. He grabbed me in the second quarter and said, "Write this down. Don't ever let me do that again."

He was a master motivator. Coaches and players would run through a wall for him. They trusted him, and they believed in him. He was relentless, and he was tough. He is the toughest person I have ever met in my life. Our team mentality was we're going to be physically and mentally stronger than our opponents.

When people played Methodist, and they lined up, they knew a couple of things: One, we would outlast them. We'd be tougher and stronger than anybody we played. And we would play until Coach Sy said stop. It didn't matter if it was four quarters or five overtimes. It didn't matter if we were up by thirty or down by forty. Our team played until he said *stop*.

"Every Snap. Every Play. Every Rep. Every Day. The Monarch Way."

That's how he coached his teams. If you brought up something, and it was an excuse, he just looked at you and said, "Just get it done."

He was a father figure to everybody, coaches and players, in that organization. Everyone sitting in this room today probably has a mentor. For the young ones, someday you'll get one. And he was our mentor. I was very fortunate — I love my dad — and I was just lucky to have two. And I know the guys feel like that.

He would say all the time, "It's not about schemes. It's not about facilities. It's about players, and it's about people. We may have chicken wire in our lockers, but we're going to win with the right people."

He did this tradition. Every season, the Friday night before the final football game, he'd grab a barrel. I had no idea what he was doing the first time. He'd grab a barrel. He'd put it out there, and he'd start ripping up pieces of paper, and coaches were handing them to the players.

He said, "All right. One more time, we'll line up together this season. You write down on that piece of paper your regrets. And we're going to light a fire. And we're going to throw them in the fire. And we're going to burn our regrets. And we're going to play ... *together*.

So tonight, the regret I'm sure my friends and I share is that he's not here. But if he were, he would smack me in the head and say move on.

Our football program was all about family. And we are. His legacy will live on forever in all those guys and everyone who played in the program. His legacy will live on in the way we do business.

He told me one time in one of our long car rides, if you can count on one hand the true friends you can call at 3 a.m. when you're up against something, you're a pretty fortunate guy. He's right. But the main thing he produced over nineteen years is a whole lot of men who I know would go running if he or Dr. Sy ever called.

When I left Methodist to get my master's degree and came back in 2000, there was a difference. Coach was always in his office. But when I got back, he had a new rule: "From noon until two is Dr. Sy time." He said, "You better get your priorities straight, and take care of your family." And I remember that today.

His family was very important to him. He talked about them all the time. Dr. Sy, his daughter Jill, son-in-law Gary, grandson Kyle — we called him *Hurricane Kyle* — his other grandson Zach, and his niece Laura. He would talk about his daughter and ... his attempt to help her in the sport of tennis.

I want to thank you for sharing him with us because in the world of college athletics, you've got to share your family. There's a lot of hours and time we put into this, and it takes away from them.

The positive impact he had on thousands of lives over his coaching career is amazing. My life is better, and I'm doing what I'm doing today because of him.

It's a great day. And I'm proud to have Jim Sypult in the Methodist University Athletic Hall of Fame.

Hall of Fame Acceptance Speech
Sharron Sypult

I want to thank Dave, our AD, VP, and MC, and those responsible for honoring Jim with this Hall of Fame recognition. He would be incredibly proud, as am I.

Let me introduce Team Sypult gathered here tonight: Jill, our daughter, played on the only National Championship tennis team at Davidson College. On Tuesday, she broke her wrist and middle finger lunging for a deep shot. The athletes here will appreciate her *sensible* decision to finish the match. Gary, her husband, is a jazz pianist. Kyle, our grandson, has *Wild-Horse Rider* tattooed on his arm. And Laura, our niece, was a Methodist cheerleader.

Jim was king of the Monarch Nation for nearly twenty years, and I was his queen.

I can't describe the grit, grime, and glory of the Sypult era from the inside. Only those who were there can. I can tell you *some* of what I know about the leader, legend, and legacy of Jim Sypult.

Once and only once, I was privileged to hear a pregame talk. The travel squad and staff were packed into a hotel meeting room at Newport News, Virginia.

"Ready ready Monarchs!" Jim roared.

"Hey!" was the resounding response.

Everyone snapped to attention and became instantly quiet. All eyes were on Jim, all ears listening intently, game faces in place.

I started to take notes; Jim had none.

Jim began slowly, his powerful voice echoing down the hall. Then the words flowed like a waterfall.

He said, "Play for the joy of playing because someday you'll be bald and fat with a snotty kid who wants to play the trombone. You'll look back on this day, this beautiful day God has given you, this gift, this opportunity, to play football."

"What's a win?" Jim asked. "Your character is first, your desire, discipline, dedication, and preparation. It's about mental toughness, toughness needed to get the job done."

He was inspired. They were inspired. I was inspired and ready to suit up.

It was the best motivational speech I've ever heard. It was *so* good, it was great!

Preseason, I rarely saw Jim. During the season, he arrived home well after dinner and worked late into the night. In the wee hours, he drank cowboy coffee and left to break down film, draw up practice and game plans, or watch a player run laps for some rule violation.

He slept little; he lived big.

Jim grew up in a coal-mining community in West Virginia, his family the only one with indoor plumbing. He loved to read and write, and he always kept journals and recorded sayings, some he used later to fire up the troops.

At West Virginia University, Jim starred as a freshman quarterback. He started and lettered on the varsity all three years and served as captain his senior year. *Bwana* was his nickname, and Bobby Bowden was one of his coaches.

Jim not only coached in the States but also coached a pro team in Bologna, Italy. He led them to the Super Bowl playoffs and beat the team that trounced them 82-0 the year before. They called him *Coach Grande* because he was *so* good.

At Methodist, Jim didn't win a single game his first year. However, a national ranking, Coach of the Year award, and conference championship followed.

There was something magical about Jim. Maybe it was his commanding voice, intensity, or integrity. Maybe it was the way he carried himself, his confidence, comfort with others, and moral clarity. His wit and storytelling are legendary. Did I say he was handsome? He was. Very. And he was in love with his wife.

He also loved football with a passion. To Jim, it was a game of discipline, dedication, and fair play. He loved the competition, clash of wills, and tests of manly strength and courage. He respected the officials and rules and taught players to do the same. "Football lives inside me. It's in my blood," he said.

Another passion was his football family. They mattered. The kind of people they were mattered. Their purpose in life mattered. Their behavior and treatment of others mattered. They played together in 100-degree heat. They prayed together on and off the field. They sang "Let the Good Times Roll" on the bus. They wore pink shoes and headbands for breast cancer awareness, and they burned their regrets every year before the last game.

If a player used a word that wasn't in the Bible, the whole team did ten up-downs. When a bus broke down or someone pulled a hamstring, a *Jeez-oh-Pete!* from Jim was more effective than any curse word.

"Do it the right way, and trust in the Lord," he said over and over.

Coach Sy, as he was known, was dedicated to playing the best football possible, and he was positive no matter what. He led by word and example. He pushed players to work hard and play as hard as they could. He believed in them until they believed in themselves. He made us all better people.

Jim knew how to make people laugh. He made practice fun, the game fun, and coaching fun. He told amusing, animated stories before meetings and tossed in a little nonsense for laughs. He used humorous nicknames and terms like GATA GATA GATA. *GATA* means "Get After Their Asses." *Ass* is in the Bible and, therefore, A-OK. Jim created the Food Club for the coaches — all big eaters. As president, he enforced its only rule: Never talk about how much anyone ate.

Some stories Jim repeated every year. But "The Wild-Horse Rider" ... that story was by far the most remembered and retold by the players. He always told it when facing a crisis.

It began with a real bang late in a game in '92. Methodist was behind, and someone was bitching and complaining. Of course, Coach Sy did what any good head coach would do: He shattered his clipboard on a dumbbell rack, and the words flew from his mouth. At the top of his lungs, he shouted, "There are five types of people: doctors, lawyers, fighters, fuckers, and wild-horse riders." He then launched into one of the greatest speeches ever uttered at Methodist

University ... or so I've been told. That, friends, is how the legendary Wild-Horse Rider came to be.

What is a Wild-Horse Rider? Well, metaphorically speaking, it's someone crazy enough to ride a wild horse. It's someone who prepares, who steps up and somehow, some way, performs and overcomes. Whatever it takes, he will do. He may not be the best player on the team, but he's the leader, the game changer, the winner. To be called a *Wild-Horse Rider* by Coach Sy was the greatest of compliments.

When Jim came to Methodist, the old locker room had no showers, heat, or air. Think about it: *no heat* or *air* or *place to shower*. When there weren't enough shirts or helmets to suit two-hundred-plus players, he sold ads to buy equipment. He painted the locker room, planted Bradford Pear trees, and cleaned toilets. Whatever needed to be done, he did — like the Wild-Horse Rider.

Over time, a code of behavior and a culture committed to purpose, principles, and pride evolved. A fellowship to mentor young players spread; and a brotherhood, *the sons of Sy*, united in spirit.

Why is Jim called the *Father of Methodist Football*? In his forty-five years of coaching, he was a father figure and role model to *gazillions!*

"I had no sons of my own," Jim said, "but I had many sons as a coach. I have been truly blessed."

He guided and cared for them like a lion king for his pride.

"Don't bitch or complain, lie, cheat, or steal," he said, "and call your mother every day. And don't make excuses!"

He hugged them. He texted them birthday cards even after they graduated. He even sang to them — John Mellencamp's "Jack and Diane," a favorite.

So many times, I overheard, "I love you, Coach" to which he replied, "I love you too."

Coach Sy's legacy? Simple: His legacy is the people he influenced and his lessons about hard work, positive attitude, and integrity. "It's *not* about winning and losing," he said. "It's about building relationships and teaching the right thing." He did both.

He was a force of good, he shaped lives and changed thinking, and his words and spirit live in those who knew him.

"My heart will be in your heart," Jim said. "My spirit will be in your spirit."

Gosh! He was good. He was *so* good, he was great!

Player Comments

Rhyan Breen

Jim Sypult is the Father of Methodist Football and the Monarch Nation. He has coached an innumerable amount of high school head coaches and assistants. Coach Sy, Papa Sy, Jim Sypult serves as an inspiration to literally every person he coached. He taught us how to play and influenced how we live.

Matt Hanshaw

Today the man who changed many young men's lives for the better was enshrined into the MU Hall of Fame. It's been long overdue, and we miss you, Coach, but I know you're coaching the hell out of some bunch of overachieving kids upstairs. I'm thankful every day I got to play for Jim Sypult and all he did for me in my life. I will never forget him.

Matt Panza

Coach Sy is the Hall of Fame!

Andrew Rusk

Wild-Horse Riders have been waiting for this — an Honor earned and an Honor that needed to be given. Papa Sy has been in the Hall of Fame for years. That's the Hall of Fame of all the hearts and minds of his boys.

Jonathan Willis

Yes, this should have happened a long time ago. When you think of Methodist football, you cannot help but associate Papa Sy's name with it. He did so much for all of us, not just teaching football, but his office was always open. I never had a thought of leaving the program under him. He made that a home for us.

Jonathan Byrd

The Hall of Fame now has the original Wild-Horse Rider.

11
More Jim Sypult Stories

Not Easy Being Fifteen

IT WAS A SATURDAY MATINEE at the Eastland Theatre in 1960. I had a romantic encounter with an older woman named Shirley. She was in the eighth grade; I was in the seventh. It was my first real date. I walked to her house, and we happily walked a good two miles to the movies ... hand in hand. She didn't seem to mind the walking. We walked everywhere then. I'm not sure how she felt about holding hands.

The movie started, and I made my move. Casually, I dropped my arm behind her chair and held it there at least fifteen minutes, hoping my arm would blend into the furniture and not fall asleep. Then, very quietly, I started to creep my fingers up the back of the chair inch by inch at a turtle's pace. I had a lot of territory to cover to reach my destination but couldn't risk any sudden move, or my intentions would be revealed. I covered the steep incline, focusing entirely on the steady, ever-so-slight movement of my fingers. I had no idea what the movie was about, nor did I care. I kept my gaze on the screen.

After much time, I reached the pinnacle of my first goal. My hand rested on the top of Shirley's chair. All I had to do was drop my fingers nonchalantly on her shoulder. My heart raced, my breathing quickened, perspiration broke out on my pimply forehead. It was now or not at all. I lowered my hand.

THE END. The movie was over. Shirley rose from her chair and left for the bathroom. For two agonizing hours, I had climbed the mountain, planted the national flag, and internally cheered my accomplishment. I had scaled my Mt. Everest and touched her shoulder — somehow a victory of no value. Thankfully, it was a double feature, but I contented myself by just holding her hand.

Forward to 2015: A fifteen-year-old boy is watching television at home. He is infatuated with the sweet smile and dimples of a blond who sits next to him at school. His nearby smartphone alerts him to a message. He switches onto Snapchat. On the screen, that very classmate appears. She is topless and reveals her naked, somewhat mature breasts ... and some other body part. After a few moments, the image disappears into space, over in seconds. Nothing left to imagine or savor like a *Playboy* centerfold.

Girls are mysterious creatures at this age, exciting, and hard to resist.

The experience in the theatre really happened. The second episode may or may not have happened. I made it up, but then again, maybe I didn't.

Recently, I teen-sat my fifteen-year-old grandson Kyle for two weeks. This experience caused me to recall when I was fifteen, some fifty-five years ago.

Despite the difference in decades, some things haven't changed. Physically, fifteen is an awkward age. There is a growth spurt, an elongation of the bone. Body movements don't match up to the feet. My grandson trips over his own shadow. So did I. Kyle's voice is starting to change, crack, and lower. Pimples appear on that once baby-smooth face, along with unwanted hair. The transition from middle school to high school is difficult. Freshmen lack the maturity, experience, and social skills of older students. And upperclassmen snap up the younger girls.

I could say life was simpler in 1960, but it wasn't, nor was it less challenging. Rich people have always gotten richer, and poor people poorer. Wars are always waged, and threats of war threaten. Governments always change. Dysfunctional families remain dysfunctional. Discrimination discriminates. Equality continues to be unequal, and on and on.

What is different now is speed. The Internet has changed everything. Google and Siri answer questions immediately. We receive instant news, and instant response is expected. The computer has hampered thought. This speed causes anxiety and stress unknown in the history of mankind.

In 1960, we enjoyed weekly dances called *sock hops* after athletic contests — no shoes allowed on the gym floor. Guys would stand near the walls with arms folded while girls danced with each other to barnburners like Chubby Checker's "The Twist" and Brian Hyland's "Itsy Bitsy Teenie Weenie Yellow Polka-Dot Bikini." Those guys with sweethearts held their partners very close, sweating profusely to songs like "Save the Last Dance for Me" and "What in the World's Come Over You?" Chorus, theater, clubs, and high school fraternities and sororities were popular. High school pride was paramount.

Now social life revolves less around school and more around smartphones. Violent video games and hanging with friends have replaced many school functions. Extracurricular activities are reserved for techie nerds or college-bound students motivated to improve their resumés.

The academic achievement landscape has changed also. While 4.0 was perfect in 1960, 5.0 is now possible with weighted classes like calculus and biophysics and advanced biology. It's an accelerated, fiercely competitive race for academic achievement to get into the *right* college — the Ivies, if possible. Ironically, overall achievement nationally is at an historic low and the dropout rate at an all-time high.

In my time, we set our sights on the state university or local college. I was recruited by Dartmouth my senior year. My family was really pumped. Three things let the air out of their expectations: Dartmouth offered no athletic scholarships; tuition was about $20,000 more than my dad's salary; and, most importantly, my ACT scores arrived. I would not be a Dartmouth man.

Even the athletic landscape has changed. In my day, we played all sports according to the season: football in the fall, basketball in the winter, and baseball or track in the spring. We played sports to have fun. Now athletes concentrate on one sport, playing year-round, going to camps, getting private instruction, joining pricy clubs, and traveling to far-off places to play. Some families spend more money preparing their kids to earn athletic scholarships than the value of the scholarship, and a high percentage of these students never obtain any scholarship at all.

My wardrobe at fifteen consisted of a church outfit, some school clothes, and sneakers for play. Most were hand-me-downs from my brother or sale items from the local department store.

Clothes today for a fifteen-year-old are a top priority. A boy's shirt has to be a popular brand: Nike, Polo, or Tommy Bahama — more costly than my son-in-law's wine tab. Otherwise, the teenager feels like an outcast from the jungles of the Amazon. And the shoes have to match.

My allowance was a quarter for school lunch that I most often used for hot dogs at the school hangout or the pinball machine: five plays for a quarter.

My grandson has a debit card replenished weekly and amply for his food and leisure.

Despite our differences of time, my grandson's challenges have led me to this truth: If I were fifteen now, I wouldn't be much different than my grandson. I would be totally connected to smartphones, and I would constantly challenge the house rules, assuming there were any. I would have a totally different perspective of the opposite sex and dating. I would buy into the present culture — clothes and all.

2015 presents challenges my generation did not experience. And I am far less judgmental as a result of my recent guard duty for my grandson.

It's not easy being fifteen now or way back when. Teenagers have a difficult time. Some things never change, and some things change a lot. In retrospect, I think my fifteenth year was better ... except for the instant naked pictures.

A Tale about Hair

It is very strange to stress about hair nowadays. My own hair is receding, and much has already left the building.

My options other than a hat? Hair implants, the God-awful comb-over, and shaving my head like a bald eagle. I could also dye my hair purple to make a fashion statement or wear a toupee, knowing full well hairpieces scream, "Wig, wig, wig. I'm wearing a wig."

In the last few years, controversy regarding hair length and accept-ability became news. Colin Kaepernick, while the starting quarter-back of the San Francisco 49ers, gained widespread attention when he refused to stand during the national anthem. He was protesting racial inequality and police brutality of non-whites in our country.

When the season ended, Kaepernick became a free agent and was *not* signed by any NFL team. Regardless of his proven abil-ity to perform, other teams blackballed him because his political beliefs *and* hairstyle were controversial and distracting from the sport. At the time, Kaepernick sported a bouffant Afro.

Michael Vick, former starting quarterback for the Atlanta Falcons, said Kaepernick needed to "go clean-cut" to be "presentable" because "perception and image are everything" to team owners. As you may recall, Vick served twenty-one months in federal prison for his dog-fighting business.

Kaepernick pushed back, and the conversation continued until Vick apologized.

In my high school yearbook, every male had an according-to-Hoyle hairstyle — short. In my college football team photo, my teammates had buzz cuts and short styles. There wasn't even a sporty mustache, goatee, or beard.

Then in the '60s, the Beatles and hippies challenged the status quo and changed hairstyles in America and the world.

As a young high school coach, I expected my players to adopt that traditional clean-cut Pat Boone look. One of my players, Gary Shaw, showed up the first day of camp with hair to his shoulders. I demanded he cut his hair; Gary refused. It was a standoff.

There was no school policy that required short hair, yet I persisted in my attempts to have Gary conform to customary standards. He refused. Then one night, my friends challenged me to defend my short-hair rule. I could not justify my position except to say short hair was a tradition. Confronted with my rather weak stance, I conceded and never spoke of players' hair again. After my silence on the matter, Gary Shaw ironically cut his hair. After Vick's apology, Kaepernick also cut his!

Thereafter, in high school and college, my players sported various hairstyles and facial hair of every imaginable design. Hair was never an issue. Except once ... when I was an assistant at Middle Tennessee State University in the late '70s. My head coach demanded short hair and banned all facial hair. He even required the assistants to measure the braids of black players. Their hair strands could be no longer than three inches. The measuring was a demeaning task and not only embarrassing for both parties but also racial. The head coach, by the way, was bald.

As a young man and athlete, I preferred a low-maintenance sheared look. When I coached in Tennessee near Nashville, however, I adopted the style of male country singers and grew long Elvis sideburns. I experimented with a goatee and beard occasionally which were not to my wife's liking. Nor mine as they itched and caught food that missed my mouth.

Recently, I was people watching in Walmart while waiting for my wife — as one will do. An older man with long gray hair pulled back and tied in a ponytail walked by. He looked odd to me, somewhat out of place. Then another older man with a huge belly waddled past. He had a full head of hair, dyed red and cut like a woman's bob. In addition, he had thick, long braids hanging over his shoulders. How I longed to have Gary Shaw's locks!

Kyle, my grandson, is always in style from hair to shoes, especially shoes. At seventeen, he shaved his head with dog clippers. His girlfriend liked the new look and said he went *Katy Perry* on her. Katy Perry, singer and songwriter, had just shaved her head. It was a return to the clean-cut look, the old style made new.

Hairstyle became a family issue. My wife and I loved Kyle's new cut. His parents, on the other hand, said he looked like a monkey. I was offended for Kyle and for me since I looked just like him as a teen. To keep peace in the family, I'll refrain from commenting on my son-in-law's hairstyle — picture Larry of The Three Stooges.

Colin Kaepernick has since shaved his head as well. He should be able to demonstrate his First Amendment rights, and he should be able to kneel during the national anthem without retaliation. He should also be able to wear his hair any way he chooses. So should my grandson Kyle.

"At seventeen, my grandson Kyle shaved his head with dog clippers."

And if I dye my hair chartreuse or don a Little Lord Fauntleroy wig, so be it!

Oh, to have hair again!

The Whole Nine Yards
Published March/April 2001 in *STOP*

Jim Sypult won the *STOP* writing contest with this essay.

Editor's note in *STOP,* a magazine about tobacco: Football Coach Jim Sypult promised God he'd quit if he didn't have cancer. He had developed blisters inside his lip and was terrified of throat and mouth X-rays. He disliked every dental hygienist who'd ever suggested tobacco was ruining teeth, and his breath reeked of tobacco! Forty years on, he realized the kids he coached were following his example by chewing and dipping themselves. He had to stop for their sake and his own.

Mail Pouch

I started chewing tobacco at the age of fourteen while growing up in the coal-mining country of West Virginia. My dad, whom I idolized, chewed Mail Pouch, a favorite brand among miners. I would *borrow* bits of my dad's tobacco and hide them behind a loose cement brick in the basement.

When I'd gathered enough for a chew, I ventured to the playground or ballpark with a protruding jaw and a tough-man attitude.

The Big Dipper

I continued to chew through high school and college and graduated to Copenhagen (snuff) in my adult life. Now I *had* to have a dip instead of a chew. Using tobacco was a social event with my friends: chewing, dipping, spitting, and spinning a yarn. I *had* to have a dip each morning when I awoke for the *zip.* It just felt right at midmorning for another zip. After every meal, it was a must for digestive purposes. Snuff went with everything. It made me feel tougher, an image that suited me well as a college football player and later as a coach.

Walking Advertisement for Tobacco

After forty years, I had a slow awakening: I was a walking advertisement for tobacco. I am the head football coach at Methodist College in Fayetteville, North Carolina, and too many of my players smoked, chewed, or dipped. Obviously, this wasn't healthy. It also created a poor image for our team. And there I was — their leader, a role model!

Team Spirit

One day, my grandson Zach asked, "Pap, what's in your lip?"

I thought, *Is Zach going to imitate me as I imitated my father?* That idea sucked. I wanted to be a positive example for my two grandsons.

I also wanted my players to understand that tobacco used in any form was detrimental to their performance and well-being. Eliminating tobacco would give them a better opportunity to win, both on and off the field. But I had to set an example, or my words would be empty.

True Grit

My motivation was strong. On December 16, 1999, I made the decision to quit using tobacco, a decision that tested my courage and discipline. It was a gut check. I missed tobacco every day. It was in my thoughts at some moment each day. I'll probably miss tobacco on some level for the duration of my life — something I learned about the nature of nicotine addiction. It is a powerful drug, and I am addicted.

Touchdown

Abstinence from chewing tobacco has improved my life. I smell better, and people no longer stand across the room when speaking to me. I have higher self-esteem and know I have the discipline to make a decision and stick to it. I have a healthier lifestyle and no longer fear the dentist or dislike the hygienist!

Jim with grandson Zach: "I wanted to be a positive example for my grandsons."

More importantly, I am an example for my players and grandsons to follow.

As a walking advertisement, I now read, "I stopped, and so can you."

I have influenced the lives of my players by demonstrating that if their coach can stop using tobacco after decades of addiction, then so can they.

To my knowledge, my team is now almost tobacco-free. I got

hooked on tobacco. I am now unhooked and glad for it. My image is just as tough as before, and maybe tougher, because giving up tobacco chewing is much tougher than just chewing.

Plain as Black and White

It's as plain as black and white: The NFL controversy about kneeling during the national anthem began as a respectful protest against police brutality and racial injustice.

NFL quarterback Colin Kaepernick started the controversy in 2016 by taking a knee during our anthem, "The Star-Spangled Banner." In effect, he brought attention to the plight and treatment of blacks and other minorities in America.

Despite Kaepernick's intent to improve racial inequality, he was accused of disrespecting the song, flag, and military — certainly not what he intended. Other players followed his lead in peaceful protest, a constitutional right of every American to voice grievances. Most agree about Kaepernick's right to protest. Many disagree about what he was protesting.

After the season, Kaepernick became a free agent but was never signed by any NFL team despite his six successful seasons in the NFL. Was he blackballed? Did team owners collude to make him an example? Did they deliberately keep him from playing in the NFL?

President Trump ignited the controversy when he called the protesting players SOBs. He said, "Wouldn't you love to see one of the NFL owners, when somebody disrespects our flag, say, 'Get that son of a bitch off the field right now'?"

"Guess that makes me a proud bitch!" Kaepernick's mother responded.

The president accused the players of being unpatriotic and insulted them with an offensive name. In so doing, Trump galvanized NFL players and politically polarized the country. The conversation changed dramatically.

The Sunday after the president's remarks, at least two hundred NFL players knelt in solidarity during the anthem in defiance of Trump's comments. Others either locked arms in support of the protest or stayed in the locker room during the uplifting song. The players displayed unity in the face of divisiveness from the President of the United States.

The motivation for the protest got lost in the national debate that ensued. Kaepernick wanted to challenge the general public to look at social injustices and spark a meaningful conversation. He was trying to do something good, and he did what he thought was right to the detriment of his football career.

Trump then sent Mike Pence, Trump's lapdog, to Indianapolis to attend a Colts game honoring Payton Manning at half-time. Pence, however, planned to leave before the game even started. He told his traveling party to stay in their vans because he would probably leave early.

The Colts were playing the 49ers, Kaepernick's team and the starting point of the protest. As expected, many players knelt during the anthem. Pence left the game, citing disrespect for the flag and military as the reason. Pence's departure was political grandstanding, a deceptive ploy Trump planned long before. The stunt cost the taxpayers $250,000.

To put this protest in perspective, Anthony Scalia, a conservative Supreme Court Justice and Trump hero, ruled that burning the flag was an exercise of free speech. On two separate occasions, Scalia made this same ruling. So burning the flag is acceptable, but kneeling as if in prayer isn't?

Of note, Trump typically holds a grudge when slighted or criticized. He always wanted to be an NFL owner. In 1964, he bought the New Jersey Generals, a USFL team. He planned to compete with the NFL and merge both leagues. He signed rookie Doug Flutie, a Heisman trophy winner, to a multi-million-dollar contract and then wanted the other USFL owners to partially reimburse him. Does that Trump tactic sound familiar?

Two USFL owners called Trump a *nightmare* and *classless buffoon*. Other owners said Trump *wouldn't listen, wouldn't shut up,* and *was without dignity.* Trump's plan failed, and the USFL went bankrupt. Surprised? Trump then tried unsuccessfully to buy the Colts, Patriots, and Buffalo Bills. Unsuccessfully! Did Trump's failures cause him to retaliate with attacks on Kaepernick and the NFL?

I grew up in a white, segregated community and played on the first integrated football team at West Virginia University. I coached high school ball in Bedford, Virginia, and experienced the first violent and explosive steps of integrating schools. By the way, Bedford is named for confederate General Nathan Bedford Forrest, the first Grand Wizard of the Ku Klux Klan.

In my forty-five years of coaching, I have mentored hundreds, probably thousands, of black players. I recruited in their homes and communities and knew their parents. I listened, tried to understand their situations and problems, and counseled them.

I had strong personal relationships with my black players and families. I have great empathy for them, but I am white in a white world, not black in a white world. I, and we, can't fully comprehend racial discrimination unless we lived it as a black.

In football, we all wore the same uniforms, fought together to reach the same goals, and cried the same tears of defeat and joys of victory.

It's time for all of us to be better. Kaepernick's protest was about racism and social injustice. It was *not* about the anthem, flag, military, or patriotism. It was *never* about what Trump claimed. *Never.*

The NFL athletes exercised their right to express political opinions in peaceful protest. Some served in the military, and many have family members who are veterans or currently serving. They love this country and are very patriotic.

Trump can't determine what Kaepernick's protest was. Nor should anyone else.

O say, does that Star-Spangled Banner yet wave
O'er the land of the free and the home of the brave?

Football and Head Injury

Editor's note: This story was written before every rule Jim Sypult suggested was implemented. All NFL players mentioned were found to have chronic traumatic encephalopathy (CTE).

Tick. Tick. Tick.

Junior Seau's time bomb exploded.

No one suspected the twenty-year National Football League veteran would kill himself with a gunshot blast to the chest.

He was forty-three years old.

There was no note.

There was no explanation.

The future Hall-of-Famer's life ended with questions and deep concerns. Was there a connection between his football career and long-term consequences of head trauma?

Seau's suicide was one of many among NFL players. Dave Duerson of the Chicago Bears took his life with a bullet to the chest. Ray Easterling of the Atlanta Falcons ended his life of dementia and depression with a note requesting his brain be studied for head trauma. Adrian Robinson committed suicide by hanging.

Seau certainly had suffered concussions and complained of headaches. Did he suffer a psychological breakdown? Was he depressed? Did he have loss of memory? Did he have severe chronic pain? Was he in the early stages of dementia? Did he have a progressive degeneration of the brain?

Seau was a warrior. He prided himself on *not* missing games due to injury. He didn't report pain to trainers or doctors. He just played regardless.

Thousands of former NFL players have filed lawsuits against the NFL and helmet manufacturers. They claim they were never warned about possible health risks while being instructed to use the head for contact.

How many ticks before the next bomb erupts?

I, too, fear health consequences of head blows. I have experience and knowledge as a player and coach regarding blows to the head. In the '60s, helmets had no padding except for the ears. An attached suspension strap could be adjusted to prevent the head from striking the inside top of the helmet ... supposedly.

As a player at West Virginia University, I had a headache going into a practice or a game or didn't have a headache and knew I would get one — every day.

My head and helmet were my weapons. My nickname was *Bwana*, which meant *Headhunter*. When I played free safety, the middle of the field belonged to me. If my opponent entered my territory, I had his head, and I used my head as a weapon.

Coaches taught us to tackle low — to hit the opponent at the knees or ankles. Physiologically, that positioned the head straight down, and contact was made with the crown of the helmet. The head (specifically the brain), neck, and spine are all vulnerable to serious injury in this position.

Going to the training room wasn't discouraged exactly, but frequent visits were frowned upon. *You can't make the club in the tub* was a popular saying of many coaches. In other words, get on the field and out of the whirlpool, or you wouldn't play.

Screenings for concussions were rudimentary at best. *How many fingers am I holding up? What day of the week is it? What's your name?* These questions were the extent of most examinations. If I answered correctly, back in the game I went.

Fifty years later, helmet design has drastically improved. The fundamentals of tackling and blocking now emphasize safer techniques. Rules have changed to make players safer from dangerous contact. Trainers have strong guidelines regarding evaluation and treatment of head injuries, and players are better educated about the symptoms of head trauma.

The game, even with these improvements, still puts the head at risk. The head will always be at risk.

Football is a contact sport. There are collisions, and many are violent. Players accept the inherent risks of the game. Contact to the head can occur in almost any sport or physical activity under the right circumstances. Falling off a bike and hitting the head even with a helmet securely fastened can cause extensive damage. In football, the opportunity for head collisions exists in every play.

The rules must change more.

- Blocking below the waist should be eliminated from the game at all levels.
- There should be a legal hitting zone for tackling. This *strike* zone should extend from the bottom of the thigh pad to the level of the armpit.
- All contact should be initiated with the front part of the shoulder pad.
- Contact with the top of the helmet, *spearing*, is currently illegal. This rule should extend to the ball-carrier when he lowers his head.

All players, whether on offense or defense, should be penalized for initiating helmet-to-helmet contact.

Enforcement of these rules will result in judgment calls by the officials, but judgment calls are a part of all sports. So coaches would be forced to teach and practice these safer techniques to prevent their teams from unnecessary penalties and head injuries.

As a coach, I was and am still concerned about the health and welfare of the players and long-range effects of head injuries. Regardless of my strong love of the game, I personally have reservations about my grandsons playing football, and this reserve pains me greatly.

We must make America's favorite game safer for the players.

Tick. Tick. Tick.

Toe the Line with Your Health
Published August 10, 2012, in the *Observer*

Editor's note: Jim Sypult was a member of the *Fayette-ville Observer* Community Advisory Board which met regularly to discuss local issues and contribute op-ed columns. Three of his stories follow.

Why was my toe hurting? I was sitting on the courthouse steps by the Cape Fear River in Wilmington, listening to a concert. My toe hurt. I took my shoe off and inspected my left big toe. It was black on the bottom. Dirt or scrape. No big deal.

On the way home, I was chilled. Not a good sign on a 90-degree, humid evening. At home, I poured peroxide on my toe. It fizzled like vinegar poured on soda. Another bad sign.

I ended up at a Primary Care. When I crossed my legs, Sharron, my wife, noticed something on the sole of my sandal — a roofing nail.

A tetanus shot followed. I swear the longest needle in the history of needles pierced my butt. It felt like a warrior spear, a javelin, a harpoon searing through my lower back to my hipbone. It hurt like *H-E-L-L*.

Next, I found myself in a podiatrist's office. He said things like *Interesting!* and *I don't want to sound an alarm, but ...* and *I need to investigate further.* More bad signs.

I'm going to admit you to the hospital. A really bad sign.

Here I learned the true color of gangrene — black, not green.

The prognosis followed an X-ray: The nail in my sandal had stabbed my toe every time I took a step, causing an infection.

The toe had to go — not a sign, a fact.

I underwent an arterial procedure to open the veins in my leg for better blood flow to my toes.

Here's the irony: I knew better.

Practice What You Teach

For decades, I coached football, and every fall I stressed the importance of foot care in my *Take Care of Your Feet* talk/demonstration. My players imitate and delight in retelling various parts of this talk to this day.

I taught my players how to treat dry feet, sweaty feet, and athlete's foot. I taught how to put on socks, how to smooth out the wrinkles to prevent blisters, and how to secure shoelaces and tie shoes.

There's much to know, such as right-footed punters tie to the left of the shoe to prevent the knot from interfering with striking the ball.

As a diabetic with neuropathy, I knew to inspect my feet daily. But I neglected what I knew and lost a valued toe.

The night before, my wife and I bid my toe goodbye.

The next morning, the doctors, and there were many, said my wedding ring had to be removed. I said the ring could not be removed. My finger had grown around the ring during many years of marriage ... and some added pounds. A nurse with the reputation of *I've never seen a ring that couldn't be removed* finally saw one.

The ring stayed. The surgery commenced. I awoke with nine toes.

Family and friends comforted me with appropriate remarks. One relative called me *Ro-bert-Toe*. A friend told me to buy a *toe* truck. My grandson wanted to know if my toe would grow back.

Take Diabetes Seriously

Diabetes and its complications are serious matters, but humor gets me through tough times.

Anyhow, here's the serious part:

- Diabetes is a disease with long-term consequences: neuropathy, heart disease, strokes, blindness, kidney failure, and more.
- 60 percent of lower-limb amputations occur in people with diabetes.
- According to the American Diabetes Association, 25.8 million people have diagnosed diabetes, and five million more are undiagnosed.
- The estimated cost of treating diabetes is $218 billion a year.
- By 2050, at the current rate, one in three will be diagnosed diabetics, and one in two will be undiagnosed.
- The increase in diabetics is dramatic. People aged fifty and sixty used to be diagnosed with the disease. Now people twenty and thirty have diabetes.

- Childhood obesity is a direct cause of diabetes and a major concern.
- In some areas, 40 percent of children under twelve have diabetes.
- A greater investment must be made regarding childhood obesity, with an emphasis on diet and exercise.

A toe may be just a toe, but I sorely miss mine. It even hurts sometimes. And so, take care of your feet.

Culture of College Athletics
Published September 2, 2011, in the *Observer*

Editor's note: This story was written when Woody Hayes was the head coach at Ohio State, WVU was in the Big East, and the UNC-Chapel Hill chancellor, athletic director, and football coach were embroiled in a scandal for multiple NCAA rule violations: e.g., players receiving gifts from agents and a tutor completing course work for players.

Is cheating in college ball new? Is it rare? Do fans care about improprieties?

No, no, and *no,* hosts Mike Wilbon and Bob Ryan answered on ESPN's *Pardon the Interruption.* They were discussing the NCAA probe of *impermissible benefits,* gifts provided by a booster to seventy-two Miami football players.

Improper benefits and academic misconduct are not new; they have been part of the college athletic scene for decades. I witnessed improprieties as a NCAA Division I player in the '60s when cheating took place but without investigations.

Nor is cheating a rarity. From Southern Cal to Ohio State to Miami, teams have been investigated, sanctioned, and punished for infractions: USC and Miami players accepted gifts from agents, and Ohio State players sold Buckeye memorabilia in exchange for cash and tattoos.

Fans want to win fairly but don't seem to care about irregularities and investigations. They don't care about cash and handouts afforded top players. They don't care about coaches and administrators behaving badly. They just love their teams and can't wait for the season to arrive. And they offer unwavering support — as long as their team wins.

Culture of Major Athletic Programs
- Money and greed: Football and basketball generate huge revenues, the backbone of every athletic D-I program. Conferences realign

for better exposure. Geographic sense now makes no sense as teams travel great distances for money: e.g., Texas schools travel to the Northeast for big paydays.

- Winning: To gain huge revenues, teams must win. Winning now means defeat of traditional rivals, top twenty-five finishes, conference championships, major bowls, and national championships. Coach Butch Davis did not achieve these coveted goals at North Carolina. Was he dismissed for his shortfall? At West Virginia University (my alma mater), Coach Bill Stewart was fired after winning the Fiesta Bowl in 2008 and achieving nine wins in three consecutive seasons. "Apparently not good enough for the Big East," one fan said.

- Excesses: Here is where the troubling *athletic tail wags the academic dog*. Huge stadiums and elaborate athletic facilities attract more fans and elite athletes. Academically borderline recruits are sought and admitted to schools. Ohio State's Woody Hayes expected his salary to be as high as the highest-paid professor. Coaches now often make more than their school presidents.

- Players: Players generate millions of dollars for their school and should be paid, some argue. They are being paid. They receive full scholarships and free educations. They also get a standard stipend to cover expenses like laundry. Anything beyond this framework resembles professional status.

- Zeal: Boosters want their team to win. So improper benefits and under-the-table money are offered to recruits and players. The naked truth is every school not being investigated fears it will be next.

North Carolina's Quagmire

Chancellor Holden Thorp and Athletic Director Dick Baddour supported Coach Davis for a year while the NCAA investigated the football program multiple infractions. True leaders advocate and practice such loyalty and stewardship, loyalties that coaches and the public expect. Thorp said he believed Davis knew nothing about improper benefits his players received, yet he fired Davis eight days before their preseason camp.

Was this firing really about academic integrity, or did the Board of Trustees strong-arm Thorp? We may never know. Will Thorp receive the same fate from the Board of Trustees or Board of Governors he handed to Davis? [Baddour and Thorp were fired soon thereafter.]

Changing the Culture

Is it possible to change this culture of cheating?

We are so enamored with college athletics that priorities have been juggled and ethics compromised.

We must put these athletic programs into proper perspective.

That *athletic tail wagging the academic dog* needs adjusting. We need to include coaches and student athletes on committees making decisions about athletics. Administrators may be stewards and leaders in higher education, but their experience and understanding of sports are lacking.

Coaches and players understand the real problems. They will cut through the bull to find solutions. I have found coaches to have great integrity and honor for the most part.

Reform is needed and needed now, even if that means new standards, rules, and leadership. What is in place is obviously not working.

We must bring back the core values of education and sport to college athletics. These values are hardly new or rare except in the sense of being lofty and fine. They are longstanding and honored and need to be embraced before they become values of yesteryear.

GPAs Don't Measure All Capabilities
Published December 28, 2012, in the *Observer*

One day I walked into the university president's office and asked for a raise. My program had generated millions of dollars in revenue for the school. I deserved a raise.

The president gave me $100 more per year. He felt good about it; I felt, well ... it was short of my expectations.

A new Cumberland County Board of Education policy requires students to earn a 2.0 grade point average to participate in extracurricular activities. Superintendent Frank Till wants to evaluate the opinions of teachers, coaches, and others before this new policy goes into effect in 2014.

Current thinking assumes students will be motivated to attain the required GPA to participate in an after-school activity. If students are denied participation in extracurricular activities, will they use that extra time to study?

Some will study, but such a requirement falls woefully short for most.

Sounds Good, But Isn't

Requiring a 2.0 GPA isn't a magic bullet for success. Academic success is only one measuring stick. Many students possess talents not associated with the classroom: artists, athletes, musicians, and creative thinkers, to name a few. Others have a proclivity for pursuits in technology, computers, and industry. Should this element of the student body be denied the privilege of extracurricular activities because of a low GPA?

Schools like Duke, Vanderbilt, and Harvard have unbelievable graduation rates. They should. These schools get the academically elite students and athletes from our high schools.

Public schools aren't so fortunate. In most schools, students from impoverished backgrounds often have poor academic skills, less than ideal home environments, questionable influences, little parental discipline, and bleak, dead-end prospects for the future. They are primed for failure.

Add to this situation many teachers who are underpaid, unqualified, unmotivated, burned out, or disenchanted with the state of education.

Public schools should require a basic standard for graduation. But being denied the privilege of marching in the band, playing soccer, or leading cheers because talents and interests are not scholarly seems shortsighted. Having the misfortune of a less-than-desirable environment should not determine the privilege of participating in the choir, chess club, or debate team.

It's not a good thing to take away the positive activities in young people's lives in deference to academic demands. Denying students activities that stimulate and excite them curtails their desire to attend school. At least, extracurricular activities surround them with caring teammates, coaches, and educators teaching strong values.

GPA vs. Success

A 2.0 GPA requirement does not take into account the Walt Disneys, Bobby Fischers, John Travoltas, and Henry Fords who weren't academically motivated and dropped out of high school. Many highly successful people didn't attend college, or they dropped out like Joe DiMaggio, Rachael Ray, Steve Jobs, and James Cameron.

Even Einstein thought learning and creative thought were lost in a strict academic regimen.

Student failure is a concern of our society, most especially to those involved. Discipline may be the motivational action needed, and students need to give their best efforts to perform to their greatest academic potential. They should not, however, be denied participation in individual pursuits that aren't academic.

Let's not come up short of student expectations and interests in educating our youth.

Let's not take away their joy and exhilaration in activities they love.

Let's not make academic demands that affect our students negatively. They deserve our best effort if we expect their best effort.

2012 U.S. Open Marathon Final

The steadfast wind was an unwelcome visitor at the 2012 U.S. Open.

The reigning Open champ, Novak Djokovic, struggled and became frustrated. The challenger, Andy Murray, weathered the wind and captured the championship.

The overall strategy was topspin to drop the ball fast into the court. The players could strike the ball forcefully, allowing the wind to slow the ball and drop safely. Wind was the issue, but in the end and in history, the only thing recorded was the win and loss.

Players

Djokovic, a Serbian and No. 2 ranked player in the world, stood stately at 6 foot 4 inches. His body fat was 6 percent. His training, diet, and conditioning, finely tuned. His flexibility, incredible. And he was as quick as a gnat. Djokovic's strokes were flawless and accurate. The ball shot off his racket like a bullet. His serve always timed above 120 mph. He wore blue shorts and a jersey trimmed in red. His beard was short and neatly trimmed. He looked grand as a proud warrior.

Murray, a Scotsman ranked No. 4 in the world, had never won a Grand Slam. He was runner-up at Wimbledon but won Gold in London. He carried all of Great Britain into these finals. Murray was the antithesis of Djokovic. His floppy, curly hair made him taller than 6 foot 3. His shirt and shorts didn't match. His shoes looked worn like everyday wear. He reminded me of Huck Finn. His physical stature and athleticism were a step down from Djokovic, but only a small step. His game was effective, and his occasional service when needed was timed at 136 mph.

Djokovic and Murray have been playing each other since they were twelve. The congratulatory handshake at the end of the match turned into a heartfelt hug.

Crowd

I expected rudeness in New York, but the capacity crowd was courteous and congenial. Getting to and from the Open was, yes, crowded, but efficient. The subway stopped at the front door of Shea Stadium, home of the New York Mets and Billie Jean King Center.

This was an upscale crowd. Half dressed fashionably in coat and tie and evening attire. I don't think they serve champagne and vino at the Super Bowl; they do at the Open.

Spotted in the crowd: Donald Trump — his hair stayed in place despite the wind. Sean Connery and Kevin Spacey pulled for their young countryman. Regis Philbin and Joy, his wife, looked healthy and rested. Andrew Garfield, Spiderman, got the loudest applause.

It was windy and cold. The temperature drop was significant with the windchill around 45 degrees. I wore shorts and a thin pullover. No jacket. I shivered and held my daughter for warmth. It was the first time I'd been cold since April.

During the fourth set, the concession stands ran out of food, coffee, and beer, so I settled for ice cream. Hey, I had to eat. Everything cost $5 and up, even water. Not a worry for these people. If our economy sucks, it's not evident in New York City.

Match

Oh, yeah, the marathon match in gigantic Arthur Ashe Stadium: It was epic. It tied the record for the longest Open final in history: four hours and fifty-four minutes.

Both players fought brilliantly and mightily. Djokovic was down 4-0 in the first set but fought back to a tiebreaker which Murray won 10-8. In the second set, Murray won 6-4. Djokovic made mistakes. Was he tired? Was he frustrated with the wind? Was he disappointed with the tiebreaker loss?

Apparently not. This fighter never quit. He stormed back and won the third set 6-2 and the fourth set 6-4. I sensed a fifth set. I wanted the match to end, so I could get warm. But I prayed for the fifth set with a tiebreaker. It was that kind of night.

After losing two straight sets and the momentum, Murray seemed done. But don't bet against Huck Finn. Murray quickly established a 3-0 lead and changed the momentum. Then Djokovic fought back to 3-2. I thought *tiebreaker!*

Fate

This is the only pro-tennis match I've ever seen. I coached my daughter in tennis until college. I coached football for nearly five decades. I'm not a real tennis guy. But sometimes you stand at the ridge of a mountaintop and only need to take another step, no matter what.

Or you get a cramp. Djokovic got a cramp. He did not fake it. He didn't want it. He certainly didn't need it. But the tennis god decided. Djokovic wasn't the same. The gallant Serbian prince now only had thoughts of playing through the pain. The Scot smelled blood and victory and pranced on the court.

Djokovic lost the fifth set 6-2. Andy Murray won his first Grand Slam.

As a fan, and now I'm a tennis fan, I appreciate the skill of a professional, the commitment, and the training. The difference between the champion and the rest of the players? The will to win, heart, fight, adaptability, and smarts. Those traits of a winner always ring true ... even in strong winds.

Suddenly

I cry suddenly. I get emotional, and tears fall from my eyes.

Not like former Speaker of the House John Boehner who mastered crying in public. Boehner blubbered when reflecting on the American dream and climb from his father's Ohio bar to his political position. I sometimes cried because he was third in line to the presidency.

I weep about other things like the loss of loved ones: Grandpap, Mom-Mom, Grandma, Mom, Dad, my sister Sally, my aunts and uncles — all gone — and three of my football players in the prime of life.

I cried when I learned my daughter had breast cancer. Thankfully, she recovered ... which made me cry again.

I shed tears at disappointments: missing a plane for an important job interview and not being selected for head coaching opportunities.

Conversely, I cry for joy: marrying the woman I've always loved, listening to her college valedictorian speech, and witnessing the birth of our child.

I also cry for beauty.

"Suddenly, a humpback launched out of the water. We were breathless, charged, silenced in a shared experience."

In London, several years ago, I saw the play *Les Misérables*. The main character sang a beautiful song called "Suddenly." His tenor voice was pure, magical, and so sweet that I wept.

Recently, on a whale watch at Auke Bay near Juneau, Alaska, we witnessed a humpback spout water from his blowhole and flip his fifteen-foot tail as he dove deeply before breaching. For twenty-five minutes, the creature surfaced, his humpback visible, his tail whipping the water, his body twisting and turning midair time and time again.

Then he magnificently and unexpectedly launched out of the water a few yards in front of our catamaran, sea spray whipping around him, fully exposing his huge body, the size of a bus. We were breathless, charged, silenced in a shared experience. Tears poured from my eyes.

On that very day, twelve miles from Juneau, we visited the Mendenhall Glacier, one of ten thousand in Alaska. This glorious thirteen-mile ice river took my breath and speech away as I watched ice melt, falling away from the glacier — what's known as *calving*.

Nearby, the Nugget Creek waterfalls cascaded three hundred and seventy-seven feet into the lake. The glacier was pure white with touches of lapis lazuli — blue ice, the bluest of blue, unreal yet real. It was stunning. I wept again ... suddenly.

Jill, Our Green Goddess

It was green, cold, and runny. It looked terrible and tasted worse.

It was cold soup, one of our daughter's first attempts at cooking. Like a good daddy, I responded, "It's delicious, honey."

Good thing. She progressed from cold lentil soup to chilled apple-melon-fennel soup to prime rib, lobster, lamb chops, beef Wellington, and *spaghetti frutti di mare*, my favorite — a far cry from that first lentil concoction.

Now she's a restaurateur, fancy name, and serves fancy food like fried lettuce wedges and pig belly ... not my cup of coffee, but people pay for it. Her cheeseburger, on the hearty man's side, was voted Best in Charlotte.

Dad's happy. "It's delicious, honey." This time I mean it.

A Foodie Is Born

Jill was a child who feared turtles and climbed to the top of my head at supersonic speed when a dog barked. She detested sand because it got her dirty, and ocean waves scared her. She refused to walk *into* my vegetable garden, let alone work.

In her teen years, we posted a *condemned* sign on her door because the room always looked like the aftermath of a hurricane. She didn't want to drive and didn't even mention getting a driver's license. Yet, at fourteen, she flew to New York City by herself to attend Alvin Ailey dance classes.

Throughout high school, she was the No. 1 seed in tennis. As a junior, she decided to skip her senior year and was accepted to Davidson College. She played on a national championship tennis team, spent her junior year studying food and politics in France, and traveled extensively in Europe and Asia.

After her graduation, Jill, her mother, and I lived in Bologna, Italy, a city that fed her culinary interests.

Now Jill is married with two sons and owns restaurants, cafes, and a catering service in Charlotte. She calls herself the *Green Goddess*. Her business has won many awards statewide, nationally, and internationally.

She no longer fears turtles and dogs.

Wife, a Liberal Democrat

Did I say my wife is a liberal Democrat? To the left, to the left, and more to the left. In 2012, Jill became the unofficial spokesperson for the Democratic National Convention's food service in Charlotte, and my wife envisioned dining with Barack and Michelle.

Not so fast. Jill served fifteen thousand media members at just one event. All the servers, about two hundred and fifty, last count, had to be background checked and approved by the Secret Service and security. The Federal Drug and Food Administration and county Health Department inspected all the food and preparation of each item, even checking cooking temperatures. An agent practically lived with Jill for two weeks.

Delivering food to the venues inside the Convention perimeter was a nightmare. Jill was pursued by the print media, radio stations, and television programs for interviews. Not a lot of time for mom and dad.

So we settled for credentials to attend the Convention at the Bank of America Stadium. After applying online, we were granted a chance to land tickets as only three hundred were available in Fayetteville. We arrived at 8 a.m., the doors opened at 10, and we snagged two Golden Tickets.

My wife did not serve Obama, but she was one of seventy-eight thousand cheering for him. She sat on his left.

12
HE SAID/SHE SAID COLUMN

Sleeping with the Enemy
Sharron Sypult

"NOBODY WILL EVER WIN the war between the sexes," Henry Kissinger said. "There's too much fraternizing with the enemy."

Jim and I had great fun fraternizing and writing a "He Said/She Said" column for the *Fayetteville Observer*. Breaking news: I am the *she*, and Jim is the *he*.

It was an offbeat start if ever there was one. Tim White, the editorial page editor, was seeking women to serve on the *Observer's* Community Advisory Board. So I sent him a letter and offered myself up.

"I am a woman, and I understand you are looking for a woman ... to join the *Observer* Community Advisory Board" my letter began. I also called Tim White *Tom*.

I said my sex alone would bring diversity to his Board. I said I was cheeky at times but altogether proper most of the time. I told him I had an archenemy — hard to believe — who would take every opportunity to lob a pie in my face.

To his credit, White screened unsavory criticism and printed our most outrageous lines no matter how risky or risqué — e.g., "You'll have to ask Anthony Weiner about his wiener." Wait. He did *not* print that line!

At any rate, I joined the mostly male Advisory Board in 2011; Jim jumped in a few months later. As a high school newspaper editor, he had learned a thing or two about journalism. He was also naturally funny and a gifted storyteller with an effortless style.

The *Observer* published several of our op-ed articles, and then the idea to become partners in print came to me like an unexpected gift. All I had to do was convince Jim to join forces.

Our first column got some pretty good reviews: *cute, hilarious, genius.* But our most valued review came from White who said our

She: Fergie's been a real pain in the neck. Earlier on, it would have been "off with her 'ead" with a blunt ax — a *real* pain in the neck. While Andrew was executing duties, Fergie was topless on the beach and in the company of other men — one photographed sucking her toe. Toe sucking wasn't very royal. Even so, Fergie's attempt to sell access to Andrew for 500,000 pounds was her undoing. Andrew was cuckolded and horn-mad, if not stark raving. She wasn't well-liked in the palace anyway. She didn't do enough bowing and scraping.

He: How did we get on Fergie? Charles, Andrew, and William ... these boys are really exciting. Just the kind I'd love to drink ale with. Anyway, why the references to Shakespeare? Since you brought him up, he had to marry Anne Hathaway who was in a family way. Shakespeare willed her his *second-best* bed. These Brits sure have issues.

She: Snap! The royals had their share of scandal over the centuries. Never mind the clergy and their in-house hookers. Henry VIII, for example, married his brother's wife Catherine. Henry tried to annul their marriage of twenty-four years so he could marry Anne Boleyn. Anne fascinated him: She had six fingers on her left hand ... and maybe three breasts, but no extra toes.

He: Too bad. I could use an extra toe.

She: Henry was on fire; his pursuit, hot and heavy ... and waist forty-seven inches. Anne kept him at bay for seven years until he promised to marry her. She became pregnant, and Henry married her, expecting a boy. He got Elizabeth I instead. A great monarch, but not a boy. Anne didn't produce a male heir, so off came her 'ead.

He: Good idea. That's just what we need to control the population.

She: Henry married Jane Seymour eleven days later. Not much time for mourning. Earlier, Henry dallied with Anne's mother and sister Mary who bore him a child or two.

He: At least he kept it in the family.

She: Thousand pities for Queen Anne and those bluebloods tortured, burned, disemboweled, hanged, and beheaded. Gracious, I have gone astray. Where was I? Oh, yeah, what's a little sex (or a lot) before marriage?

He: You have gone astray. I was talking about unwed mothers and royalty, and then someone got disemboweled and beheaded.

She: As soon as Kate and William marry, they can stop swanning about and begin birthing babies they aptly dodged for the past decade.

He: For Kate's sake, I hope they have boys.

She: By the by, Prince William doesn't have a last name.

He: What? We all have last names, don't we?

Yes, Dear, I Miss Oprah Too!
Published May 26, 2011, in the *Observer*

Editor's note: Prince William wed Kate Middleton April 29, 2011. *The Oprah Winfrey Show* ended May 25 of the same year. This star-studded, daytime talk show was the highest rated in history.

He: Let's keep the subject light.

She: Light? As in Donald Trump's wackadoodle run for president? Or the Obama birther nonsense? Or the need to see Osama bin Laden death photos? Isn't it enough we shot Osama in the head and threw him in the ocean?

He: If that's light, we might as well talk about politics, pandemics, and nuclear meltdowns.

She: Something will be funny about them ... in time.

He: America needs light, I tell you. Popcorn, sports, the royal nuptials.

She: Well, William and Kate's fairy-tale wedding is over, and Camilla is really 'appee, 'appee, 'appee the Diana hype has come to an end. Breeding is Kate's main function now. Pause. Pippa, Kate's little sister, drew much praise and press for her slinky, buttons-to-the-bum dress.

He: Jeez-oh-Pete! Pippa was stunning. I liked her toilet-paper party dress better. Party on, Pippa!

She: Two other sisters, apparently the tacky princesses of the royal family, were likened to Cinderella's stepsisters because of fashion faux pas at the wedding. Eugenie wore a dreadful dress, garish and hard on the eyes; and Beatrice strutted about like a pea-brain peacock in the worst hat ever.

He: You want some popcorn?

She: That hat was over-the-top ugly. It looked like a door knocker pasted to the befuddled girl's forehead. Don't the royals have *tasters*? You know, advisors with good taste.

He: Apparently not. I'm tired of the royal wedding. I'm tired of people like Regis and Oprah leaving us.

She: They're not *leaving* leaving. Not forever like Osama.

He: It's so depressing. Every week, someone gets voted off *American Idol* and *Dancing with the Stars*. Every week, Donald Trump fires somebody, or somebody quits.

She: They're all gone like Susan Lucci of *All My Children* (after forty years) and Coach Taylor in *Friday Night Lights*. Garrison Keillor of Lake Wobegone may be leaving us too. Woe is we in these woebegone days!

He: I think it all started when John Madden left *Monday Night Football*. That's just me.

She: Madden? Never heard of him.

He: Madden, he invented a video game. Ahem. What's up with Oprah?

She: Oprah, the talk-show queen, just ended her show, taking Stedman with her and leaving women adrift. Now I am depressed, and I feel an ugly cry coming on.

He: Stedman?

She: I remember the first time I saw Oprah: She was a young television reporter in Nashville — so excited about interviewing Charlton Heston. He was a huge celebrity at the time; but she was the star.

He: The first time I saw Oprah, she weighed 125 pounds. The next time, she weighed 180. Then 140; later 230. I thought she had a twin sister.

She: No, no, no. You're thinking of Oprah's half-sister. Oprah's best friend, Gayle, is like a sister. Oprah asked the difficult questions and opened conversations about weight and weighty issues like child abuse, alcoholism, and sexuality — transgender, transvestites, gay, bi ....

He: How about *tri*? I'll *try* anything.

She: I'm serious. Thanks to Oprah, we can talk about the *N-word* and *va-j-j*.

He: *Va-j-j*? Holy macaroni! I missed that episode.

She: Think about Oprah's *aha* and teachable moments, moments that resonated and impacted women ... and some men. Think how she connected, touched, and inspired us with possibility. Think about all those subjects we wouldn't be talking about if it weren't for Oprah.

He: Some things are better left unspoken. Deep sigh.

She: What about her book club, wildest dreams, and famous and infamous guests? Who can forget her wagon of fat? Tom Cruise jumping on the couch? Or her car giveaway? *You get a car! You get a car!*

He: I didn't get a car. I mentioned the fat already, and Tom was jumping with joy for landing Katie Holmes. Just saying

She: Who's going to talk about money, makeovers, and mad cow disease? Health, hair, and happiness?

He: Howard Stern?

She: It's so hard to say goodbye. It's too much to bear. How will women cope? Oprah was our advocate. She supported us ... and I'm not talking about good bras and Spanx.

He: Whatever you say, dear.

She: For twenty-five years, Oprah helped women deal with heavy issues. She's been our advocate, role model, and friend. She brought us together in a sisterhood of life.

He: Maybe ... definitely. Yes, dear, I miss Oprah too.

She: Subtle. You're just saying what's prudent to get sex.

He: I hope that doesn't end too!

Women's Issues vs. Football
Published August 31, 2012, in the *Observer*

Editor's note: A decade ago, the GOP waged a War on Women to restrict their reproductive rights. The platforms and actual events are worth revisiting.

She: Women are tired of offensive backwoods remarks, tired of being politicized, and tired of politicians making decisions about our health care and rights. We want to make our own decisions.

He: Calm down, honey. Think of diversions like NASCAR, road trips, and football ... ah, what a great sport!

She: What are you saying? And don't call me *honey*.

He: I'm just saying I love football, and football is here again. Fans wait, wait, wait, and then wait some more for the season to begin ... like shopping with women.

She: Shopping? Really?

He: Ahem. Fans are hungry for the sport — the roar of the crowd, big plays, and swagger of it all.

She: Uh, huh.

He: I'm just saying summer was a prelude to football.

She: I'm just saying the GOP platform and ticket are far, far right of mainstream thinking in America. They want us to step back in time before Roe v. Wade, before the pill, before ....

He: I want to talk football.

She: I want to talk about why women are so upset. The Vatican called nuns "radical feminists." Nuns!

He: Hmm. How do you think Notre Dame will do this year?

She: A North Carolina minister wants to lock gays in facilities surrounded by electric fences until they die.

He: Will the Tar Heels have a winning season?

She: A Pentagon report called rape in the military "an occupational hazard." A Fox News pundit said our female soldiers should expect to be raped.

He: You think this territory is too risky for me and I'll shy away, don't you? Well, I'm as *bold* as Paul Ryan.

She: Ryan is dodging questions about *forcible rape* bills he co-sponsored. Forcible? AARGH! What about the forced transvaginal ultrasounds for women?

He: Well, maybe I'm not so bold.

She: Ryan and the GOP want to ban all abortions even for rape and incest victims.

He: I'm not going there.

She: Congressman Todd Akin, ironically a member of the House Science Committee, thinks women have some superpower to prevent pregnancy in the case of *legitimate rape.* Geez!

He: Maybe Akin doesn't know how babies are made.

She: A GOP mega-million-dollar donor oafishly offered a method of birth control: Bayer aspirin between women's knees. How do you spell *ignoramus*?

He: You just did.

She: Birth control is a health issue that somehow became a religious and political issue. A congressional all-male panel on birth control refused to allow a Georgetown law student to testify about contraception.

He: Uh, oh! You're on a tear. Might I suggest a *pregnant* pause?

She: Rush Limbaugh called this law student a "prostitute" and "slut" for talking about contraception. Was Limbaugh fired like Don Imus? No, Limbaugh was inducted into the Missouri Hall of Fame. Now authorities fear someone will spit on his new bronze bust ... or worse.

He: Rush! The Richard Petty Experience — now that's a rush: three laps at 170 mph.

She: Flush Rush! Mitt Romney wants to get rid of Planned Parenthood that provides health care for millions of women, 90 percent preventive like cancer screenings and prenatal care. He wants to cut women's health services while cutting taxes for the rich. Geez!

He: We're not talking about football, are we?

She: No wonder Romney avoids discussing women's issues while campaigning; he just wants them to go away.

He: No, we definitely aren't talking football.

She: I am not going to address Romney's golden gaffes, Cadillacs, or car elevator in his new house. Or dog him about strapping his dog Seamus to the top of his station wagon.

He: PETA alert. Anyhow, Romney and Ryan looked good in matching plaid shirts and jeans in Wisconsin ... but then they cried.

She: So did Seamus. He didn't want to ride atop the family car again.

He: I'm starting to cry. Can't we talk just a little football?

She: I wonder about Romney's memory. When he was eighteen, he and five buddies shaved the head of an allegedly gay man. They tackled and pinned him to the ground. Romney can't remember this brutal attack; his friends can't forget it. Who could?

He: It's hard to trust someone who can't drink a beer, especially while watching football on TV.

She: The GOP keeps denying there's a War on Women, but it sure feels like a war. Forces hostile to our best interests keep attacking us. The extreme element in the Republican Party does not speak for us or to us. It's our bodies and our choice.

He: Football is not your choice today.

She: A growing number of women see Republicans as goobers, blockheads, Neanderthals. Come to think of it, many have receding foreheads and prominent brow ridges.

He: Did you just say that?

She: I don't expect you to answer for your sex.

He: If you want to talk about sex, I'll stop talking about football. Deal?

World-Class Pigs and Weiners
Published July 11, 2011, in the *Observer*

Editor's note: Before the *Access Hollywood* tapes and sexual assault allegations against Roger Ailes, Bill O'Reilly, and Bill Cosby, there was Anthony Weiner, a New York congressman. He resigned for sexting explicit photos to various women — one was a minor. A new chapter in the men-are-pigs annals was added. Actually, the connection between the two dates back to Homer's *Odyssey* when Circe transformed men into pigs.

She: Are men pigs?

He: Define *pigs*.

She: Fiddle-dee-dee! You know what I'm talking about. And it ain't *Gone with the Wind*.

He: Men and pigs? Frankly, my dear, I don't know what you're talking about.

She: In a pig's eye! You know *exactly* what I mean, and don't call me *dear*. The jokes about Anthony Weiner are everywhere.

He: Oh, those pigs! Cheating goes back to Biblical times. Remember David and Bathsheba? David sent Bathsheba's husband to die in battle, and David was one of God's favorites.

She: Uh-huh. Another David, David Petraeus, cheated on his wife. He even gave classified information to his lover while he was the CIA director.

He: *Today a peacock, tomorrow a feather duster.*

She: Bill Clinton said he didn't have sex with Monica, but her dress with DNA said otherwise. Of course, Clinton's definition of sex blew us away.

He: *Blew*? Right! You can't be spreading DNA around.

She: John Edwards cheated on Elizabeth ... when she had cancer. Classy! Then he lied about his affair and love child and persuaded an aide to take credit for fathering said child.

He: Good ol' John Edwards ... from White House to outhouse.

She: Arnold Schwarzenegger cheated on Marie Shriver with his housekeeper, and a love child was born. The betrayal and other woman — not a beauty queen — shocked us.

He: The list of cheaters goes on and on.

She: Jesse James blindsided Sandra Bullock with a tattooed girlfriend. Tiger Woods made a pig of himself in lots of sties. Mark Sanford disappeared for days to *dally* with his *soulmate* in Argentina. Dominique Strauss-Kahn sexually assaulted a hotel housekeeper ... allegedly.

He: Viagra probably helped. Hmm. Wasn't Strauss-Kahn called a *rutting chimpanzee*, not a pig? Of course, in France and Italy, having a mistress is like owning a poodle.

She: The famous and powerful are *not* more prone to indiscretion; they just think they can get away with extramarital affairs.

He: JFK, Dwight Eisenhower, and Thomas Jefferson got away with it. Babe Ruth, Eddie Fisher, Barry Bonds, and Ashton Kutcher did not.

She: They're like the thief who isn't sorry he steals but is mighty sorry he's going to jail.

He: What about the guy who steals, doesn't get caught, and ain't sorry?

She: Newt Gingrich asked his wife for a divorce while she was dying of cancer.

He: Such wholesome stories.

She: Let's not forget Eliot Spitzer, New York's *Luv Gov*, who resigned amid a prostitution scandal, his wilting wife at his side. So much for his wholesome image.

He: Weren't whips and chains involved?

She: Right! Back to Anthony Weiner and his penis tweets. He squealed like a pig about hoaxes and hacking and then confessed to lying and sexting.

He: Wheek! Wheek! Wheek!

She: Why do men think a penis picture will impress women?

He: Brett Favre thought so.

She: Brett Favre texted nude photos to a woman who was not his wife.

He: Such titillating details!

She: Talk about de-pantsing the powerful. They de-pants themselves.

He: Now there's a word you don't hear every day.

She: Weiner's wife was pregnant at the time which makes him a world-class pig. Is sexting cheating? Please stop making those pig noises!

He: Remember the days when cheating meant actual sex?

She: Sexting is more than Jimmy Carter lusting in his heart. Desire can throw reason to the wind. The next thing you know, men stick their *noses* where they shouldn't.

He: OK. I don't know about that *nose* comment.

She: Men having affairs leave telltale signs ... like a sudden interest in health foods, jogging, and Just For Men hair dye.

He: Not to mention lipstick on the collar ... and elsewhere.

She: Women want to know why men cheat. Rose in *Moonstruck* said men cheat because they fear death. What does that mean?

He: I don't know. Cheating on your wife might lead to death?

She: Men link self-image to sexual vitality and youth, I've heard. Affairs make them feel younger — an ego boost.

He: Sex does seem to be key. For every cheating pig, there's a willing woman, but we don't call her a *sow*.

She: Uh-huh. We've heard all the *reasons* men cheat — actually excuses: a mistake, need for something new, poor sex life, strong sex drive, sex addiction. Leave it to someone, probably a man, to turn immorality into a medical condition.

He: You might be onto something. The *wild boars* of this world thank you.

She: I know what you're going to say: Men can't help themselves because of the vasopressin receptor gene.

He: The what?

She: That gene supposedly determines whether men are faithful or bent on pollinating every flower. Probably some pigheaded man came up with that theory.

He: We cheat because of our DNA? Will this theory hold up in divorce court?

She: Not funny. In the words of Emily Dickinson and Woody Allen, who married his adopted daughter, *The Heart wants what it wants ....*

He: It's not just our hearts!

She: That reminds me of a joke: If you want to lose two hundred pounds, divorce your husband.

He: Hey, that's not funny!

She: Bad behavior at the top trickles down. Public figures influence behavior and serve as role models. We become desensitized and think everyone is cheating.

He: The trickle-down effect — Reaganomics.

She: Uh-huh. Reagan also cheated on his first wife. The Weiners of the world hurt those who love them most. Pigs, I tell you, *pigs*.

He: Try not to mince words, dear.

Prelude to Football
Published September 2011, in the *Observer*

Editor's note: Jim Sypult loved football ... and eggplant to a far lesser degree. He did a dance for each. His appreciation for eggplant existed long before it became a penis emoji:

He: Praise be and pass the eggplant! Football is upon us.

She: Great balls of fire! Here we go again.

He: What do basketball, baseball, soccer, golf, and tennis have in common?

She: Balls.

He: True, but they're sports that entertain us *between* football seasons.

She: *Between* football seasons? Balls!

He: Baseball used to be America's game. Too slow, too boring. Players were traded daily and changed teams. Who cares?

She: Baseball fans.

He: Golf lost Tiger.

She: No, Tiger lost golf ... not to mention his game, endorsements, fans, and a few billion bucks.

He: Granted, his wife was really teed off when she battered him and his Escalade with a nine iron. Yes, we are semi-entertained by other sports.

She: Like the Women's World Cup, Hope Solo, and victory over Brazil?

He: We were captivated ... briefly. Soccer fascinated us like a shooting star.

She: You seem to enjoy relaxing at the beach.

He: Yeah, I think the bikini-clad girls would make good cheerleaders — excuse me, bikini-clad *women*. Of course, the *women* who return my glances now have AARP cards.

She: Well, those bird-watching binoculars come in handy.

He: We have to look out for sharks: the ones with big sharp teeth and little red eyes. It's the sharks *on* the beach that are the most dangerous.

She: Snap! Well, there's fishing. What about the morning you caught seven fish?

He: Monsters all.

She: Deep-sea fishing?

He: Oh, those monster waves. Rocking back and forth. Rocking. Rocking. Rocking. Excuse me while I puke.

She: Swimming with the dolphins in Mexico?

He: Now that was amazing.

She: What about your passion for food and eggplant? You even do a food dance.

He: Yes, eggplant is a wonderful diversion. I love eggplant. I have more eggplant recipes than Bubba Blue has shrimp recipes — you know, *Forest Gump*.

She: You have been known to post pictures of eggplant on *Facebook*.

He: Well, they're sort of shaped like footballs! And more wholesome than Anthony Weiner's posts.

She: Other matters seemed to capture your attention this summer ... like WD-40.

He: Who would have thought WD-40 would relieve arthritis? A local woman at Walmart shared that jewel with me ... while I was waiting for you to finish shopping.

She: I don't know about the arthritis, dear, but WD-40 gave you an instant tan.

He: Remember the farmers market when I balanced a straw on a watermelon to determine if it was ripe?

She: How could I forget? What causes a straw to turn 180 degrees when a melon is ripe is the darnedest thing. What's also amazing is the crowds your straw demonstrations draw.

He: Fans have to kill time waiting for football to begin. We wait, wait, and then wait some more ... like shopping with women.

She: Well, bless your heart! Eggplants and melons and shopping all lead to football, football, football.

He: I love football.

She: You do at that. What's so special about it?

He: What do you think?

She: I like the shoulder pads and tight pants.

He: Uh, huh. Fans are hungry for the sport. Every Saturday is like Christmas to me: the anticipation, excitement, and joy.

She: The mascots, tailgating, celebrations in the end zone, fans covered in school colors — fun to watch.

He: It's competitive, high intensity, and unpredictable. The sacks and tackles and swagger of it all. It's three hours of pure pleasure.

She: Or longer. Please don't start reciting starting lineups.

He: The tests of manly strength, the big plays, and the cheering

Jim Sypult: "West Virginia meets St. Petersburg, Russia. Peter the Great sired three hundred children. Sounds like my Grandpap!"

crowd. I can't say what it is exactly. But football is unto itself.

She: On the edge of glory? No, that's Lady Gaga. Dang! I've got that Gaga song stuck in my head.

He: I'm just saying that summer is a mere prelude to football.

She: Ballsy and Balzac!

He: Balzac? Is he a tight end?

She: You somehow remember plays from twenty years ago.

He: Fifty years ago! Memories of playing football get better with age like cheddar cheese or whiskey. The game is universal like music.

She: Universal? The Cheeseheads and Ducks? I get the Fighting Camels, I suppose, but Fighting Bishops and Fighting Okra?

He: Fans are connecting in costume ... and waiting like bears in hibernation, dreaming of the season to begin.

She: Fortunately for you and millions of football fans, we're past the prelude and NFL lockout and into the first movement.

He: Ah, football! The sweat, crotch irritation, and foot fungus — small matters to endure. It's a tough game for tough people.

She: I know what you're going to say next: "Football is the greatest game ever created."

He: Touchdown! Fishing, food, bird-watching, and other sports — all warmup acts at a Black Eyed Peas concert.

She: The Peas or football?

He: No contest.

She: Careful, dear, you're about to break into your football dance ... again.

He: Wrong dance. My eggplant supreme is ready.

13
SONS-OF-SY TRASH TALK

Alumni Bowl, Flag Football
November 2, 2019

QUINCY MALLOY, HEAD WHISTLE
I just want to make this clear, guys. I don't care if you put the jersey on for one year or four. If you support the Methodist football program and what a Wild-Horse Rider means, then you are a Monarch for life. What we are building is a brotherhood that will help mentor these young players on what it takes to put on that green and gold!

Trayfer Monroe
Quincy, you sound like Coach Sy after a hard practice. You playing?

DeCarlos West
He has no choice. We are doing two-minute drills like we used to do on Thursdays.

Matt Panza
Will there be a trainer? Cause I'll need one at some point.

Andrew Rusk
I need one just thinking about it.

Quincy Malloy
The hospital is open twenty-four hours IMAO.

Tavares Hunter
Icy Hot will be on deck to accommodate muscles, aches, and pains.

Chris Gauntlett
Is there an AED on-site?

Josh Cook
Will there be oxygen and IVs on the sideline?

Mike McDermott
I don't remember, does the bookstore sell heating pads and Epsom salts?

Jonathan Byrd
I'm good for about five plays. Hope we have some depth.

Tavares Hunter
I'm going to play the hell out of that one down I'm in.

Damon Sloan
I'm going against you for that one play.

Tavares Hunter
We have one shot at this. We'll lean on each other and call it a draw.

DeCarlos West
I'm going to need more than thirty minutes for warmup.

Jeremy McSwain
Be ready, young bucks!

Travis Smith, Sr.
Oh, it's on!

Andrew Rusk
We old guys may not be able to run as fast, but like Will [McPhaul] said, "We'll show 'em how to get it on in a parking lot."

Todd Holmes
I like that. Time for an old-school beat-down!

Antonio Mcgregor
I'm getting tired just reading this post.

Dustin Daniels

Pretty sure I pulled a hamstring while scrolling through this.

Nicholas Liles

9-1 — still the squad.

Quincy Malloy

I'm not trying to start anything, but I just got confirmation MU ALL-TIME RECEIVER VAUGHN CROSS HAS COMMITTED TO PLAY! I'm just saying, OLD MC, y'all might have your hands full.

Vaughn Cross

Either double me or lose. Lol.

Jonathan Byrd

I'm down. I'm more likely to get hurt playing flag football.

Tavares Hunter

Flag football is for the skinny boys.

Andrew Rusk

Boys, it's about to get real. Old MC got the band back together.

Matt Panza

I got at least two good hits left in me.

Quincy Malloy

DeCarlos West and Trayfer Monroe, OLD MC ALL-AMER-ICANS, will be playing. Two of the best offensive and defensive players to come through Methodist! No one is too old or too young to participate.

Will McPhaul

Truth, I'm only attending for the parking-lot portion.

Trayfer Monroe

Me and #2 got unfinished business.

DeCarlos West

You correct, Trayfer. That's Sypult all the way.

Will McPhaul

I'm just going to smoke cigars.

Gary Futch

Can I sign up for that job?

Tavares Hunter

Wait! Are you saying I've got to get in shape? Trainer!

Jesse James Iversen

First ever Methodist University flag football game in honor of my late, great Head Coach Jim Sypult.

Video Challenge by Jamar Brown before Alumni Bowl (The Wild-Horse Rider Closed *Facebook* Group)

Yo, people! What's going on?

You know I don't go live often, but we got this football game coming up this weekend. And for those of you going against me, I want to show you I'm out here working out. I don't work out like regular. Forget weights. Forget running. Forget all that cardio. I lift logs. See all these logs I'm lifting [huge logs in bed of pickup truck]?

That's how I get ready for the football game because I'm still [pounds chest with fist three times] man of steel.

Those of you who want something this weekend, just know I'm ready. And I'm prepared. I don't care if this is flag football. This is tackle.

I'm lifting these logs to get ready to smash heads.

So run up on me if you want to try and catch a ball in front of me. See what's going to happen.

Let me get back to lifting these logs because that's how I roll. Because I exercise. That's how I get ready. That's how I get down.

The SyPole Fishing Pole, Anthony Cassone

Some of you saw the SyPole fishing pole with *Sy* on the rod at the flag football game. On the butt cap, there is a helmet sticker Coach

Sy gave me. He never gave the caps out much when I played, but he gave this one to me.

Editor's note: Coach Sy, a Fishing Club member on Hilton Head Island, carried a bat in his car to do battle with gators when he reeled in fish.

Camp and the Dreaded Hill

Todd Holmes

As stated by many players and coaches, the '97 camp was most likely the toughest camp any Monarch ever completed. Scorching hot, two- and three-a-days, late meetings, sleep deprivation, people *dropping like flies*, jungle rot — you name it. It was hell. Coincidentally, it was also our best year ever record-wise. That camp made the rest seem easy because we would all say, "Well, it ain't anything like the '97s." Coach Sy knew what he was doing, and we all left that year as men.

Jimmy Summers II

I remember those camp days, and three-a-days made a man out of me.

Josh Cook

Those camp days! In some sick way, I miss them.

DeCarlos West

Aye, that hill was brutal! After a physical practice!

Randal *Chuck* Webster

The blisters I accumulated just from that walk in cleats!

Mickey Jordan

Coach Sy still lives on in each one of us! The impact that man made in our lives will last until we meet him again inside those Pearly Gates! We all stayed, and we became champions in life and many other things! God knew what he was doing when he put us in Coach Sy's hands to mold and make us the men we are today! So glad I never jumped on that night train that ran right behind the practice field!

Mike McDermott

The Midnight Train to Georgia!

DeCarlos West

All I know is a lot of players hit I-95 before camp was done! Especially after those twenty-four eighties in the heat.

Matt Panza

Don't forget the gassers!

Jimmy Summers II

Yes, gassers overtime.

Brandon Spiece

Every kid I've ever coached knows about gassers and overtime.

Quincy Malloy (with Momma Sy): "Jim Sypult was a father figure to me. The Malloy family loves his family so much!"

Darrien Tucker

Only the strong survived. Made men out of all of us — the ones who stayed and paid the price. Jim Sypult lives on. I always tell my guys, "Don't show fatigue." I can hear him saying that while we were running those gassers.

Randal *Chuck* Webster

You gotta PUSH-SH-SH yourselves!

Andrew Mullis

I'm loving this! Makes cold chills run up my neck just thinking about those days. That hill, the thermometer nailed to the pine tree that would inevitably read 114 degrees in the shade, and worst of all, having to tackle that hill more than once at practice because we forgot to weigh in!

Shannon Yount

I dreaded that hill after practice during camp but would give anything to be a part of it again. Coach Sy was right when he said those who stayed would be champions — not just about being a champion in football, but in life as well. Coach wanted to make sure we were prepared to take on whatever we decided to do in our life. If we could make it through his camp and season, we would make something of ourselves in life.

Wes Thompson

Hated that hill. I want to share this with my players. Dealing with a bunch of doctors and lawyers instead of Wild-Horse Riders.

Brandon Spiece

I can remember Shaun Jones and I making it up the hill, around the track — you didn't walk across the field — and over to the bleachers. We fell asleep with our gear on and woke up just in time to get to the next meeting!

Andrew Farriss

I never thought I would *like* anything that had to do with preseason camp! But looking back on it, I wouldn't trade those experiences for anything. I can still feel exactly what it was like to get up so early and ol' Scotty coming out to play. Thanks, Coach, for four great years that will impact the rest of my life.

Darrien Tucker

I remember being in camp and hearing Coach Sy yell from the offensive side of the field, "DON'T SHOW FATIGUE!"

Matt Panza

You never forget the sounds the cleats made walking down to practice and back up after. Nowhere in life have I heard it since. Many things went through my head during camp, but quitting was never one. I never had any illusions about being the best; I just pushed myself to help out. Crazy thing is I don't so much remember the plays, but I remember the craziness of my teammates. Mickey Jordan throwing up during a run play, Coach having the QBs hang from the trees, the D-line being up-downed to death every practice. Shuffle shuffle jab jab.

Jon Sherman

Would go back to camp right now if I could!

Fred Van Steen

Coach ran great camps and taught us all some great lessons more about life than football. I am grateful every day for the experiences and lessons and try to pass along that knowledge to my young players every chance I get. When I think about those days, it brings a smile to my face and gets those juices flowing.

Corey McGuire

If anyone ever said *Chattanooga,* Coach Sy would get all fired up and say in his Coach Sy voice, "Did someone say *Chattanooga?*" We loved getting Coach fired up.

Dave Eavenson

I recall Coach Sy using that reference when someone decided to quit the team, saying they are taking the Chattanooga Choo Choo out of town. It definitely got him angry when guys quit the team.

Jimmy Summers

From a standing position, can you still jump vertically over a six-foot guy?

Antonio McGregor

I might be able to jump over a little person ... well, maybe, if he squatted down.

Fast Track, Kick Ass, Darrien Tucker

Methodist players were much faster than Salisbury State, so they didn't cut their grass, trying to slow us down. We had way too much team speed. Coach Sy said he'd have the grass cut low, and then "We're gonna kick some ass!"

Coach Sy: "Monarch fed. Monarch bred. We'll play them anywhere! Down back or in the parking lot!"

Bob Swank

Two or three road games in a row, our bus broke down on I-95, and we ended up practicing at the bus repair shop.

Terrance *BigAbe* Abraham

It was the hills, I tell ya — that and Damon Sloan and Tavares Hunter.

Damon Sloan

I'm sorry, Terrance *BigAbe* Abraham. I don't think you got *BigAbe* from being small.

Tavares Hunter

Damon Sloan loses weight and forgets his head alone outweighed us all.

Prince of Darkness, Fred Van Steen

Here I sit at Bridgewater College ready to watch my son play, and my two fondest memories are Dan *Bam Bam* Dunham knocking out the Prince of Darkness and *Big Bake* [Jeff Baker] doing the same to some unfortunate D-lineman. The Prince of Darkness, a strong safety, KO'd two or three wide receivers of opposing teams and was running his mouth in the paper about putting someone from Methodist into darkness. Too bad for him. He ran headfirst into Dunham, and the Prince went to sleep for the rest of the game. They sure remembered the Monarchs that day — well, two of them, at least.

14
BEST RECORD EVER

IN 1997, THE MONARCHS GAINED NATIONAL RANKING (20th in Division III) but weren't invited to the playoffs.

They were a well-conditioned, disciplined squad. The players ran twenty-four eighty-yard sprints at the end of every practice, and six players bench-pressed over four hundred pounds.

Randal *Chuck* Webster, a 6-foot-7 offensive tackle, might have been the largest player in D-III football. His exact weight was never determined as the school scales stopped at 350. "It's easy to run the rock," Coach Sy said, "when it goes your way, Chuck!"

Trayfer Monroe, a defensive powerhouse, played strong safely, cornerback, and outside linebacker. He holds the career record for tackles with three hundred and seventy-three and game tackles with twenty-one. According to Coach Sy, Monroe found something good to say about any adversity.

DeCarlos West, a 5-foot-7 tailback, weighed 165 pounds and played half the season with a sprained ankle. A video called *How the West Has Won* highlighted West's speed and ability to squeeze through wafer-thin holes.

When Methodist beat Davidson, *the other team,* Coach Sy said it was the best day of his life as a coach. The Monarchs spoiled Davidson's Homecoming and 100th Anniversary. Brian Turner threw a spiraling twenty-six yard pass to Leonard Bellamy with a minute and seconds left on the clock to win 19-16.

Methodist crushed powerhouse Frostburg State 40-12. Coach Sy said that game was as much fun as he ever had in coaching. They were huge and unlike any team MC ever played, he said, but when the Monarchs walked down that hill and entered the stadium, it was like "a lightning strike."

Methodist's only loss was to Ferrum at Ferrum. Coach Sy referred to them as the *F-team* thereafter. Of note, Frostburg State beat Ferrum 31-0, but Methodist beat Frostburg 40-12 (stats from *Fayetteville Observer*).

Dave Eavenson, MU Athletic Director, former Head Coach and Assistant

One thing I can say about the '97 team is how mature they were. We did something most college teams do not do. Coach Sy made a decision about halfway through the season to stop practicing in pads. We spent most practices in helmets and very little in shoulder pads. He felt we needed to keep our team healthy and they would be mature enough to handle it. It was one of the boldest and best coaching decisions I have ever seen. No doubt in my mind that decision helped lead to our success. That was a fun year. Great players, great coaches, and great people!

Matt Eviston, MC Sports Information Director, 1995-1999

1996 was a special year too. We were 6-4, and it was Methodist's first winning season in the program's history. Hurricane Fran wiped out the scoreboard before our first game. It was a wild way to start the season. More adversity. Another mountain to climb.

Fullback Keljin Adams won the *College Football Chronicle* Unsung Hero Award, and Leon Ché Clark was an honorable mention. Clark was Methodist's own Superman and not just because he liked to wear a Superman T-shirt. He was a great student, great football player, and superior leader on and off the field. He was also elected student body president two years in a row. Those were great days! And Coach Sypult was the best!

Randal *Chuck* Webster

We were 9-1, the best record in the school's history. Many of the players were D-I talent. Much of our success was due to the development under Coach Sypult's program. We had great leadership on that team by the likes of DeCarlos West, Leonard Bellamy, Trayfer Monroe, and me, just to name a few. Coach Sypult did a masterful job of keeping us focused, determined, and DETAILED that season. We didn't make many mistakes on either side of the ball which had a lot to do with our overall success. We were a very disciplined football team.

PlayerSpeak

DeCarlos West

Summer school started it all! The rising seniors worked out daily in over 100 degrees. The coaches did a great job preparing us for the tough games that we won in the fourth quarter and OT. The brotherhood and closeness of that team are what Coach Sy bred in us. He was doing it, and we had no clue.

Sigmund Platt

I remember the season like it was yesterday. That Fayetteville heat was in the house during camp, but we had worked hard that summer on conditioning. Elmore Lowery pushed us to the limit and made us laugh during workouts. Lowery joined the Marines in the off-season, and he came to camp straight from boot camp wide-open. He sang the "Devil Dog Marine" song all the way through the mile runs, finished before everyone else, and joined in to try and run for everyone. When we went to do man makers, he lead the group and talked so much trash that he kept on going even though he was supposed to stop for a break.

Nicholas Liles

Elmore Lowery also intercepted a ball with one arm while wearing a cast on the other to win a game for us on the last drive against Ferrum in '96. We all had words with their crowd on the track because they had been talking smack the whole game.

Elmore Lowery

I recall intercepting a last minute pass which led to us winning a close game! Coach Sypult had a unique way of bringing a hundred and twenty-six dynamic players from all over the country together. He made us work as a unit! During my Methodist career, I cost the team several fifteen-yard penalties for late hits and trash-talking!

Coach Sy always fussed at me for something. When we were playing in Tennessee, it was a rough game, and I got into a fight with a fan. Coach was not happy in the least! During half-time, he was looking at me, and I was saying to myself, *He's going to bench me!* Coach surprised me by saying, "Elmore, that's the way you fly around out there!" I'm thinking maybe he didn't notice that late hit cost us fifteen yards we couldn't afford. Coach was an awesome and outstanding leader of men! I love him because he allowed me to be me.

Leon Ché Clark

The wrecking crew. If you need to move a mountain, that's the crew to call.

Mike McDermott

I remember Anthony Fairlamb, a giant offensive tackle, scoring a touchdown [in '95]. I remember coming home from an away game and rushing to the supermarket to get beer before midnight — I was legal — and running into Coach Sy in the beer aisle. I remember the elation of the entire team when we beat Davidson and the grin that didn't leave Coach Sy's face. I remember DeCarlos West receiving the ball for a return and ROTC guys firing a little gun about twenty feet behind the end zone. West dropped the ball, and the other team scored another TD in a matter of seconds. ROTC was never at a football game again.

Editor's note: Randal Webster reportedly did an end zone dance after Fairlamb's touchdown, which Webster denies: "No, I was too cool for that."

Patrick P'orye

I framed my game pants as a reminder that no matter how bad life gets — it's never as bad as sitting on a colony of fire ants.

Leon Ché Clark

I've had this '97 T-shirt for twenty-three years, three continents, seven countries. It still fits, still breathes well, still makes the old chest swell up when I wear it. Important meeting coming up? It has been known to go on under the shirt and tie. Some football programs place their players on a high horse. Our Coach taught us how to ride wild ones.

Jonathan Willis

Now we know what was wrong with Coach [Carl] Funderburk. Lack of sleep. Maybe he was a nice person when he could sleep! Just kidding.

Damon Sloan

I remember those days — some of the best days of my life.

Antonio Mcgregor

The PASSION! No one can take that from us EVER. Thanks, Coach Sy! Suddenly I'm ready to hit the field!

Jimmy *the Beast* Summers II

I remember those camp days and three-a-days made a man out of me. Thanks, Coach Sy. The toughest game to me though was the ICE BOWL in '98. It was so cold and icy, we could only score field goals. Our toes and hands were frozen, and at half-time, we were trying to warm them on a furnace.

Celebrating the first victory over powerhouse Frostburg State, the last game of '97, and the best season ever in the history of Methodist football.

DeCarlos West

After Friday night walk-throughs, Coach Sy always said the opposing teams were coming to *The Methodome!*

Leon Ché Clark

Of all the things I learned in school, playing football prepared me most for life.

Tony Bugeja
You guys were the original wild ones.

Richard Pope
From someone who was there for all of the 2-38, I can say if you didn't get fired up to play for Coach Sy, you didn't have a pulse.

Tavares Hunter
All I remember about the Catholic game in '99 is Coach Sy's half-time speech: "Grab your nuts, and be a man out there. They are a better team than we are, but we have more fight than anybody. Fight, dammit, fight!"

William *Ray* Ray
Coach Sy could light up a room. He was our driving force in the locker room and in our personal lives!

Randal *Chuck* Webster
I remember Ray Ray [William Devon Ray] being extremely hard to tackle after the catch — had legs like a horse and would humbly smile when he was out there killing DBs.

Darrien Tucker
In practice, we used to battle it out during one-on-ones, and Leonard Bellamy, Ray Ray, and all the other receivers used to compete. It made games easy.

Trayfer Monroe
Ray Ray was a WR/RB/TE/FB all in one. Defensive nightmare!

Coach Bob Swank
Don't forget punt blocker.

Jason McCarty
And triple jumper!

15
USA SOUTH CONFERENCE CHAMPS

I N 2005, THE MONARCHS WON THEIR FIRST Conference Championship, an honor denied the year before because of a loss to Shenandoah. In '05, Methodist crushed Shenandoah 35-0 and beat Christopher Newport 35-28.

Quarterback Chris Roncketti, a four-year starter, played nearly every offensive play from 2002-2005 and was "the best quarterback in the conference," Coach Sypult said. He could "run well and throw well and take a bad play and make it good." Daryl Lawrence, the inside linebacker and defensive quarterback, starred as a sophomore (*MC Football Media Guide*, 2005).

The season was jam-packed with passes, dashes, and fourth-quarter heroics. In the Guilford game (42-25), the defense recovered three fumbles, and Mike Hill scored after two long runs. Against North Carolina Wesleyan (31-20), George Sands' touchdown capped a seventy-three-yard pass play. At Maryville, Methodist scored three times in the fourth quarter to win 28-24.

In the first minute of the Emory & Henry game, MC scored twice: a safety and fifty-nine-yard run by Roncketti. In the second half, Jeremy McSwain returned a kickoff for ninety-seven yards. Patrick Larkin kicked three field goals, and the game ended 55-21, the most points scored by MC since Gallaudet (73-14) in '94.

Three touchdowns came in the last 2:20 of play at Averett (29-28). Mike Hill scored, pulling Methodist ahead 23-22. Seconds later, Averett took the lead 23-28. Then after a fifty-nine-yard drive, Roncketti scored with twenty-six seconds remaining.

Against Christopher Newport, the Monarchs chalked up thirty-five points in the first half, which Coach Sy said he never dreamed possible — although he had nightmares about that game. MC beat CNU for the first time in five attempts.

At Shenandoah, Roncketti passed for three of five touchdowns, amassing over five-hundred yards which included a record ninety-three-yard pass to Chuck Howard. Among the records set in '05,

Roncketti passed two thousand, two hundred and thirty-four yards, Hill rushed for a thousand and fifty-four yards, and Patrick Larkin kicked thirty-eight PATs (stats from *Fayetteville Observer*).

The Season, Chris Roncketti

The 2005 team was an experienced team that came close to the championship in 2004. Before the season, Coach Sy asked the seniors to find something that showed what we wanted to accomplish. In the Methodist gym, there were banners from all the sports teams that have won various championships, but football didn't have a banner because we had never won a championship. So we decided to get a blank one that we would see every day. We had no doubts it would eventually go up in the gym with 2005 on it. There were some close calls along the way, but the team never believed we were out of a game.

The first game that comes to mind is at Averett in the pouring rain. It was a mud bowl and a game I almost missed. I was living off-campus, and my alarm never went off that morning. I famously missed the bus to the game. One of the assistants showed up, and I arrived about forty-five minutes before kick-off. We picked up a couple of crucial fourth downs late in the game before I scrambled in for a score with only a few seconds remaining. That game helped us put 2005 on that banner.

We lost the first game of the year to a good Salisbury team, but that loss turned out to be a good thing for our team. In the second half, we utilized a spread offense and realized we were built for that style. We had a great group of young wide receivers and a couple of running backs who could really operate. That game set the tone for how we would play the rest of the season.

We felt we let one slip away in 2004 when CNU beat us at our place. We didn't let that happen in 2005 when we exploded for thirty-five first-half points. That CNU win was one of the most satisfying we ever had.

We got off to a slow start against Maryville. We were down double digits late in the game inside our own five-yard line before we marched down the field and scored. Maryville made a huge mistake and decided to send in an all-out blitz, leaving a corner one-on-one with Patrick Doleman. He caught an easy slant and outran everyone to the end zone with only fifty-four seconds left. That was a wild comeback with a hundred and eighty-plus passing yards and two passing touchdowns in the last five minutes of the game.

Unfortunately, we did lose one conference game. We played Ferrum on a Friday night after a seven-hour bus ride prior to kick-off. They ran the triple option. Both games we lost that season were to teams that ran the option. It was the only night game we played in my four years. And Mike Hill, our leading rusher and Methodist's all-time leading rusher when he graduated, missed the game. We struggled

Coach Sy with Chris Ronichetti. "Winning masks a lot of problems. In our championship season, the problems were still there. It was just easier to handle them when the atmosphere was positive."

early and spotted them twenty points before we eventually tied it 28-28 to make a game of it. Another game we showed we wouldn't quit as we came back in the second half before losing a high-scoring game. That game I wish I could redo because it prevented us from the playoffs, and Coach Sy deserved to coach a playoff team.

We finished the season by beating Shenandoah for the first time in school history in a blowout. It was a great way to end the season and the most fun I ever had playing football. We set a goal to win it all, and we achieved it. We beat two teams for the first time ever and scored at least twenty-eight points in every game. Mike Hill set the record for most rushing yards, and I set the record for passing yards and total offense in a season. Coach Sy was the perfect coach for that team, and he had a great group of assistants who got the most out of that group. It was an honor to be a part.

PlayerSpeak

Brandon Hayden

The Cape Fear Baptism Speech before we beat CNU was one of the best pregame speeches ever given! Coach Sy talked about the weapons they had and the game plan we had. It was a normal pregame speech to the defense until Coach said we had the Cape Fear River water on our side. It is what we had. He then went to the locker-room sink and soaked himself with water. I don't remember every word he said, but the defensive players followed suit, and we soaked ourselves in the same sink. At this point, we were loud and proud, and no brick wall could stop us. I remember offensive players looking at us coming out of the locker room with that what-the-hell-just-happened? face. This was also one of the best games I ever played.

Jon Sherman

In '04, we beat Emory and Henry 36-27 at their place with a long field goal. What made that game stay in my mind was the joy and excitement of the whole team. Our opponents had us dress in an indoor-pool facility, and every player jumped in that pool celebrating the win! Coach Sy just laughed. In '05, we had no business coming back against Maryville, but we did. We kept fighting till the end. We beat CNU and were up 35-0 at the half — crazy.

Irrington Roberts

We came so close to losing the Maryville game. At the end of the Guilford game, we blocked a kick to seal the win ... and we all went crazy. I saw George Sands do backflips in full uniform at varsity games. Now that's impressive!

Matt Panza

Coach Sypult trained us to fight for every second and every inch until the whistle blew. Ten seconds is a lifetime.

Chris Roncketti

Coach Sy is the sole reason I went to Methodist. After transferring from West Point, I visited a few schools, but it only took five minutes talking with Coach to know I had to play for him. His passion for the game was evident, and I would have played a game on Ramsey Street if he told me to. He put a lot of pressure on me, but he also believed in me more than any as well. I worked my tail off every day to prove him right and to ensure I never let him down. I loved every minute of my time at Methodist, and I'm forever grateful for Coach and everything he did for me.

Rhyan Breen

The defense only gave up four sacks in 2005 which is great considering how many people wanted to hit Roncketti.

Jonathan Willis

I wish I could go back and do it again. In 2005, that camp brought us all closer as a team. Offensive and defensive players hung out. There were no separations between the groups.

Antwin Shuford

When teased about collecting Social Security, Shuford, an Iraqi veteran, said, "I might be old [twenty-six], but I'm better and faster, so I win."

Jonathan Byrd

I won damn near every award there was to win as a player, but nothing comes close to Poppa Sy telling me I was a wild-horse rider.

Matt Panza

Jonathan Byrd is the only man I ever saw throw up during a play and continue to play.

Sunrise Service with Coach Sy

Andrew Rusk

The camp Sunrise Service was the worst because you had to practice all day after getting up at 5 a.m.

Matt Panza

I had to run at 6 a.m. I know we got in trouble, but I can't remember what for. I can remember Grady hitting the Porta John though.

Jon Sherman

A mile around the track without stopping was the run test my first year, and then it changed to a number of laps around the track based on the position. The run test was no joke!

Jeremy McSwain

I had Sunrise Service for missing practice, almost fighting, and letting my roommate oversleep. Something happened in practice but was quickly resolved by my standards, but Coach made sure to teach me a lesson — a 5:45 a.m. lesson.

Matthew Sposato

I had to hit the good ol' Sunrise Service for taping my ditty shorts up in practice so I didn't chafe. I don't think Coach Sy knew why. After that morning, I never did it again.

Kyle Smith

I had Sunrise Service one time because I said some things to Averett fans, and they ratted me out to the AD — thus making me accountable for my words. Lesson learned. Needless to say, what I said did not meet the NCAA code of ethics. I remember exactly what I said! However, it's best I not repeat it. At Sunday workout, Coach pulled me aside and said these words: "I'll see you in the morning — Sunrise Service." I didn't ask questions. Sunrise Service we all feared during the season. It wasn't the running that scared us. It was letting down Coach Sy.

Andrew Geddie

I had it only three times — for missing breakfast or sleeping in class too much — but I still get flashbacks. Those runs were the worst, but they made my grades shoot way up, and I developed a classroom work ethic. Something I still use to this day.

Brett Morton

Sunrise Service was punishment for not conducting ourselves the way Coach Sy expected us to. "Don't be that guy," he would say. A line delivered with such effectiveness, it made us understand we needed to make sure we had our crap together. He treated us like men and expected us to uphold his standards.

The Big-Guy Run

Jonathan Willis

I would try to stay seven steps behind Roncketti to set the huddle for y'all.

Jonathan Byrd

I would start jogging to where the huddle would be.

Jonathan Willis

Damn right! Chris Roncketti was too fast for us to keep up with. But I would always spot the touchdown signal. Byrd, I recall you doing a few big-guy runs as well when Chris would get outside.

Jonathan Byrd

I know that move.

Rhyan Breen

He did the fake big-guy run, where you sort of swing your arms really hard but don't move that far.

Jonathan Byrd

I'm sure Willis watched as they ran.

Chris Roncketti

I didn't like getting hit, so I ran away from people like my life depended on it.

Brandon Spiece

As I get older, it all means more to me than ever. Coach Sy was one of the greatest men I ever knew.

Justin *Bo* Gray

I think about Coach Sy all the time — what he taught me as a young man — and still to this day, I am a wild-horse rider.

Matt Panza

Fall makes me think of helmets and mouthpieces, shoulder pads, and fresh paint on the grass. Taping my ankles, icing my joints, and sucking wind between whistles. Bleeding, hitting, line 'em up, ready, go.

Blitzing, sacking the quarterback, calling the defense and GATA — *Get After Their Asses.* Reading guard, smashing the fullback, and shuffle shuffle jab! Dropping to the flats.

I miss the violence. I miss hitting, tackling, facemasking, getting mad, and letting the monster out of the basement for a walk.

The game will pass us by, but I'm not complaining. Just miss strapping on the helmet with the boys and smashing folks in the teeth. Coach Sy was right: Football did far more for me than I ever did for football.

Coach Sypult

Those who stay will be champions!

16
THE GREEN ZONE

COACH SY: Everybody else calls it *the red zone,* but we call it *the green zone.* [Methodist's colors are green and gold.]

Jim Sypult Coaching Clinic

The Jim Sypult Coaching Clinic began in 2019 with a group of former players who wanted to get together and talk. John Sherman identified some core values of the Clinic: "We value others above ourselves. Build each other up. Be a team that cares about each other."

Jon Sherman, the Driving Force

The Clinic is growing. Those who come understand what this Clinic is all about: remembering Coach Sy and what he taught us, bringing us together, and just being a Monarch because of his vision. We plan on recognizing all members of Coach Sy's tree.

The highlight in 2020 was a legend panel of three, talking about how they have achieved success. Donnie Kiefer, head coach at West Ashley High, wanted to express how Coach Sy impacted his life while coaching at Davidson.

David Abernathy

I had the honor of speaking at the 2020 Jim Sypult Coaching Clinic. Coach Sy gave me my first opportunity to start my two-year college career as a player and coach. I looked forward to honoring him and my former coaches and teammates.

Jonathan Byrd

Jim Sypult pushed me to be a better man and is one of the major reasons I'm a coach today. It was an honor to speak and help with the Clinic. His legacy lives on with many former players coaching all across the nation.

Sy Helmet Decals

In 2018, the Methodist football team honored legendary football coach Jim Sypult by wearing a *SY* decal on their helmets. Coach Sypult served as head coach of the Methodist football program from 1992-2010. His 1997 team finished 9-1 and was nationally ranked, and his 2005 squad won the USA South conference crown — a program first.

Methodist Athletic Hall of Fame

Jim Sypult is the all-time winningest coach in the history of the program. He guided the Monarchs through some of the most celebrated seasons and was chosen the Dixie Intercollegiate Athletic Conference Coach (DIAC) of the Year in 2000.

The *Father of Methodist Football,* Coach Sypult impacted the lives of many young men over a coaching career that spanned four decades. His memory and legacy will live in the hearts of former players, coaches, and football alumni (*mumonarchs.com*).

Hall of Fame Recipients

DeCarlos West, 2004
Trayfer Monroe, 2007
Quincy Malloy, 2011
Chris Roncketti, 2012
Jim Sypult, 2019

Jim Sypult Coached Eleven All-Americans

Rich Jinnette (1992), Britt Morton (1994), Tony Bugeja (1996), Keljin Adams (1996), Leon Ché Clark (1996), Trayfer Monroe (1997 and 1998), Randal Webster (1997), DeCarlos West (1997), Jason Marion (2000), Quincy Malloy (2000 and 2001), and George Sands (2006).

State Championships

1996, 1997, 1998, 2000, 2001, 2003, 2004, and 2005

Memorable Methodist Wins
  Chowan, 1993, 16-13, first win
  @Davidson College, 1995, 16-14
  Davidson College, 1996, 42-13
  Frostburg State, 1997, 40-12; and 1998, 20-14
  @Jacksonville, 1998, 35-26
  @Ferrum, 2003, 37-34, comeback win
  @Christopher Newport, 2005, 35-28
  Campbell University, 2008, 32-21
  Christopher Newport, 2009, 10-9

Great way to end the '09 season: In the last two minutes of play, CNU scored, Anthony Cassone blocked the extra point, and Tyler Mosko kicked a field goal to win 10-9. Coach Sy with Mosko.

Wild-Horse Riders Closed *Facebook* Group

Editor's note: In 2015, Coach Sypult created a closed group on *Facebook* called *Methodist University Football: Wildhorse Riders, 1992-2013.* He wanted to reconnect, offer support to the Monarch Nation, and share stories, memories, and information. "It is a fellowship to keep in touch and look after each other," Jonathan Byrd explained. Posts range from T-shirt photos to the installation of lights at Monarch Stadium to memorial tributes for Stacy Cook, #62, former team captain and line coach.

Fred Van Steen

If Methodist had lights in '92, Coach Sy would have had us practicing at midnight.

Andrew Rusk

We definitely would have been under the lights instead of moving to the basketball courts when daylight savings hit.

Stacy Cook

Loved every minute I had of Coach Sy's coaching.

Tavares Hunter

Quincy Malloy and I try to keep alive the House that Jim Sypult built. I swear we have that man's blood running in our veins.

Coach Sy's last game at Monarch Stadium. Pictured with seniors Josh Cook #42, Matt Hanshaw #7, Anthony Autry, Corey McGuire #21, Josh McKenzie, and Chris Nuta #50.

Matt Panza

Remind the new MU football players that those who stay are a part of a brotherhood that means so much more than the game. Those two-a-days in the *Fayettenam* heat, hours in the weight room in the off-season, and gut-busting sprints at the end of practice created a bond and a lifelong family that nothing can break. It's easy to be family when you're winning, but during the rough times is where those bonds are forged. No one else on that campus will be tested the way we have been. Ready ready Monarchs! Team!

Brandon Spiece

The bond formed with teammates and coaches is special. Hard to put into words. Dr. Sypult, Coach Sypult's wife, taught us all how to write and to be better students. She wrote more on my papers than I did! Lol. Coach Sypult, the original Wild-Horse Rider and Father of Methodist Football, taught us how to play the game the right way and to be better men. As it turns out, molding all of us into better people was the Sypult family business. I am forever grateful.

Extra Points by Coach Jim Sypult

In 1973, I coached one year at Fairmont State. We had a volunteer student assistant we nicknamed *Crazy Fred*. Turns out *Crazy Fred* is Fred Phelps, father of Michael Phelps! True story, I think.

I put my team through some flexibility stuff during two-a-day practices. I felt like an aerobics teacher up there.

How about the time in '98 when we stopped that big Frostburg running back half an inch from the goal at the end of the game!

We practiced between the baseball and softball fields which was great. We could watch the softball and baseball games at the same time.

It took me a few years, but I finally solved the missing helmets problem. Then it was the socks! And who stole the XXL T-shirts in 2005?

Remember the *Barber* defense. Named after John *the Barber* Shaw. Got that defense from John Madden on a *Monday Night Football* game and installed it the next day. Now I sit around and do yoga.

My yoga teacher had me breathing through my knee today. I must have missed something along the way.

17
TRUTH BE KNOWN

EDITOR'S NOTE: On November 11, 2002, seven Methodist football players were wrongfully arrested, charged with hazing and sexual assault, and punished for an incident after a game in the locker room. The players' pictures and names were plastered everywhere, and they were treated like criminals — largely because of a reckless campus investigation and vindictive report by the student dean. All charges were dropped after a thorough sheriff's investigation, but their innocence was never made known to the public.

Insight and Context by Rhyan Breen, Attorney

If the intent is to provide insight into Coach Sypult, it is important to include his account because it provides more context as to who he was and presents an inside look on the handling of similar situations by universities.

Jim Sypult Account of Lockergate

In 2006, three Duke lacrosse players were accused of assault and rape. The media found them *guilty*. The administration and faculty found them *guilty*. The court system found them *not guilty*. The Duke players were innocent but guilty in the eyes of the world ... until high-powered lawyers proved their innocence and vindicated them.

In 2002, seven of my football players at Methodist College were accused of hazing and sodomy. The media, administration, and faculty found them *guilty*. My players had *no* money and *no* lawyers, and, unfortunately, *no* vindication. The legal system saved them from going to jail, finding *no guilt* and dropping all charges. However, they were humiliated, their lives and reputations severely damaged, and their innocence never made public to the world.

Play by Play

A few days before our last football game in 2002, my athletic director walked into my office and shut the door. "This is big," he said, sitting down. He had trouble written all over his face.

He then gave me the most disturbing and bizarre news. "I just came from the president's office," he said. "Yesterday, after practice, seven of your senior football players tackled, stripped, and sexually assaulted a freshman player by jamming a *Sharpie* pen into his anus."

I was shocked, ashamed, and overwhelmed by the enormity of the situation. These seven were my captains and leaders! They were respected and admired on campus: student body officers, dorm counselors, choir members, honor students, a Homecoming king. How could this be?

I was given a *gag* order and told *not* to talk to the media or anyone. In effect, I couldn't talk to the press to defend my players. I was instructed to direct all questions from the media to the public relations director and to suspend the accused from the team immediately. I didn't know what happened, but even I thought an assault had taken place — at first.

This much I knew: In the ten years I was the head football coach at Methodist, there was never an incident in my locker room, never a complaint of any unacceptable behavior, never a hint of impropriety. I stressed character and integrity and held my players to high standards and good conduct. So I put my trust in the Lord and the truth.

I brought each of the accused seven into my office and temporarily suspended them as directed and per my team policy. Each player denied the accusations and claimed the event was simply locker-room *hijinks* — no harm intended and certainly no sexual assault. Just laughter, hollering, and good-natured horseplay. A senior was trying to write *seniors* on a freshman's butt.

One of the accused told me he had spent most of the previous night with the alleged victim who wanted to talk to me. I agreed hoping to get to the crux of the matter. I alerted my athletic director about the request; I wanted him to witness what was said. He called the campus chief of police who vetoed such a meeting, arguing I would *taint* the evidence.

The alleged victim showed up in my office anyway, saying he was "confused and never intended for this incident to go so far." I was ordered *not* to talk to him. And so I lost the opportunity to learn the truth at the outset.

By the end of the day, media vans with attached satellites bombarded our campus. *Someone* had leaked the story, *someone* close to the situation who had *inside information*. Every local television network carried us as the lead story. National coverage followed: ESPN, ABC, CBS, NBC, Fox, C-Span, CNN. My telephone never stopped ringing for weeks.

I wanted to talk to the press but was silenced by the school administration, an agonizing silence that made my players look guilty. The news coverage continued for months.

The president's concern was the school's public image and Board of Trustees. He and I had heated meetings, and one ended in a shouting match.

The dean of students, George Blanc, was handling the case, a fact that did not bode well. The year before, I had challenged his punishment of some students — punishment that was *improper,* according to the student handbook. He was not a friend.

The campus security was under Blanc's supervision. He ordered a disgruntled security underling to conduct an investigation to which I strongly objected because of past conflicts. On three separate occasions, I had filed *complaints* against her: She had called my black players *boys,* shoved and bullied others, and wrongfully issued parking tickets to players parked outside the locker room. She was anything but *impartial.*

One tenured faculty member, Michael Colonnese, a close friend of the dean, vehemently demanded the players be expelled and head coach fired. This English teacher and I had many conflicts in the past about his dislike of football players, a matter he openly boasted to students and other faculty.

Colonnese was rumored to be giving information about the allegations to *Fayetteville Observer* sports reporter Brett Friedlander. He had a bulldog reputation and pounced on the story with a passion. His daily reporting was so harsh and far-reaching he lost all professional integrity. He resented me because the previous year, I had refused to release my educational credentials ... out of principle, not fear.

As it were, the dean, campus security officer, faculty member, and reporter were clearly connected and certainly biased.

For the next seven months, Friedlander wrote story after story with unbelievable accusations made by *anonymous sources. Anonymous sources!* Every day, new details, rumors, and *Sharpie* jokes emerged.

Friedlander's stories were one-sided and inaccurate. It was never-ending, a horror show, an explosive story that grew and would not stop.

All seven players were arrested, handcuffed, and treated like criminals. They were charged with *hazing* and *assault*. Their mugshots appeared on the front page above the fold of the *Observe*r. A few letters dominated the editorial page, demanding the players be severely punished and the head coach (me) fired. These young men were more victims than the *alleged* victim.

There were over a hundred players in the locker room but *no* eyewitnesses to substantiate the alleged victim's claims.

The campus security recorded a video of the players who were in the locker room at the time. These witnesses either didn't see what happened or denied a sexual assault took place.

Dean Blanc concluded I was at fault since the assault took place in the locker room. In a written report I did not see until months later, he accused me of creating a culture of hazing on the team. In bold, all-capital letters, Blanc stated, SYPULT KNEW OR SHOULD HAVE KNOWN.

This document created a real problem for the school's liability insurance company, and I was assigned my own lawyer. My lawyer visited frequently, examining the details again and again. He was prepared and wanted to defend my character and the false allegations in court.

Lawsuits were filed against each of the accused, the school administration, and me. These seven young men were found *guilty* by the press and the public, and so was I.

Summary of the Aftermath

Hundreds of students and community members supported the accused players and gave testimony about their outstanding character. *Hundreds* that were largely ignored.

The alleged victim was taken to the hospital after the incident, and the medical report showed the player had minor bruises but was *not sodomized*. The dean and campus security had this report early on, but it was *never* made public.

- After the school's investigation, six of the players were put on probation, and one was suspended for the school year. I was given a hefty fine, a fine I paid to prevent my staff from being fired. But I never admitted any guilt.

- Two months after the *alleged* assault, the lawyers for the *alleged* victim dropped the charges, fearing complications of "church and state laws." They requested the district attorney handle the case.

- The district attorney discarded the dean's findings and campus security report. He then ordered the county sheriff to perform an investigation, a real investigation by an objective professional. It was a break in the case — a *miracle.*

- The sheriff's investigation was thorough and unprejudiced. Every member of the football team was questioned. The investigator, Jimmy Black, thanked me for our cooperation. He revealed that Dean Blanc warned him I would be *uncooperative.* The dean denied making such a statement and called the sheriff a *liar.*

- Black determined *no criminal act* had taken place and *no hazing.* In my presence and for me to see, Black tossed the dean's report and campus security report into the trash.

- Black turned his investigation over to the district attorney. Because of the sensitive nature and high public profile of the case, the DA handed it over to the grand jury.

- Much later, the grand jury ruled *no probable cause* and found *no guilt.* Finally, all charges were dropped.

- Friedlander's reporting of the *alleged hazing* stopped. A short article appeared on the back page of the local newspaper about the court's decision. Thereafter, the lawsuits against the accused players were also dropped.

- The lawsuit against the school was *settled.* My name was never mentioned. The suspensions and probations against the accused were never reversed. The fine I paid was never returned. The toll the locker-room *incident* took on us is hard to assess.

Presumption of guilt and rush to justice are very dangerous in alleged sexual assault cases. The zeal to condemn and punish is troublesome. Those who can afford legal representation like the Duke lacrosse players fare much better than those who can't.

Methodist owes those seven young men and me an apology — at the very least.

Editor's note: Some insider leaked the story to the *Observer* and fed Friedlander information. Coach Sypult refused all interviews with Friedlander thereafter. In 2005, Friedlander lost his job at the *Observer* for inaccurately reporting a sports story.

Book I Intended to Write

"Fuck you!"

This was the high-intensity moment. My editor and wife, the best writing teacher I know, suggests telling a story with the most intense point first and then work back with flashbacks, dialogue, and description of events.

I had prepared and prayed for this occasion. My job and possibly my career were on the line. I was meeting with the president of the college regarding an alleged hazing incident by the football team and my future as its head football coach.

"What am I going to do with you?" Dr. M. Elton Hendricks, the college president, asked. "I'm getting pressure from the community, faculty, and Board of Trustees to fire you. The only reason I've not done anything yet is because Bob McEvoy [the athletic director who was also at the meeting] believes in you, and you are a man of integrity. But what to do?"

"I'll tell you what to do," I said. "Tell the public that something happened on this campus, and Jim Sypult is my head football coach. He'll figure it out and handle it. Jim Sypult is my man."

"I wish I could believe that."

"Fuck you!"

What did I just say? It's over. I just told the president to get fucked. I'm done. I thought.

I got up to leave.

"Wait a minute," Hendricks said. "I didn't mean that. Let's talk this out."

I thought that time would heal all the bitterness. After *ten* years, I thought he would know my character and integrity. I would think *ten* years was enough time. Apparently, it was not. It creeps back to me every day in a thought. I then dwell on it.

First, the mishandling of the entire episode wrongly hurt seven student-athletes. They were singled out for wrongdoing but had all criminal charges dropped by a grand jury. All legal cases were dropped by the alleged victim. Yet these young men were prejudged and punished by the school and embarrassed by the media (namely Brett Friedlander, a sports reporter for the *Fayetteville Observer*). Second, I was fined and punished by the school for an alleged incident that was determined not to have happened.

I am not writing this book as a personal attack on members of Methodist University (Methodist College when the incident occurred). Namely, Hendricks, then president of the college, and George Blanc, vice-president of student services. I'm convinced personal attacks were aimed at me.

This is a book to right the wrong committed against seven students whose reputations were sullied and to show how college administrators protect themselves and their reputations as well as rush to judgment. Grievous mistakes were made, a campus investigation was botched, and innocent lives were affected. I also hope to shed light on the serious consequences locker-room behavior can have on our current culture, however innocent.

Further, I myself was incorrectly punished as a result of a false but often-used expression — *on your watch* — which was used as an explanation and condemnation.

The media is also to blame for this injustice, and it is my contention that sex sells and some reporters have no scruples when advancing their journalistic careers.

This is an honest and accurate account of the events.

18
As Told By ...

DAVE EAVENSON, JR., former Dickinson College Athletic Director
I want you to know the tremendous admiration I hold for Jim. What he did for my son David was so unbelievable. In a large part, where David is today is a credit to Jim. For him to take David under his wing to teach him about coaching is more than I could have ever asked. I always thought Jim's relationship with David was more like father and son than mentor and coach. Coach Sy always made me feel a part of the Monarch Nation.

Dave Eavenson (son of above), MU Athletic Director, Vice President, and former MU Head Coach
I love Coach like a dad. The other day, I tried to count approximately how many lives Coach touched in his forty-five years coaching football, and the number is staggering. My guess is over ten thousand.
He impacted my life in so many positive ways, and I would not be doing what I am doing today if it were not for Coach Sy.

Steve Barrows, former Head Coach at Anderson University
I love him and cherish the many memories of watching the Monarchs play and spending time with him at the AFCA conventions. I am blessed with his friendship!

Gary *Gunny* Cunningham, Assistant Coach at Chamblee High and former MC Assistant
Coach Sy was a true champion, and I know because he never stopped believing in me. I thank God for Coach being in my life!

Steve Frank, former Head Coach at Hamilton College
I loved Big Sy. He was a friend, colleague, mentor, and role model. We met at Davidson College in 1979. From the beginning, I could see Jim's professionalism in the way he addressed his staff and

interacted with all individuals in the program. He treated everyone with respect and expected it in return. He never felt any job was too big or too small. Football coaches were all coaches, no rank, no order — just people working towards a common goal.

Jim treated players with love and expected them to maintain team rules and perform to the best of their ability. Every player had a role in the program, and all roles were equally important. They knew where they stood, their relationships built on honesty and transparency. Jim was a coach all parents want their kids to play for and the coach all coaches should aspire to be.

Dave Eavenson: "Coach Sy is a legend and the Father of Methodist football."

Carl Funderburk,
former MU Assistant and North Carolina Central Coach
I learned more valuable lessons from Coach Sy than from all the coaches I have worked for combined! He will always be the standard I strive for every day of my professional and personal life.

Keven Gregg, MU Head Coach and former Assistant
Even though I only worked for him one year before he retired and didn't know him as well as most, he still texted every year on my birthday at 6 a.m. Coach Sy is a man who cared about everyone he met and had an impact on all. His lesson is one I try to embody every day in my life now by messaging people first thing in the morning on their birthday. I'm just not as good at it as he was.

Jerry Hogge, former MU Director of Golf Management Program

Glad to have known such a great storyteller, leader of young men, and giant of a man. Heaven just got a lead angel. He made everyone better.

David Holloway, former MC Team Chaplain and Elizabethtown Presbyterian Minister

In 1998, I accepted a call to serve an inner-city church in Fayetteville. I knew absolutely no one there except Jim Sypult who had been an assistant at Davidson College when I served as chaplain. Jim invited me to lunch. We talked and laughed about some of the crazy things that had taken place at Davidson. Then Jim asked if I would be the chaplain for the Methodist football team. Of course, I accepted his offer. Some of the happiest moments of my life were standing on the sidelines with the Methodist players and coaches.

Once after a funeral for a player who was killed in a car accident, Jim called me. "We have to talk, Holloway," he said. "It's very important!" We agreed to meet at a McDonald's close to the campus.

"Those folks have something I don't have," he confessed. He was referring to the family of the young player who had died [Justin Gambrell in 1999]. "I want to know what they've got and how I can get it." Jim and I spoke of spiritual things right there at McDonald's. We even prayed together as Jim recommitted his life to the faith of his childhood.

Eight weeks later, Jim preached a powerful message at the church I was serving. He was a true friend and more special to me than I can ever express. I am forever grateful that God brought Jim Sypult into my life.

Ed Holly, Head Coach at Westminster Christian and former MC Assistant

Not a week goes by that I do not use something I learned from Coach Sy in my program. It is amazing how many things remind me of him.

Dave Eavenson (aka *Yankee Dave*) and I speak on the phone regularly, and when one of us has a dilemma, it always comes back to one of Coach Sy's sayings. It is amazing how many sayings Coach had for every situation. What is even more amazing to me is even though I never played for him, he always made me feel like family.

Ralph Isernia, Head Coach at Rensselaer and former MC Assistant

Coach Sy turned boys into men. Not just the players, but coaches too. I am proud to be a part of this coaching tree and forever part of his family.

The legacy he leaves is the players he coached, the coaches he mentored, and the lives he has forever impacted. We are who we are because he was who he was. Near or far, Dr. Sy and Coach Sy will always be a huge part of our lives.

Matt Kelchner, Associate Athletic Director and former Head Coach at Christopher Newport University

Coach Sypult is a great man and an honest man. You may not realize what he has done for you now, but you will in ten to fifteen years.

Editor's note: At Coach Sy's last game of his coaching career, Kelchner asked to talk to the MU team. He then presented the game ball signed by the CNU players to Coach Sy.

Tony Lerulli, Head Coach at Limestone University and former Head Coach at Maryville College

One of my closest friends in the coaching profession. We had eight great games against each other when I was head coach at a school in Tennessee. We would call each other often and spend most of the conversation just laughing.

One of the very few coaches I considered a mentor and friend ... always there when I needed advice on important issues. Jim mentored me throughout my time as a head coach for which I will always be grateful. Going to miss this great man. He was the winningest coach in Methodist Monarch history.

Editor's note: Lerulli, a college coach for over forty years, presented Coach Sy a rocking chair upon retirement.

Bob McEvoy, former MC/MU Head Basketball Coach and Athletic Director

Coach Sypult and I arrived at MU (then MC) in early 1992. We hit it off from the start. He grew up in West Virginia, and I grew up in Ohio. We shared stories of familiar places, events, and people from our neighboring states, and our common childhood memories made for amusing trips down memory lane. He loved to laugh, and I always enjoyed my time with him.

One September, we hosted an Appalachian State junior-varsity football game. It was one of those 90-plus days in Fayetteville, brutally hot, and the humidity so thick you could taste it. Kickoff was set for 1 p.m.

Coach Sy and I settled into our seats in the little shade we could find. We dressed over ninety JV Monarchs. During warmups, I noticed App State only suited twenty-five players. I kept waiting for more to appear. None did. Our Monarchs led 10-7 at the half and went to the locker room to hydrate. The App State guys found a couple of shade trees behind their bench, took off their helmets and shoulder pads, and pounded down the water.

A few minutes later, one of our student trainers ran up to Coach Sy and said, "Coach, the App State team is getting ready to go home. They say it's way too hot to finish the game."

Coach Sy looked at me and, without a word, walked through the crowd and across the field to the shade trees. He must have given App State the best five-minute pep talk of all-time. They not only played the second half, but they beat us with a last-minute touchdown! Coach Sy was a great motivator and teacher of life lessons ... even for our opponents! Classic.

Bob Swank, Head Coach at Chamblee High and former MC Assistant

Thanks for everything you have done for me and all of the coaches and players you have come across at Methodist. You have had one heck of a run and touched the lives of thousands.

David Turner, Assistant Coach at University of Florida and former Davidson College and Italian Player

When I was a freshman at Davidson College, I met a coach who would impact my life — Jim Sypult! He had a way of coaching that made me know he cared. He gave me an opportunity to see, play, and live in another country — Italy. My fondest memories are traveling with the *Griswolds* — Coach Sy, his wife, and daughter. So much fun.

Over the years, Coach would call just to see how I was doing. I would check *Facebook* to see where he and his wife were traveling, and it always seemed as though I was there with them.

Everything about Coach Sy recommended him: e.g., his enthusiasm for football and love of the game, shrewd game play and attack, strong recruiting record, and gift to lead. He demanded much of himself and his players and was a rigorous football strategist, gifted speaker, and teacher of what is good in sport and life.

As I'm writing this, tears are flowing because I wish I could talk to him one more time just to say thank you for coaching me. Thank you for taking me to Italy and allowing me to live a dream. Thank you for always calling at the perfect time. And thank you for your love! You have affected hundreds, if not thousands of lives. You are a big reason I do what I do. I love you, Coach Sy.

Rich Trogdon, VP City Executive at First Bank

I want to thank Coach Sy for the opportunity to work for him. I learned a lot about leadership, integrity, and fight that I use on a daily basis in the business world. I can't explain, and did not realize it at the time, how much I learned from him and my experience working with him.

Rita Wiggs, former MU Athletic Director and USA South Commissioner

Hiring Jim was one of the best decisions I ever made, and he never failed to thank me on each year's anniversary. His legacy will live on through the many athletes he coached over the seasons.

Kirbie Dockery, MU Senior Director of Advancement Services

I loved our USA South football media days. The other conference sports information directors always agreed Coach Sy was a favorite, partly because of his stories. He didn't take himself too seriously and made us all laugh when most of the other coaches were worried about giving away team secrets.

I interviewed Coach Sy for his farewell story. It was the hardest interview I've ever done, hands down. I will always remember it because he had me in tears. How do you say goodbye to a program you've given so much to?

As Told By ... Davidson College Players

Kirk Gavel

Coach Sy was one coach I was fortunate to have in my life. I owe so much to him. I loved him. He was a great leader and teacher to all of us. In our last game against Wofford in 1984, we won, and I had a pretty good game. Everyone was celebrating, but I had tears in my eyes, and he saw it. Later, the head coach gave Coach Sy the game ball. He then gave it to me. [Gavel still has that football.]

One year, I had an open wound on my forehead that would not heal. Blood ran down my face at practice every day because we were banging heads every day. I still have a scar. Before the Bucknell game, we came in from the pregame warmup and took a knee, hats off, listening to Coach Sy. I always looked him right in the eye and listened to every word he said. Coach eyeballed each player. When he looked at me, he came over and kissed me on the forehead. He loved his players, and we could tell.

We had this pursuit drill called *perfect play*. We took our angle of pursuit to the sideline and broke down in a football position, feet chopping. If someone didn't get his pursuit lanes right or took a lazy step, we'd do it again. It could be tiring at the end of practice. Anyway, I actually liked this drill and always got it right ... except one day. Coach Sy held up the ball to his right, which meant I had to hightail it for the left sideline, about five yards downfield. I tripped over my own feet and landed, sprawled flat on my face. I got up as fast as I could and started chopping. Coach Sy ran over to yell at me, but I looked at him and said, "These things happen sometimes, Coach." He just laughed, blew his whistle, and ended practice. I am thankful he was a part of my life.

Andy Hunt

Coach Sy was always so full of life. I suppose I subconsciously half-expected him to live forever. He was my coach for only two seasons, but it always felt like so much more. My life is so much richer because he was in it. His spirit will live on not only with his real family, but also with his football family. We'll carry him with us every day. I love you, Coach!

It's fitting Coach Sy passed while doing something epic! I think this Hunter S. Thompson quote is applicable to his life: "Life should not be a journey to the grave with the intention of arriving safely in a pretty and well-preserved body, but rather to skid in broadside in a cloud of smoke, thoroughly used up, totally worn out and loudly proclaiming 'Wow! What a Ride!'"

Ken Nazemetz

Coach Sy believed in all of us. I still remember and love his speeches and the way he fired us up. He'd scrooch down and say, "Gotta have mo" and "Katie bar the door, cuz we are comin!"

Carrick Pell

Coach Sy was my secondary coach at Davidson College. I was a 170-pound freshman, and he put me in the second series of the season because the corner in front of me missed two tackles. He BELIEVED IN ME. Didn't take me out the rest of the season. I never missed a tackle, and I played my heart out for him! He was a legend and has had a lifelong impact.

Ben Pope

I go back before the Wild-Horse Rider days, back being *wild* like a *wildcat* and hearing Coach call for some *fr-ay-shmen* to get in the drill. I was at Davidson for the 1981-84 seasons, and Coach Sy was a big part of me hanging in there. Loved that guy! We never gave up because of Coach Sy. He related so well to the players and made it so much more fun. Bite the medulla, Coach!

I remember when my mom called Coach Sy at Methodist, to get his address to send him a wedding invitation. At the time, his QB was also named Ben Pope. When my mother told him who she was and why she called, he replied, "My QB can't get married!" But he was there for the wedding in May 1993! Honored me by attending! A great coach and better man, much loved by the Davidson Wildcats and Wild-Horse Riders alike!

Keith Rawlins

In my mind is a vivid memory of how Coach Sy would get freshmen to practice kick-offs and kick returns. He pronounced *freshmen* as *frayshmen*. It cracks me up to this day. I still share stories of this awesome coach and a few of the ways he amused us. His heart and how much he cared for his charges were always evident.

Colleen Brannen

I was a football equipment manager at Davidson College and thought Jim Sypult was a wonderful coach. My junior year, I was dating the wrong guy — not a football player. The following summer, the football coach from my high school set me up on a blind date with a guy who played football at Davidson five years ahead of me. We dated for two weeks, but I was headed to summer abroad in London. I snail-mailed Coach Sy to say this guy seemed awesome, but was he a good guy or just a charmer?

Coach Sy snail-mailed back ASAP to say this guy, Rob, was one of the finest young men he had coached. Fast forward, we celebrated twenty-eight years of marriage this fall — four kids. Coach was right, and I am so grateful he took the time to write me a letter thirty years ago. But that is who he was. He was the best.

As Told By ... Bologna Towers

Toni Manigiafico, Assistant Coach in Italy

Here in Bologna, my Carolina amigo left a beautiful memory. We all loved him and appreciated him both as a person and as a coach. He will remain forever in the heart of the Bologna Towers American football team.

Mauro Anteghini, Player
Grazie per tutto quello che mi hai dato.
Translation: Thanks for all you have given me.

Andrea Tugnoli, Player
It was an honor to know him.

Massimo Terracina, Player
Coach Sy was my mentor of the oval ball and an example of how to relate to guys as players and men. When I meet with old friends, we talk about Coach Sy and past adventures. There are no words to describe hm. I carry his friendship in my heart.

"Could I, by chance, turn the Bologna Towers around and win?" Coach Sy wondered. "Emboldened by many bottles of Chianti, I could ... and I did."

As Told By ... Friends and Family

Gary Tinder, Best Friend
You're asking the wrong guy about memories. I forget my dreams before I wake up. Jim and I were just a couple of little guys growing up in a mining community. It was an easy life. We didn't go to town that often. We didn't know anything better. We threw rocks and played ball all day every day until dark and after because that's what

we did. Everybody had a busted head some time or other.

Every year, we had one good baseball in the group. When we lost it in the woods, we rolled up paper as tight as we could and covered it with mining tape — electrical tape. We used that ball until some big guy at bat busted it.

As for storytelling, there were no stories to tell. If something happened to us, we told everyone. We passed stories down, but we mostly told stories whether they were true or not.

Machiko Tinder, Close Friend

So many people came to Jim's service. So many football players were there, and one by one, they told their stories, how Coach Sy changed their lives and made them better men. It was an unreal, wonderful day, and I found out Jim was a big hero!

Rick Corwin, Best Friend in Grade School

I always thought of Jim as the big brother I never had. We did what young boys do — mostly sports — passing a baseball or football but also hanging out in the neighborhood. We played tackle, just the two of us in his backyard, and basketball in a dirt court in the neighborhood after school and on Sundays. We played at the Old Armory on Jackson Street and went to teen dances and tried to meet girls. I remember Jim could always outrun and out-juke [fake] me. I could never beat him at any sport. Maybe that's when I realized sports were not for me.

Larry Hill, Good Friend

I remember Jim fondly for all he meant to me and those whose lives he touched and made better. I greatly admired his compassion, enthusiasm, humor, dedication, and commitment to do the right thing.

Jim and I became friends in high school while playing football and running track. He was the quarterback, and I the center. He called me his "protector."

In 1973, we found ourselves on the same coaching staff at Fairmont State College. We worked incredibly hard that year developing a new defensive scheme that paved the way to a conference championship and Coal Bowl win.

It was truly one of the best experiences of my forty-five years coaching college sports. It reinforced our friendship that lasted a lifetime. I love you, man.

Kathy Fleischman, Member of Scribblers, a Hilton Head Writing Club

It took only one meeting and one story to know Jim Sypult was a gentleman. If he used an *unladylike* word to further his narration, he always stopped before he uttered it to offer his apologies to the ladies present. His writings were poignant. He was effective in making conclusions. He taught us all so much, beginning with his boyhood in a small town ... to what he considered the importance of training his teams in more than just the intricacies of football ... to amusing tales of his travels. He was obviously a model for his chosen profession and a prominent and valuable member of Scribblers where he served as our most amusing president for several years.

John *Blinky* Lucente, High School Teammate

Jim and I played football and basketball and ran track together at East Fairmont High School. We had great teams with his leadership and determination. He was always a gentleman, a great student-athlete, class president, and editor of the school paper.

Jill Sypult Marcus, Daughter

I have wished my dad were here for guidance at times like this. I know he would have told me this: "Get your head out of your ass and lead." So that is what I pledged to do with my organization.

Grandson Kyle: "Pap is in my heart and on my arm. I got this tattoo because he represents what a Wild-Horse Rider is, and I want to be just like him."

Kyle Marcus, Grandson

My pap was the greatest grandpa a grandson could ask for. He was the best storyteller in the world and a great man. He taught me so much and will always have a special place in my heart.

Zach Marcus, Grandson

He was "Pap" to me for as long as I can remember—a loving grandfather, an authority figure when I needed one, and a comedian if that's what the day called for.

Pap had this tell when he was about to tell a story (as he was wont to do). He'd purse his lips, roll his left shoulder, and entertain with a mixture of animation and earnest that was his own. I wonder if he had the same tell when speaking to teams he coached. Pap was there for me as he was for so many, and I'm glad others got to experience, learn, and be inspired by him.

Robert Sypult, Brother

It is very special for me to know Jim's thoughts. Of importance is that Jim was also my *hero*, and his career was an inspiration, as it was to all who knew him.

I remember Jim playing basketball at EFHS, and, when possible, I would come home on leave from the Marine Corps to watch him play. To think it all started on a dirt court next to the Groseclose's house in Jordan, West Virginia.

Ted Cline, Brother-in-Law

Jim Sypult was my mentor and hero growing up. He taught me many things about life and the importance of sports and friendships associated with them. But, most especially, he taught me his sense of humor.

When I was little, I watched my sister Cheri run and jump on Jim's lap for a quick hug and kiss. I dreamed of finding a wife like that.

Later in life, we worked together siding a beach house in oppressive heat. Ate hotdogs and danced in the rain. He was a wonderful person to be around, and he loved his family and friends with a passion. He was my brother and friend.

Cathleen Campbell, Sister-in-Law

My sister [Cheri/Sharron] was lucky enough to find her Prince Charming at fourteen, and to me, they were the perfect couple — he, the quarterback; she, the head cheerleader. Best friends, partners, parents to Jill, and grandparents to Kyle and Zack.

Laura Henry, Niece

My Uncle Jim was one of a kind! I will always admire so much about him. I have many memories, and all of them involve laughter because he had a great sense of humor. He was a great athlete, writer, cook, giver of advice. Above all, he was a great husband and father. I will always be inspired by the relationship he had with Aunt Cheri.

Rachel Cline, Niece

My Uncle Jim was always my hero growing up. He was smart and funny and by far someone who molded me into the person I am today. When I was around five, we had two uncles named Jimmy in the family, so he said, "Rachie, just call me Aunt Himmy. OK?"

I remember when he'd wrap a towel around his head, become a swami, and perform card tricks. I cherish his hugs, laughter, and sarcastic honesty; birthday calls and call when my son was born; and drinking beer and playing bocci ball at the beach. I will always love him and think of my Aunt Himmy.

Ash Cline, Niece

In 2000, I accepted the East Fairmont High School 1963 Career Scoring Leader Award for Uncle Jim. I remember a lot of people cheering and telling me what an incredible athlete he was. What I remember most is feeling so proud to have family with that type of accomplishment — especially during a time when I didn't seem to have a lot to be proud of.

Melissa Nicoletti, Niece

I remember talking about faith with Uncle Jim. He was always easy-going and easy to talk to. I loved he always had a smile on his face. And he was quite fond of his wife. He was a wonderful man. Blessed to have him in our lives.

Faith Mayle, Cousin

I remember seeing Jim's high school picture on Cheri's nightstand when we were girls and thinking what a handsome boyfriend. It was truly true love and has lasted for all-time.

19
JOURNAL ENTRIES

Reflections

I WALKED DOWN THE SIDELINE away from everyone and prayed: "Please don't let me ruin it for this team" [after a come-from-behind win at Davidson College during the 1997 9-1 season].

It is still a difficult road. I still stumble, and I have been tested. I have had to make tough decisions as a coach.

After Justin Gambrell was killed in a car accident in 1999, Chris Price died right before our eyes with a brain hemorrhage in 2000. In 2001, we almost lost Will McPhaul to an unexplained fever.

My character and integrity were challenged in a 2002 alleged hazing incident. My players were wrongfully accused, all charges were dropped, but their innocence was never made public. There was great pain.

Standing by the truth makes me strong.

Listen to your pain. It will find a way to love. God is sending you pain to show where the truth is. Every blow has a divine meaning.

Holding resentment toward others binds us to them.

"I am just one person, but I am one."

However good or bad a situation, it will change.

If we stay the path and remain loyal, good things will happen. If we become arrogant and selfish, bad things will happen.

You wear a lot of hats as a D-III coach.

To impact others, I must be worthy of that assignment.

Just be me. Do what I can and look for doable things for people.

Be chaste, morally pure in thought and conduct, decent and modest.

Stand for something — ideas, dreams, principles.

Do not compromise what you believe.

Read, study, talk to successful people. Get knowledge. Have quiet time. Listen to music. Think thoughts of excellence.

Be bold. Boldness is one of my defining traits.

Know what has to be done and the balls to get it done.

You can't run from who you are.

Train players so hard, they are relieved the game is here.

Be tough as hell, but love them.

Train players for four years to prepare them for the next forty.

Work hard, but also relax and enjoy — balance.

There will always be the dumb-jock stereotype. You have to be tough to ward off criticism ... like a horse swatting flies in summer.

The human body may fail; the human spirit must never fail. We are nearest to greatness when we are great in humility.

Start with love. Love your friends and your enemies. To love is to serve God.

Love is the only reality, and it is not a mere sentiment. It is the ultimate truth that lies at the heart of truth.

Loving is a powerful source that abides forever.

All that matters in the end is that you loved.

People pay attention to how you live. Be credible.

Focus on kindness and justice, not wealth.

Treat all people special. Search for the value of every person. Look deeper. Treat all well, even if they don't deserve it.

How can I use my talents and gifts to help others? How can I sincerely help others improve and succeed? I will make it a goal to seek out someone every day and help that person.

Get outside every day. Miracles are waiting everywhere.

Love and faith are the most powerful.

Faith

We think religion is comfortable. We commit and think some big grandfather with a white beard will wrap us in his arms and hold us. That when we die, we go to some retirement community and play golf for eternity. Something was missing. I went to the library and found books that focused on obtaining God's grace and receiving it.

At the core, the very core, there is a power, a force, I want to know.

By the grace of God, I made a choice to commit to the Lord Jesus on January 16, 2000, when I was baptized in the Second Baptist Church and professed my faith. I am humbled by my experience, by the grace of God.

The path I am on will not result in fame and national recognition, but it has resulted in a growing relationship with the unseen and invisible presence.

My belief needs to be so strong that my heart does not doubt but believes if I ask, it will be done.

Holy living? Never confuse piety with righteousness.

God contains no wrath. We are his joy and delight. When we look upon another man

"Life after football is finding a passion and doing what I never got a real chance to do ... like Tai Chi, fishing, biking, and writing."

and see a blemish (a fault), it's our own imperfection we are seeing. That is what we must correct.

Use the power of faith for the welfare of others. It is my destiny to serve other people. All my work, all my life, is done with the power and for the glory of God.

Followers tend to be dependent on the leader. Leaders are expected to be dramatic in leading, but Jesus says it doesn't need to be dramatic. Small things can give results — small, positive, useful actions.

Lead with the power of the golden mustard seed (Matthew 13:31-32). Plant well. Plant as many seeds as possible. Practice the mustard-seed power. One small act can make a difference.

Coach Ralph Isernia

We knew Coach Sy was a man of faith, but he never imposed religion on us coaches or players. He allowed us to find it for ourselves. Self-realization is more powerful than being forced to the end result.

Epilogue

EDITOR'S NOTE: Coach Jim Sypult, the original Wild-Horse Rider, died in Cusco, Peru, on January 8, 2018, at the end of a six-week family vacation. He was tough even in his final play. His last journal entry, a few days before his death, was a quotation by Thoreau: "Go confidently in the direction of your dreams. Live the life you have imagined."

Amazon and Teddy Roosevelt
Jill Sypult Marcus

Did my dad ever tell you he always wanted to go to the Amazon like Teddy Roosevelt? Well, he finally made it to Peru with our family over the Christmas holidays. He and my mom explored the Madre de Dios River by boat near Puerto Maldonado looking for anacondas and caimans. We spent some time in Cusco, the Sacred Valley, and Machu Picchu. The altitude really affected him at eleven thousand feet. His heart gave out at the airport in Cusco on their way home. I am happy he left us on yet another adventure in his life, of which there were so many.

Jim, exploring the Amazon before his final touchdown in Cusco, Peru: "I did not worry to be born; I do not worry to die."

What Was Was Epic
Sharron Sypult

I don't know how to thank those who came to celebrate the life of Jim

Sypult on February 25, 2018 [Memorial Service] — except by saying thank you.

My heart was full, and I was in a place where there are no words. I felt ever so proud and loved, most especially and profoundly by the Wild-Horse Riders and Monarch Nation.

You honored Coach Sy by coming, some traveling great distances. You honor him in the way you live and in the remarkable men you have become. You helped me and each other deal with grief, and your emotion was palpable.

For those who weren't there, let me give you a taste of that extraordinary day.

It was sunny and above 80 degrees at the Spring Lake Pavilion on Hilton Head Island, overlooking a lake with birds swooping and diving.

The minister, The Rev. David Holloway, welcomed the crowd, former players, and fellow coaches en masse, standing room only, three deep in the back, ready to recount memories that made everyone laugh out loud. Applause followed every speaker.

Jill recounted her dad's discipline, repetition, and toughness — which the players knew all too well — while he coached her in tennis.

Grandson Zach, who attended his pap's first football game when four days old, talked about fishing together. They never caught much, but it wasn't about the fishing.

Niece Laura Lester Henry read Coach Sy's "Wild-Horse Rider" story. A few f-bombs went off here and there, and the crowd exploded in laughter.

Dave Eavenson, MU's AD-turned-comedian, told stories that needed no embellishment. Coach Sy made everyone laugh uncontrollably, set the tone, and was always fun even in tough times, he said.

Quincy Malloy, impressive; Bob Swank, dignified; Ray Ray, Matt Panza, and on and on. Each one shared stories that took place on the field and off — vivid, moving, powerful, electric.

One by one, they told of Coach Sy's influence and character and emphasis on getting good grades, calling your mother, and being good men.

Some were overcome with emotion — like Chris Ronchetti, quarterback of the 2005 championship team, and Carl Funderburk, an ex-Marine who began forcefully but ended one sentence later, unable to speak.

After two hours of tributes and tears and laughter, the minister stopped the storytelling that could have continued for hours.

Southern fare followed: crab bisque, shrimp and grits, ham biscuits and sausage gravy, beer, Bloody Mary's, peach champagne, caramel-apple hand pies, and s'mores! Pink and orange flowers on raspberry tablecloths and silk linens with gold-rimmed china. The caterer — Jill, Coach Sy's daughter.

A jazz trio played. The players sang MU's "The Fight Song." Sypult's Disypults trophy was awarded — an irreverent award for the player with *big balls*.

The camaraderie, emotion, and love evident and shared; the pain, tangible; the man who loved, guided, and influenced so many, remembered and cherished.

The stories honored Coach Sy and rekindled and recaptured his spirit in our hearts and in the room.

We were touched by the man, his life, and impact. So much love; so much lost.

I will never forget the experience, nor will any who attended. It was epic.

Lead the Parade
Jim Sypult

When you leave, it's better to lead the parade than let a posse run you out of town.

People get up every day and go to work. I got up every day and went to play. Of course, it was a lot more fun when we won.

What's important to me is that my tombstone reads, "Here lies Jim Sypult. He made a difference in young men's lives." That's how I want to be perceived, and that's my standard.

James C. Sypult

ABOUT THE AUTHOR

Jim Sypult was born in a West Virginia mining camp in 1945. He was a star quarterback in high school and three-year starter and captain at West Virginia University. As a graduate assistant, he earned his master's, and, at twenty-one, became the youngest head football coach in the country.

At Elkins High in West Virginia and Liberty High in Virginia, Jim, aka Coach Sy, turned losing programs into winners before coaching in college as an assistant at Fairmont State, Middle Tennessee State, and Davidson College. In 1986, he accepted the head coaching position of a pro team playing American football in Bologna, Italy—a team he took to the Super Bowl playoffs.

In 1992, Jim became the head football coach at Methodist College/University in Fayetteville, North Carolina, and inherited a program struggling to survive. Although he didn't win a game his first season, a national ranking, conference championship, and Coach of the Year award followed. Sypult, the winningest coach in the school's history, is called the *Father of Methodist Football*.

Jim's journals, which he began as a boy, underscore his ingenuity, hallmark humor, and gift for telling stories. His editorials appeared in the *Fayetteville Observer*, and his memoir came to be while he was president of Scribblers, a Hilton Head writing club.

ABOUT THE EDITOR

Sharron Sypult, a college valedictorian and graduate fellow, earned a doctorate in English and taught literature and all manner of writing.

Her teaching career is wide-ranging: high school (two years), Middle Tennessee State (TA), Motlow State, University of North Carolina Charlotte, Fayetteville Technical Community College, and Methodist College/University. In addition to a normal course load, Sharron taught night classes and juggled academic demands while producing the student paper, student print and online magazines, media guides, and a grant proposal. She also started the journalism program at Methodist.

Sharron has published op-eds in the *Fayetteville Observer* and non-fiction in *Reflections*. During Covid, she edited Jim's stories and compiled tributes that document an incomparable football era and preserve a living, breathing record of the legendary Coach Sy.

Coach Sy and Dr. Sy beaching it.